"Pauline Kael is my favorite movie critic . . . She writes superbly; she has seen and remembers almost every film ever made; she knows where all the bodies, artistic and financial, are buried . . . I care about her humanist sensibility, her emphasis on the collaboration between meaning and technique, her savage style . . . I care about Miss Kael's criticism as literature. Her reviews can be read before, immediately after, and long after we have seen the movie that inspires or exasperates her . . . She is superior to most of what she analyzes."

—John Leonard, **The New York Times**

"I am devoted to the work of Miss Pauline Kael. She is not afraid to read the news, to tell the truth at decently garrulous length about what she saw, experienced and thought later . . . [the book] is so much the finer for being a kind of continuing diary of reactions, with periods for reflection."

—John Coleman (**New Statesman** film critic), **Book World**

GOING STEADY by Pauline Kael, author of Bantam Film Books **Kiss Kiss Bang Bang** and **I Lost it at the Movies**

Going Steady

Pauline Kael

BANTAM BOOKS · TORONTO · NEW YORK · LONDON

A NATIONAL GENERAL COMPANY

GOING STEADY

*A Bantam Book / published by arrangement with
Little, Brown and Company in association with
The Atlantic Monthly Press*

PRINTING HISTORY

Little, Brown edition published February 1970
"Trash, Art and the Movies" appeared originally in
HARPER'S *Magazine*
All other pieces in this book appeared originally in
THE NEW YORKER

Bantam edition published May 1971

*Bantam Books are published by Bantam Books, Inc., a National
General company. Its trade-mark, consisting of the words "Bantam
Books" and the portrayal of a bantam, is registered in the United
States Patent Office and in other countries. Marca Registrada.
Bantam Books, Inc., 666 Fifth Avenue, New York, N.Y. 10019.*

PRINTED IN THE UNITED STATES OF AMERICA

Foreword

Movies which might seem, of all arts, the simplest to write about, may be the most difficult to write about because they encompass so many different kinds of effort and are susceptible to so many influences. In the last few years they have been changing and moving into new areas so quickly and new young directors have been reshaping the art in such extraordinary ways, that it isn't easy to know what's going on, or to offer an informed account of what's going on, unless one really stays at it. To be a casual critic of movies is to be no critic at all, and for one whose interest is more than casual, it's painful to write about movies just occasionally, or to order. What is missing is the connection—or context—in which movies are a continuing art. In such frustrating circumstances each review one writes has to take for granted a whole succession of unwritten reviews that would have established the basis for one's criticism.

Although I had been writing and broadcasting about movies since 1953, I had never had a regular weekly column and I had just about given up hope that it was really possible to be a movie critic when *The New Yorker* offered me one, starting in January 1968. This book which is my work since that date, is, I think, in some ways the best writing that I've done because I had for the first time in William Shawn an editor who loves movies and who never said those obscene words: "Our readers won't be interested in all that." He gave me the space I needed to develop a sustained position from week to week, and, for the first time, that total independence from advertisers and from anxieties about reader response that makes criticism possible.

I have kept the writing in sequence, including an article I did during the summer months, because this way the reader can follow not only what was evolving in films during a crucial period of social and aesthetic change at the end of the sixties, but follow the reviewer's developing responses. Someone recently sent me a copy of a college magazine with an article called "Art as Transformed Subversion—The Elusive Aesthetics of Pauline Kael." I will accept the first part of the title, but I hope *Going Steady* will make the aesthetics considerably less elusive.

Contents

CONTENTS

CONTENTS

I

Movies by the Week: First Sequence

Movies as Opera

Movies have been doing so much of the same thing—
in slightly different ways—for so long that few of
the possibilities of this great hybrid art have yet
been explored. At the beginning, movies served
many of the functions of primitive theatre; they
were Punch-and-Judy shows. But by bringing
simple forms of theatre and great actors and
dancers and singers to the small towns of the world,
they helped to create a taste for more complex
theatre, and by bringing the world to people who
couldn't travel they helped to develop more advanced audiences. When Méliès photographed his
magic shows, when D. W. Griffith recreated the
Civil War or imagined the fall of Babylon, when
Pabst made a movie with Chaliapin, when Flaherty
went to photograph life in the Aran Islands or the
South Seas, they were just beginning to tap the
infinite possibilities of movies to explore, to record,
to dramatize. Shipped in tins, movies could go anywhere in the world, taking a synthesis of almost all
the known art forms to rich and poor. In terms of
the number of people they could reach, movies were
so inexpensive that they could be hailed as the great
democratic art form. Then, as businessmen gained
control of the medium, it became almost impossibly

difficult for the artists to try anything new. Movies became in one way or another remakes of earlier movies, and until inexpensive pictures from abroad began to attract large audiences the general public probably believed what the big studios advertised— that great movies meant big stars, best-seller stories, expensive production. The infinite variety of what was possible on film was almost forgotten, along with the pioneers, and many of those who loved movies lost some of their own vision. They began to ask what cinema "really" was, as if ideal cinema were some preëxistent entity that had to be discovered; like Platonists turned archeologists, they tried to unearth the true essence of cinema. Instead of celebrating the miltiplicity of things that movies can do better or more easily than the other arts, and new ways and combinations, they looked for the true nature of cinema in what cinema can do that the other arts can't—in artistic apartheid. Some decided on "montage," others on "purely visual imagery." (There was even a period when true cinema was said to be "the chase," and for a while audiences were being chased right out of the theatres.) They wanted to prove that cinema was a real art, like the other arts, when the whole world instinctively preferred it because it was a bastard, cross-fertilized super-art.

"Cinema" in a pure state is not to be found, but movies in the sixties began to expand again, and so quickly it's hard to keep up with them. In France men like Jean Rouch and Chris Marker are extending movies into what were previously thought to be the domains of anthropologists, sociologists, and journalists, while in "Masculine Feminine" Jean-Luc Godard made a modern love lyric out of journalism and essays and interviews, demonstrating that there are no boundaries in the arts that talent can't cross. Not even the grave. In "China Is Near" the young Italian director Marco Bellocchio now brings back to startling life a form that had been laid to rest with modern ceremony—that is, with a few regrets, kicks, and jeers. The new, great talent—perhaps the genius—of Godard brought chance into the art of movies. Bellocchio's talent—so distinctive that already it resembles genius—flourishes within the confines of intricate plot. "China Is Near" has the boudoir complications of a classic comic opera.

Among the five principals in "China Is Near," who use each other in every way they can, are a pair of working-class lovers—a secretary and an accountant who scheme to marry into the rich landed gentry. Their targets are a professor, Vittorio (Glauco Mauri), who is running for municipal office on the Socialist ticket, and his sister, Elena, a great lady who lets every man in town climb on top of her but won't marry because socially they're all beneath her. Vittorio, the rich Socialist candidate, is that role so essential to comic opera—the ridiculous lover, the man whose mission in life is to be deceived—and Bellocchio, who wrote the film (with Elda Tattoli, who plays Elena) as well as directed it, has produced a classic modern specimen of the species: a man who's out of it, who doesn't get anything while it's going on. The fifth principal is their little brother, Camillo, who is a prissy, sneering despot—a seventeen-year-old seminary student turned Maoist who looks the way Edward Albee might look in a drawing by David Levine. Camillo provides the title when he scrawls "China Is Near" on the walls of the Socialist Party building—his brother's campaign headquarters.

Bellocchio uses the underside of family life—the inbred family atmosphere—for borderline horror and humor. His people are so awful they're funny. One might say that Bellocchio, though he is only twenty-eight, sees sex and family and politics as a dirty old man would, except that his movie is so peculiarly exuberant; perhaps only a very young (or a very old) director can focus on such graceless, mean-spirited people with so much enjoyment. As the pairs of lovers combine and recombine and the five become one big, ghastly family (with a yapping little house pet as an emblem of domesticity), Bellocchio makes it all rhyme. He provides the grace of formal design. The grand manner of the movie is hilarious. I found myself smiling at the wit of his technique; it was pleasurable just to see the quick way doors open and close, or how, when the scene shifts to a larger, more public area, there's always something unexpected going on—surprises that explode what has seemed serious. Bellocchio's visual style is almost incredibly smooth; the camera glides in and out and around the action. He uses it as if there were no obstructions, as if he could do anything he wanted with it; it moves as simply and with as much apparent ease as if it were attached to the director's forehead. In "China Is Near," as in his first film ("I Pugni in Tasca," or "Fists in the Pocket," which was made in 1965 and is soon to open in this country), he probably exhibits the most fluid directorial technique since Max Ophuls, and I don't know where it came from—that is, how he developed it so fast.

"Fists in the Pocket" must surely be one of the most astonishing directorial debuts in the history of movies, yet it is hard to know how to react to the movie itself. The material is wild, the direction cool and assured. "Fists in the Pocket," which Bellocchio made fresh from film schools in Italy and England, is also about a prosperous family, but a family of diseased monsters. And as epileptic fits multiply between bouts of matricide, fratricide, and incest, one is too busy gasping at the director's technique and the performances of a cast of unknown actors (Lou Castel, with his pug-dog manner, and Paola Pitagora, looking like a debauched gazelle, are the best strange brother-and-sister act since Edouard Dermithe and Nicole Stéphane in "Les Enfants Terribles") to doubt his directorial genius. But the movie is a portrait of the genius as a very young man. It is so savage it often seems intended to be funny, but *why* it was so intended isn't clear. Though "Fists in the Pocket" is exhilarating because it reveals a new talent, not everybody cares about movies enough to want to see a movie—no matter how brilliant—about a family cage of beasts, and to a casual moviegoer "Fists in the Pocket" may seem as heavily charged with misguided energy as one of those epileptic seizures. But in a few years people will probably be going to see it as, after seeing Ingmar Bergman's later films, they went to see his

7

early ones. After only two films, Bellocchio's characters already seem his, in the way that the characters of certain novelists seem theirs—a way uncommon in movies except in the movies of writer-directors of especially individual temperaments. Bellocchio's characters are as much a private zoo as Buñuel's.

It was not just coincidence when, a few years ago, first one young French director broke through, then another and another; it was obvious not only that they took encouragement from each other but that they literally inspired each other. Bellocchio was preceded in this way by another young Italian, Bernardo Bertolucci, who at twenty-one directed "La Commare Secca" and at twenty-two wrote and directed the sweepingly romantic "Before the Revolution," which also dealt with a provincial family and sex and politics, and which suggested a new, operatic approach to movie-making. Both these young directors refer to opera the way the French refer to American movies; they not only use operatic structure and themes but actually introduce performances and recordings of operas—especially Verdi operas—into their work. (The bit of opera performed in "China Is Near" is the damnedest thing since "Salammbô" in "Citizen Kane.") In the analogy they draw with opera, they seem to glory in the hybrid nature of movies, and to Italians movies may seem almost an outgrowth of the hybrid art of opera. If Verdi wrote a larger number of enduring operas than any other composer (perhaps a fifth of the total standard repertory), it's not only because he wrote great music but also because he filled the stage with action and passion and a variety of good roles for different kinds of voice—which is how these two directors make their movies. Maybe, too, these directors are saying that sex and family and politics in modern Italy are still out of Verdi. Both these young Italians are different from the older Italian directors—even those just a little older, like Pasolini—in the way that their movies move. Men like Fellini and Antonioni developed their techniques over the years, laboriously, and their early movies attest to how long it took them to become Fellini and Antonioni. This is not to put them down—most of us take a long time and never become anything—but to contrast them with Bertolucci and Bellocchio, who started their movie careers with masterly techniques, proving that it doesn't take decades of apprenticeship or millions of dollars to tell planned and acted stories, and that there is still joy in this kind of movie-making. I think Godard is the most exciting director working in movies today, and it's easy to see how and why he is influencing movie-makers all over the world. But chance and spontaneity and improvisation and the documentary look are only one way to go—not, as some have begun to think, the only way. The clear triumph of "China Is Near" is that it demonstrates how good other ways can be.

January 13, 1968

Celebrities
Make Spectacles
of Themselves

There are many movies that are worse than Norman Mailer's "Wild 90"; there was one just a week ago, called "The Wicked Dreams of Paula Schultz." But "Wild 90" is the worst movie that I've stayed to see all the way through. Unlike poor "Paula Schultz," it's terrible in ways that are portentous. And, grindingly boring as it is, it has something going for it: our curiosity about what Mailer is doing in it, and why, and what he thinks he's doing. The gangster character he plays is called the Prince. Lording it over his unappealing chums, he's a growling, grunting, waddling little star, a miniaturized big-brawler who looks and sounds surprisingly like Victor McLaglen in "The Informer." It must have taken a Harvard man many years of practice to achieve that low-life effect; he didn't acquire it just for the movie. And surely it isn't the Mafia man he pretends to play but Mailer the fantasist who gets punch-drunk from shadowboxing. And it's Mailer the great lover who, in a scene with his wife, rivals the Burtons at embarrassing us. And it's Mailer the professional madman who must assert himself even with a dog—barking at it until it leaps at him.

Many European writers have made movies (Malraux, Cocteau, Pagnol), and many others have worked for the movies—worked in the real sense of writing well for the medium (Gide, Giraudoux, Marcel Aymé, Raymond Queneau, to name just a few). But in Hollywood best-selling mediocrities were publicized for prestige, and writers like Faulkner, Fitzgerald, and Nathanael West were employed as hacks. They wrote movies for money to live on while they did their own writing; they rarely got even a solo screenplay credit. West wrote Westerns for Republic Pictures, and, according to Joseph Blotner's biographical study, Faulkner wrote between forty and fifty treatments and screenplays, some of them running over two hundred pages, and only a handful of them were filmed. When Norman Mailer worked in Hollywood, he didn't get *any* of his writing onto the screen; and what was done to the two novels of his that were filmed was to remove *him*—his way of seeing—from them. The movie versions of "The Naked and the Dead" and "An American Dream" were hardly recognizable as Mailer, and this sort of thing is not unusual in film versions of important American novels. Ironically, we often get less sense of the writer in the movies based on his books than in the movies on which the writer was employed as a hack among other hacks. There is more feeling of Fitzgerald in "Three Comrades," or even in "Winter Carnival," than in the movie version of "Tender Is the Night." As hacks, the writers were a step closer to the final film than they were as authors of the originals; there was more chance for their dialogue, their kind of invention, even traces of their sensibility to come through than when other hacks, often in relays, used their plots as

11

starting points. The closer you get to the final screenwriting and shooting, the better chance you have of using the medium as your own.

The chances for American writers and directors have never been as good as they are this year. Almost twice as many movies will be made in this country in 1968 as were made in 1966. The element of financial risk in low-budget productions has suddenly been diminished by prearranged or possible future sales to television. This planning in terms of television may, in the long run, be disastrous to the art of movies, but there are short-range benefits. Men who have been trying for years to line up money for projects are now being financed—usually not for what they want to do, but at least they're working and hoping. And, with the new college market for experimental films (and new possibilities for foundation financing of them), why shouldn't writers who have wanted to make movies take the plunge? And who more likely to do it and to bring it off than Mailer? Almost all writers from Joyce on have been influenced by movies, and for decades now Americans have been writing with their eye on the screen. The writers who particularly influenced Mailer—Dos Passos and James T. Farrell—had written novels in the form of scripts. And last year Mailer's play about the movies, "The Deer Park," which was constructed like a movie, was performed. He called it an "existential play"; perhaps the bells that timed scenes were supposed to make it as "existential" as a prizefight. Now novelists could stop dickering with their agents for a job in Hollywood and, instead, assault Hollywood with a different kind of movie-making. Again, who more likely than Mailer? Wasn't he as tough as Cocteau? But maybe he isn't. You have to hand it to those skinny, wiry guys—they're stronger than they look. Mailer as a movie-maker is all blubber. With his famous instinct, however, he's on to something that will probably pay off commercially. (It should be noted that his instinct is famous because it's so often bad.)

"Wild 90" wasn't written ("Not a line," Mailer says, as if we would think written dialogue a cheat) and it wasn't directed. Mailer made a movie by setting up a situation (three Mafia men hide out from other gangsters and are visited by friends, wives, the police), with himself as star and some cronies supporting him, and he hired D. A. Pennebaker to film it. That's as different from really making your own movie as a movie star's telling her story to a hired ghostwriter is from writing. And, just as whatever "style" there is in ghostwritten books is the ghost's, and generally much worse than if the supposed author were doing her own writing, here it's Pennebaker's, and almost a parody of his usual techniques (which were pretty much a parody to begin with). In a sense, Mailer the employer has done just what Hollywood did to writers: he turned Pennebaker into a hired hack. He hired Pennebaker to do more than a cameraman does when there is a director, because Pennebaker had to decide what to shoot, yet it isn't Pennebaker's film, either, because although it was acted out for him to catch as he could, his techniques are devised precisely to catch what's *not* acted out for the camera. Although almost all of "Wild 90" takes place in one room, with Mailer and his friends sitting around talking, Pennebaker used the *cinéma-vérité* camera style (camera hand-held or mounted on the shoulder) with the grainy texture, the rapid pans and zooms and closeups that are acceptable only on what cannot be caught or revealed any other way—on riots or disasters, on the unexpected. Part of the craft of a movie director is to make movement mean something, but the movement in this film is wholly meaningless. Simple, clear photography would expose how static the material is, of course (it's as static as in a Warhol film), but that would be a great deal more honest toward this material. Basically, Mailer uses *cinéma-vérité* methods as a shortcut—a way of making a movie without going to too much effort, and of providing the raw look of "life." As a *writer*, Mailer wouldn't fake things this way; he knows what one goes through to arrive at an apparently spontaneous passage, or to become a truly spontaneous writer.

Cinéma vérité is a fast way of shooting made possible by the development in the last decade of lightweight cameras and sound-recording equipment. Two men (or even one man) can walk (or run) with the camera and the synchronized tape recorder. This has liberated camera reporting, but, technically, the results are not all that might be hoped for. The sound is generally poor or inaudible, the images are dark. These will, no doubt, improve. There are other disadvantages, though. Since the cameraman selects on the run what it is he will shoot, the footage tends to be visually monotonous, with a lot of arbitrary motion as the cameraman whizzes around focussing on pointless details, because he loses or cannot find what is interesting in a situation. Good editing can clean it up, of course, and since *cinéma-vérité* cameraman often shoot in a ratio of twenty to one (that is, use only a twentieth of their exposed footage, they can later give the footage shape or reduce it to the moments of revelation. Such moments can seem like personal discoveries for the audience when they are part of an undramatized texture. The audience that has learned to groan at conventional dramatic preparation for each climax may take these moments to be more revealing than they are. As they're not explained or related to other moments, there's a tendency to over-interpret someone's spilling his coffee or looking at himself in the mirror.

"Cinéma vérité" is one of those terms (like "consciousness-expanding drugs") that gain general acceptance even though as descriptions they are questionable. The term implies getting at something more "true" than is possible in rehearsed, acted situations. But "real people" do act, and at the same time in almost all fiction movies the camera records much that isn't consciously acted, and many stars make their fortunes on what they are or seem to be as camera subjects rather than on their acting. And conventional filmmaking often includes documentary footage of cities, sports, shops, hotels, and so on. Even though the "real-life" participants in a *cinéma-vérité* documentary are "unrehearsed," this does not mean that their actions are unpremeditated in terms of the camera; the filmmakers them-

15

selves often contrive the situations, in an attempt to produce a tense or volatile movement. For example, William Jersey, who made "A Time for Burning," arranged a meeting between an Omaha minister and a Negro barber, precipitating the events that he photographed. The major difference between conventional filmmaking (which has begun to use lighter, more portable equipment) and *cinéma vérité* is becoming the *deliberately* rough look of the latter, and even this is being taken over by fiction films (like "A Hard Day's Night," "The Knack," Privilege," and parts of "The Graduate") that want that "with-it," "spontaneous" feeling.

There is an element of fakery in *cinéma vérité* that Mailer can use. The darting, catch-as-catch-can images are bound to seem more "true," more "real" than carefully lighted and composed photography. Spontaneity has become a goal, even an ideal, for a great many people—a test of sincerity as opposed to "phoniness." Some *cinéma-vérité* filmmakers dramatize the weaknesses of their technique— retaining out-of-focus shots and confusing shifts in location—in order to make the camera and the mike appear to be eavesdropping. The method can be used to give audiences a look at celebrities that *seems* to be less slanted and more truthful than an analytical, clearly edited view. *Cinéma vérité* can be used as a new way to tell backstage stories about celebrities; the camera can follow the hero like a slavish fan, and dull conversation can seem like inside stuff if it's "overheard"—just barely picked up. The celebrity subject may—indeed, almost certainly does—control the reporter who uses the camera; then *cinéma vérité* becomes just another form of corrupt journalism. So far, the audiences who reject the slick kinds of commercial manipulation are not as much aware of the manipulation that looks amateurish and spontaneous. They concentrate on the "stars," and *cinéma vérité* depends more on celebrities than well-composed documentaries do—depends on an already created interest in the subject, and generally on the subject's doing something different from what he became famous for, like Truman Capote receiving friends at home, or Timothy Leary getting married.

Cinéma vérité can be used as a trompe-l'oeil technique, and Pennebaker used it that way in the much praised Bob Dylan picture "Don't Look Back." Part of the praise seemed to originate from the notion that the roughness of the film was necessary (though many films made in far more difficult conditions are clearly photographed and well organized). Sequences that in a Hollywood movie would have been greeted with snickers—like Bob Dylan in the throes of composition—got by because of the rough look. The technique of "Don't Look Back" also prevented instant recognition of the traditional Hollywood theme: the young idol suffering from all the attention he is getting. Audiences seemed to accept the new *cinéma-vérité* convention that the camera was an intruder in the idol's life, though it must have been obvious that Dylan had arranged to star in this film (which listed his manager as producer). There is a danger in movies, especially in *cinéma-vérité* footage—and this, too, may appeal to Mailer—in that audience responses are not altogether predictable. The young audience for "Don't Look Back" was on Dylan's side, not just because of the music but because he looked frail and sensitive, because he looked like one of them, because his narrow shoulders were appealing to all those hunched-up kids who show their opposition to war by not developing their muscles. (In the new youth culture, it's the good weak guys against the bad strong guys.) But perhaps they want their psychodramas more romantic than was supposed, and watching this movie they may have turned from Dylan to Donovan (who appeared briefly), because Donovan wasn't threatening. Dylan the movie star was a witch-boy, ethereal, with his fluffy hair in the halo of lights, but frightening, too; his put-downs were bad magic.

It is one of the ultimate fantasies to star in a *cinéma-vérité* movie, to show the world "the truth" about yourself. Norman Mailer not only took Pennebaker, he took the Dylan look—fluffy halo and all—for the ads for "Wild 90." Mailer's recent long, rambling essay "Some Dirt in the Talk: A Candid History of an Existential Movie Called 'Wild 90' " (written, apparently, to help publicize the movie, although it should, if there is any justice in the arts, long survive the film) has some passages that are as good as anything ever written about movies, and a few paragraphs on Hollywood and acting that are unequalled. But when he explains what he is doing in "Wild 90," he is self-serving. As a solution to the problem of awareness of the camera in documentaries, Mailer proposes what he calls "existential" acting, by which he means im-

18

provising within given roles in a given situation. He may not know of many ways in which improvisation has been used in Europe in recent years; he may not have seen Godard's films. But hasn't he even seen "Pull My Daisy" or "Shadows"? Or even heard of them? It's a bit like a man who has just written his first poem and announces the discovery of free verse. The people in "Wild 90" are *less* interesting than they might be playing in their own roles in life (although Mailer has picked people whose current purpose in life may be to be part of his entourage—humoring him—which is not altogether different from what they do in the movie). They sit around or stand around trying to think of something interesting to do for the camera. Mailer considers this a new kind of "psychological reality." When unconcealed awareness of the camera, hesitancy, and self-consciousness become proof that people are real people instead of actors, that they represent "real" values as opposed to "artificial" ones, bad, self-conscious acting becomes more "true" than good acting. Television commercials use this fake "real-people" approach, and perhaps it's best left to them. Mailer, a good actor himself, shouldn't throw out the art of acting to provide a justification for bad acting. (It's inappropriate, too, since most of the leads in his movie are actors, although they don't look as if they'd had much training in improvisation.)

Mailer's approach in "Wild 90" is tangential to the art of movies, but, awful as the probability is to contemplate, I think it may work commercially. "Wild 90" would be a *sure* commercial success if

19

the people in it were more amusing. Not because the statagem of pretending to be someone else helps people to reveal more about themselves but because it provides a chance for celebrities—as it does for Mailer in this film—to play at low life, to entertain themselves for a few evenings as whores or gun molls, race-track touts or gamblers. Mailer not only has found a painless, fast way to make movies but has invented the new celebrity-party-game movie, combining the advantages of scavenger hunts, masquerades, and so forth. People can pretend for a few nights what George Plimpton works at for long stretches. And, once they get talented at it, they can interact, and swap roles, and everything. These movie parties will make money, and the celebrity producer won't have to pay to advertise the pictures—the mass media will do it for him. It may, for a season, be the biggest thing around.

January 20, 1968

Ciphers

Does anyone who is even moderately interested in movies need to be warned off "How to Save a Marriage—and Ruin Your Life"? That seems as superfluous as warning a gourmet against canned spaghetti. The producer and co-writer of "How to" is Stanley Shapiro, who was also a co-writer of "Pillow Talk," "Lover Come Back," and "That Touch of Mink." (For the first he received an Academy Award, and for the others Academy Award nominations.) Its director is Fielder Cook, a veteran of over two hundred television shows, whose last movie, adapted from one of them, was "A Big Hand for the Little Lady." It's as clear as the label on the can.

A handsome, sophisticated, rich bachelor (Dean Martin) mistakes an honest, hardworking department-store employee (Stella Stevens) for the mistress of his rich married friend (Eli Wallach). "How to" is from an original screenplay that could well have been a Doris Day reject; it has the same pathetic running joke of the consummation postponed again and again. Now that the Motion Picture Association Production Code has been revised, Shapiro's obsession with virginity makes him seem rather stubborn. Really, not all the old ways were the best. The dialogue has the desperate, strained sound of burned-out gag-writers' dialogue; the wisecracks come out sourcracks—nastiness pretending to be low-down wisdom. "How to" isn't one of those happy accidents, like "The Oscar," in which bad taste transcends itself; it isn't flamboyant enough. Perhaps it was picked for the Radio City Music Hall in the same way that some people buy art to go with the furniture—that is, in order to blend with the stage show (a unicycle act, a comic xylophonist, the Music Hall Ballet Company in Grieg's "Symphonic Dances," the Symphony Orchestra playing a "Jerome Kern Fantasy," and the famed Rockettes in "Beauty and the Beat").

As for "Sebastian," moviegoers have almost no way of knowing what to expect. Despite such names as Dirk Bogarde, Lilli Palmer, Susannah York, and John Gielgud in the cast, it's a trivial little movie, a London-set comedy-thriller about espionage and code-breakers, with not much in the way of comedy and less in the way of thrills. It's just classy pulp, but the whole thing goes by before one has time to begin to hate it. This film is also from an "original screen story"; it was written by men who are known primarily for their work in English television, and it was directed by David Greene, a television director here and in England. The suspense never gets going, but "Sebastian" employs the more mannered acting of English television, and there's a certain appeal in this. The gentlemen are literate according to a peculiarly illiterate theatrical convention: they make references to mythology and "the classics," and from time to time they express their thoughts in florid, "literary" language. A few small jokes come off, or maybe we laugh just because they're so very small. When the picture tries to be Mod and posh and sexy, it's very bad; "Modesty Blaise" did what Greene and Company seem to be just barely considering.

The director of "How to" uses the clumsiest, crudest kind of obvious television technique; he shoots a relentless succession of closeups of the speaker shouting the gag line (with back of head of listener), *despite* the fact that his cameraman is Lee Garmes, one of the old Hollywood great ones, who at least keeps the color more subdued than is customary in this garish genre, just as Michel Legrand keeps the score more gentle. The director of "Sebastian" is, in television terms, clever. "How to" is bad even of its awful, opulent kind; "Sebastian" is almost, though not, amusing. I haven't singled out the television background of the makers of these movies in order to be snobbish; most movie directors under fifty have come to movies by way of television, because that is just about the only route that is open. I've pointed to the television background because, different as they are, these movies have some things in common and these things, I think, relate to the influence of television. Neither film has any resonance—it doesn't connect with our lives or any lives we can imagine—and in a year or two, when these movies turn up on TV, we may sit down to watch them again because we don't remember a thing about them.

It has been a familiar complaint about movies that they are usually derived from novels and that they should be based on material written directly for the screen. The complaint has been made, of course, in terms of ideal conditions for the development of screen art. Now we're getting "screen originals," but in a very different way; the playwrights who have been working directly for the TV screen are beginning to write directly for the movie screen (which is but a step on the movie's primrose path to TV). Television directors developed their styles working with thin, one-dimensional characters and situations, almost continuous dialogue, sharp visual contrasts, quick jabs at the emotions, and lots of climaxes. They tried to be "effective." Some of them got pretty good at it. Being concerned primarily with plays and material written directly for TV, they generally didn't learn how to use novelistic detail, and in terms of what works best on television they didn't really need to know. But almost all memorable movies are based on novels or biographies or some kind of book—"The Birth of a Nation" and "The Treasure of Sierra Madre" and "Jules and Jim," and almost any other movie that comes to mind, though it's to the point that the books don't readily come to mind, because the best movies are based on second-rate or obscure books. Great novels or very important ones seem to be too difficult—too constricting—for a director. What made them great was, very likely, the writer's way of seeing, and the film director cannot do justice to that. The great overpowers him, but the obscure or the second-, third-, or fourth-rate can stimulate him. He can change it freely; often, if he is good, he can improve on it. He can *use* it to make a good film, or even a

24

great one. Plays present difficult problems, because the dialogue and the action are conceived for the stage; and because dramatic writing is a process of refinement that eliminates the details of environment, plays don't give a movie director what he needs. But the older generation of movie directors often worked easily and well with novels, which provided atmosphere and detail and layers of observation. This helped the screenwriters and directors give their movies the illusion of a world surrounding the events of the story. Even when they worked from a screen original, they usually thought of the movie medium novelistically. Television-trained directors, even when they're making movies, and even when they're working from a novel, tend to use only the screenplay, as if it were a television original. There's nothing underneath the situations, nothing behind or around the foreground action, no sense of a life going on to support the events.

There's almost nothing to say about the actors in this kind of film, because they have so little material with which to build a character and almost no chance at a full characterization; they're often better in the roles if they don't struggle with them. If in other kinds of films one empathizes with the writers and the directors, "the creators," sensing what they were trying to do and how they failed or were hampered, in these movies one identifies with the actors, because they are the human material caught in this mechanization, and they are stuck there on the screen, hideously exposed. If there are so few new stars, it may be because it's so hard for an actor to score in these virtually unwritten roles. Even in

25

the best recent example of this kind of film, "Divorce American Style," there was the discomfort of seeing one of the beautiful wasted actresses of the screen, Jean Simmons. Her suggestions of sensibility—what she embodies—were too fine for the world of that movie. Her presence made the movie she was trapped in seem uglier. The actors in "How to" and "Sebastian" don't have any acting to do; they function as celebrity names for the financing of the pictures and for the marquee. Dean Martin is a master of casual, relaxed timing, so he comes off pretty well, but those who are trying to act look like fish struggling to get off the hook. Eli Wallach becomes frenzied, Betty Field (as a landlady) becomes grotesque. Actors who try to earn their pay by giving professional readings to lines nobody could say just make the lines stand out more blatantly. There is a sad-patsy quality about Stella Stevens' performance; she seems a victim in more ways than the script intended. Her talents wasted for a decade, she "stars" as a replacement for Doris Day. With a forced, ticky little grin, she pushes out her front the way Doris Day stuck out behind. Cleavage is cleavage, whether it's coming or going. In "Sebastian," Gielgud, as urbane as a wax effigy of himself, walks through smartly while half a dozen good actors make fools of themselves trying to act. And in this case it isn't because he's a greater actor but because they are caught in roles that require preposterous behavior and they are trying to supply characters suitable to the behavior, whereas he, like Dean Martin, only needs to play on his public image—to cool it.

If no character in a movie seems to have a past, one can be pretty sure it was written and/or directed by people from television. The characters are not likely to have much present, either. In movies based on novels, the details of character may originate in observation or in imagination, but the novelist rooted them, made them seem authentic. When details are thrown into a script to help "work up" the characters, the actors can't make the details appear to grow out of the invented situation. Some of the most revealing scenes in movies have taken place in offices or factories or soda fountains. In "How to," the salesgirls stand at military attention when the department-store owner walks by, and we wince, as we wince when Gielgud and Bogarde go through an antique cultivated-gentlemen bit, discussing, at Oxford, the subject of botany. When scenes like this are so witless and so inaccurate, we lose one of the incidental charms of movies—the little things we pick up about other people's jobs and lives, about how things work. The big decoding room of "Sebastian" doesn't even tell us anything about decoding operations. TV directors don't think in terms of the variety of pleasures possibly in movies. When we travel now, we are not *surprised,* as travellers a century ago must have been; we view so many places in terms of a movie-made *déjà vu* (the Venice of "Summertime," the Côte d'Azur of "To Catch a Thief," the Paris of "Funny Face," the Istanbul of "Topkapi"). From the theatre we can get a sense of human passions, we can learn what is *in* men, but we don't get the sense of man's environment that we get from movies. Movies can give us the setting in which the drama takes place (or a studio-made re-creation of the setting in which it might take place, or a mixture of the two); the theatre gives us only the drama itself. This isn't clear-cut, it's not an aesthetic law; it's just a generally observable difference. And it isn't clear-cut, but it's also observable, that television-trained men don't know how to open up the environment. When they have shot an adventure series or a spy series outdoors, they probably used the countryside or the city simply as a backdrop for the action. What movies lose when they are "television movies" is the texture of life, the thickness and the richness that movies as an art form took over from the novel.

As part of the audience at a movie, we may laugh or light a cigarette, we may even get up to leave, and the action on the screen is not affected. We can return to the movie house the next week and the lovers are still going through the same cycle of passions. Like a dream or a nightmare, a movie has a life of its own, and this contributes to the "mythic" quality of movies. A movie can be like a recurrent dream; we can go back to it again and again and it will be the same. Lovely. But if movies go on independent of our presence, this also means we cannot dismiss a bad picture with the thought that it will disappear shortly. It will be around earning residuals—a recurrent universal nightmare. Can we dismiss these movies with the same easy contempt when we know that for generations to come, in God knows how many countries, Stella Stevens will be holding out her arms to Dean Martin, smiling that frozen, pert smile, and Dirk Bogarde will be snarling "Don't rupture yourself" at kinky, smirky Susannah York?

January 27, 1968

Intentions

Everything that one may object to in the English film "Poor Cow" can no doubt be explained as intentional and serious and high-minded. The objections may still be valid. Joy, the Poor Cow, is having a baby pulled out of her and is crying in pain as the movie opens, and Donovan is singing Christopher Logue's words "Be not too hard/For life is short/And nothing is given to man. . . . Be not too hard/For soon he'll die/Often no wiser than he began," and I had a hunch that I should take the warning and walk out of the theatre. One comes away no wiser about Joy or her husband or her lover than when the movie began. Trying to be a modern, unsentimental slice of life, the movie becomes impersonal. This, too, may be intentional. A decade ago, René Clément gave us Zola's good-hearted Gervaise, working to support her children, mistreated by her lover and her husband, coarsened and defeated by the squalid conditions of working-class life. Two years ago, Darling, who thought only of her own pleasure, drifted upward. Joy, the Poor Cow, is somewhere between: a barmaid and demi-whore, she takes care of her child, all right, as she drifts along, mostly downward. Nell Dunn, the author of the novel on which the picture is based, seems to conceive of Joy in terms of the sensuality and happiness possible within her degraded life. The director, Kenneth Loach, seems rather more interested in using Joy as an example of modern urban anomie.

As Joy, Carol White is made up to look so much like Julie Christie that at times one forgets she isn't; John Bindon is the cloddish burglar who impregnates and marries her; and Terence Stamp is the thief she takes up with when her husband goes to prison. The acting of the three leads is subdued, and they are photographed as part of the film's compositions—minus the star lighting and placement within the frame which usually enable the principal performers to stand out. This, together with the sensitive writing of the insistently ordinary lines they speak, makes them seem lifelike. The trouble with actors when "you hardly know they're acting" is that they don't hold your attention. Several of the minor players show a more theatrical zest for their roles, and, seen against the stolidly modulated, undramatic acting of the principals, these conventionally acted bits stand out like music-hall turns—which makes them a welcome relief for the audience. The style of the film is semi-documentary, with frequent candid-camera closeups of working-class faces. What are the connections between the thieves and the work-hardened faces? What is one group saying about the other? Shot with different lenses, the manual workers are obviously cut in, and it isn't even clear where they are physically in relation to the actors, but they give the movie a look of authenticity and promises of social comment, which

31

are then not fulfilled. The hard-bitten faces are used decoratively. The color is rich, with echoes of debauchery and domesticity out of Degas and Vermeer; it's all carefully beautiful, in a way that is both unobjectionable and totally uninteresting. The low life is suffocated in tastefulness. The style signals us unmistakably that the intentions are high, but they are unfortunately never clear. Joy herself doesn't move us to pity or delight or envy. She's just another girl, and, despite the packaged foods and the short skirts and the telly, there's nothing especially modern about her anomie. She's an unlucky poor-man's Darling, but her life wouldn't be much different in another period or if she were proper working class or if the milieu were moved up a notch to the middle class.

When the director of "Poor Cow" did this kind of "fictional human document" on English television, it was considered innovative. On television, where the standard fare is banal make-believe, those principled few who try to treat social problems have to fight for their convictions, and their victories are so rare that banal social comment sometimes passes for art. And there are so many things that television writers and directors may not say or show that what isn't permitted can easily seem to be the most important things to try to do. "Poor Cow" is full of "frank," "adult" touches and talk—full of "daring" television and what would be too daring for television. But in movies plain speech and semi-nudity have already come to seem just a new convention. In these days of accelerated change, even Loach's borrowings from Agnès Varda's "Cleo from 5 to 7" and

32

Godard's "Vivre Sa Vie" seem old-fashioned, but this is probably because Loach uses them so clumsily that he makes them old-fashioned. Techniques that were invented for speed are used in a movie that is almost stately in its rhythms. Joy is treated as a "frank" case study—but of what? If she is just one more example of aimless humanity, neither good nor bad, simply living and taking pleasure where she can, why single her out for our attention unless through her we can see more of others and ourselves? This the movie in some insanely steadfast way refuses to make possible: it never attempts to give us a revelation, a vision, or even an intuition. It doesn't even have a point. It sticks to the ordinary. Because of the determined, conscientious avoidance of the unusual and the surprising—as if that would be "false to life"—the movie is vacuous. The makers of this film mistake predictability for fidelity to life. (Is anybody's life as predictable as this?) An artist working within the method of naturalism surprises us, and convinces us of the truth of what we would never have foreseen; he shows us how much there is in an "ordinary" person, and even why that person appears so "ordinary." To praise Loach for the integrity or "realism" of his conception would be to praise him for his failure as an artist.

Movies, perhaps, are not the great popular art they could be precisely because the mass audience shares this movie's shallowly realistic view of life. The mass audience probably thinks, as Loach seems to think, that being a poor cow *is* all that life is, and that's why the members of the mass audience want to get away from it when they go to the movies.

How many times have you heard something like "When you see life as it is and that people are animals, you go to the movies to escape—you want romance"? There is a temptation for those who have made an ambitious flop to decide that the public won't buy anything "honest," and to use this as a justification for swinging over to making the usual commercial, opportunistic pictures. There are lots of movie hacks who say they made a work of art when they were young and nobody went to see it. They didn't make a work of art. The ones who did don't talk like this, because their old commercial failures are still showing in colleges and film societies all over the world.

February 3, 1968

Making Lawrence More Lawrentian

If you're going to see a movie based on a book you think is worth reading, read the book first. You can never read the book with the same imaginative responsiveness to the author once you have seen the movie. The great French film critic André Bazin believed that even if movies vulgarized and distorted books they served a useful purpose, because they led people to read the books on which the movies were based. But when you read the book after seeing the movie, your mind is saturated with the actors and the images, and you tend to read in terms of the movie, ignoring characters and complexities that were not included in it, because they are not as vivid to you. At worst, the book becomes a souvenir of the movie, an extended reminiscence. (Girls read "Doctor Zhivago" so they can "see more" of Omar Sharif.) Bazin didn't live to find out that reading the book after seeing the movie would become such a mass-audience phenomenon that movies not based on novels would be "novelized" for additional revenue, nor to find out that college students, taking up "film as film," would increasingly reject the whole reading experience as passé. There is a new generation of moviegoers which believes that a movie is *sui generis* and that a critic is betraying a

literary bias—and thus an incompetence at dealing
with film as film—in bringing up a movie's literary
origins. Last year Brendan Gill discussed this problem in relation to "Reflections in a Golden Eye,"
and it recently came up in a symposium on movies
at the New School for Social Research, where the
participating critics were dumbfounded to discover
that some of the younger members of the audience
did not believe that even Albert Camus' "The
Stranger" was relevant to a discussion of Visconti's
film version.

Even if one hadn't read D. H. Lawrence's "The
Fox," it would enter into a discussion of the movie
version, because from the movie one would almost
inevitably assume that Lawrence was to blame for
what seems dated. There are moments in "The
Fox," as there are in "Reflections in a Golden Eye,"
when one is likely to smile a little patronizingly at
dear old D. H. Lawrence, as at poor little Carson
McCullers. As the creaking Freudian wheels turn,
one is tempted to say that nothing dates faster than
the sex revelations of yesteryear. It wasn't until
these movies were over that my head cleared and I
realized that what had seemed so ploddingly literary
that I had automatically blamed it on the original
authors wasn't in the books at all. It seemed so
"literary" just because it wasn't the author—wasn't
Lawrence or McCullers—but an attempt to moder-
nize or clarify the author and to "fill out" the author's material. Lawrence's 1923 novella, like
McCullers' short novel of 1941, is still too subtle to
be made into a movie aimed at a large audience
without "bringing it up to date," which means

bringing in the sexual platitudes that—in movies—are considered Freudian modernism. This has the odd result of making both these movies seem novelistic when they depart most from the novels.

The movie "The Fox" is about two young women—sickly, chattering ultra-feminine Jill (Sandy Dennis) and dark, quiet, strong March (Anne Heywood)—who are trying, rather hopelessly, to run a chicken farm in Canada. A gentle but powerful man (Keir Dullea, in a fantasy portrait of Everywoman's dream) who used to live on their farm returns and puts things in order (thus demonstrating that farming is really man's work). But his proposal of marriage to March awakens the lesbianism dormant in the girls: Jill uses her weakness to make March feel protective, and the women become active (at least, kissing-in-bed) lesbians. Though he and March go out to a convenient little shack and shack up, Jill is still dependent on March; he eliminates Jill, in a scene of implausible and clumsy contrivance, by chopping down a tree so that it hits her. There is also some symbolism about a fox that March has somehow been unable to shoot, although it has been wrecking the girls' farming plans by raiding the hen coop; the man kills the fox and, of course, raids the hen coop himself. The symbolism seems rather quaint and rather extraneous to this triangle—which is pretty much "The Children's Hour" in a woodsy setting—and rather confusing; the ads therefore explain that the fox is the "symbol of the male," and the trade press "clarifies" things even more by explaining that the "shotgun, axe, carving knife, tree, pitchfork, etc." are "phallic symbology." The movie

37

(again like "Reflections") has a solemnly measured manner, which one might assume is the result of following a "classic" in an honorably respectful but too literal-minded way; one seems to wait for the next development rather than enjoy what's going on.

But D. H. Lawrence's "The Fox" is a story about two spinsterish, educated, and refined English ladies, approaching thirty, in the year 1918; the ladies are, as people used to say, attached to each other. The fox of the story does indeed represent the male to March—but to a sexually repressed March. And the male who comes into their lives, and whom March immediately identifies with the fox, because of his smell and look, is a boy of twenty and, instead of a nice big farmer, primarily a hunter. And it's because he is a hunter—in that same mystic sense of willing the death of his prey which reappears in Norman Mailer's recent novel "Why Are We in Vietnam?"—that he is able to kill the inconvenient Jill, doing so right in front of the poor girl's parents. (The parents are one of those "details" that movies eliminate when they want to keep certain characters sympathetic—in the same way that Perry and Dick in the movie of "In Cold Blood" still kill four people but no longer deliberately swerve their car to smash a dog.) This hunter-boy, far from giving March a sexual sample of what she has been missing, is rather afraid of so-much-woman, and at the end of the story D. H. Lawrence undercuts the simple, "Lawrentian" male-female stuff with some impassioned second thoughts about the whole thing. Married to the boy, March is not the submissive female he had hoped for; she is independent and unsettled and unhappy. The fox may have outfoxed himself; he wishes he had left the two women "to kill one another."

The central problem of "The Fox" as a movie is the problem of adaptation. The adapters (Lewis John Carlino and Howard Koch) are neither incompetent nor stupid, but is there a mass market for a story about repressed spinsters in 1918? That being highly questionable, they have made "The Fox" a modern story. But you can hardly make it modern without making it more explicit, and if it's all spelled out, if everyone is sexually aware, if March is the kind of girl who sings a bawdy song like "Roll Me Over" and proceeds to roll around and thrash about in an experienced, if bewildering, way in that shack, you no longer need symbolism. The sex sequence not only makes the symbolism superfluous but disintegrates the characters, because if March is a swinger like this, if she isn't afraid of sex with men, what's she doing in the woods playing house with that frumpy little Jill? The force of the novella is in what Lawrence treats symbolically—the hidden power of sex in the women and the ambivalence of the male. The movie not only brings the hidden to the surface but resolves the male ambivalence in banal male strength. One kind of schoolgirl crush gives way to another. I wonder whether we could watch "The Fox" feeling so relaxed and patronizing about the author who used to be considered sensational if the man were still Lawrence's *boy*.

To take this a step further: My guess is that "The Fox" will meet with less critical opposition than "Reflections in a Golden Eye," just because it is so

sexually explicit that it is tame and "healthy,"
whereas the stifled homosexuality of Marlon Brando's duty-bound Major Penderton is grotesque and
painful. Although Brando's character could hardly
be taken as a cue to go and do likewise, "Reflections" was condemned; the ban became an embarrassment, because where but in the seminaries are
there still any considerable number of *repressed* homosexuals? The scenes of Elizabeth Taylor and
Brian Keith making love in the berry patch could
hardly shock a modern audience, but the fat, ugly
Major putting cold cream on his face, or preening
himself at the mirror, or patting his hair nervously
when he thinks he has a gentleman caller, is so
ghastly that some members of the audience invaria-
bly cut themselves off from him by laughter.
Lawrence's scared boy with a latent-lesbian bride
might have made them laugh, too. Both these movies are about homosexual drives and how they lead
to murder, and I think it's fair to say that neither of
them would have been made even just a few years
ago. And yet it's already too late to make these
movies the way they have been done. "Reflections"
has been furbished with *additional* fetishes, as if the
original weren't Southern and Gothic enough. The
horsewhipping that Elizabeth Taylor gives Brando
—which doesn't appear in the book—is a new antique, and so is the conversation that follows, in
which she explains that the whipping cleared the air
and that he is more agreeable now, so that we are
cued to crank out the Freudian explanation "Oh,
yes, he wanted to be beaten," as we crank out "He
hit the horse because . . ." There is much heavy

cranking to do in both these movies. Is there any reason, then, to see them instead of just reading the slender little books, with their glimpses of character, and an author's distinctive voice, and prose that carries one along? Despite everything that is laboriously wrong with "Reflections," the visual style—like paintings made from photographs—is interesting, and the director, John Huston, and the actors were able to do some extraordinary things with Carson McCullers' conceptions. One cannot imagine earlier reigning idols of the screen (Gable? Tracy?) playing the Brando role, and though his performance doesn't completely come to life—maybe because the Major doesn't have much life in him, and Brando subdued is Brando partly wasted—it nevertheless shows our greatest actor in a serious, complex role, and there are moments when the performance *does* work and Brando shows how good he is. And then Brian Keith does, too. And Elizabeth Taylor is charming as a silly, sensual Southern "lady"—a relief from the movies in which Burton ostentatiously plays down to her and she valiantly tries to act up to him and they're both awful. "The Fox" doesn't have such striking performances, and although it is probably that not very many rising young stars would care to risk the whining Sandy Dennis role, one might uncharitably point out that she had already made an acting style out of postnasal drip. "The Fox" is monumentally unimaginative, but it certainly has been mounted; the color photography is banally handsome, and there's a tricky Lalo Schifrin score to supply excitation. Maybe it is because the adapters and the director,

Mark Rydell, are so plainly wrestling with Lawrence in terms of their commercial idea of honesty—making Lawrence more Lawrentian—that the movie has a simple-minded fascination. It's easy to sink into and soak up, and it may be a popular success, because many people will enjoy the sexy romance, which is pretentious enough to pass for a serious treatment of a classic. This would be no more foolish than to take a detective thriller like "In the Heat of the Night"—which is entertaining because it's a good racial joke about the black Sherlock Holmes and a shuffling, redneck Watson—and inflate it to the status of important drama, as if that inflation was necessary for one to enjoy the picture. Lawrence once sent his Friend a picture of Jonah and the whale, with the caption "Who is going to swallow whom?" This may have some small relevance to his unresolved novella. There's no doubt about the movie's swallowing the book; will moviegoers who then read the book be able to see Lawrence through the blubber?

No matter *how* a movie like "The Fox" might be done—even if it should be done with artistry, and even if Lawrence's conceptions should be retained—it would be unlikely to have the kind of impact that Lawrence's writing had when his books appeared. The movie of "The Stranger" is set in the correct period, the thirties, but that doesn't help to relate it to what Camus' great modern statement of the concept of alienation meant in its period—which, conceptually, was the forties. The picture might be more imaginative, the hero better cast, and so on, but how can the historical impact and importance of the novel be communicated when the idea of alienation has already become conventional—has been reduced to the cut-rate "Cool Hand Luke"? "The Stranger" is a beautiful movie, but it is not an "important" one; it functions on the screen not as a definitive new vision but as a simple story with intelligent overtones—a factual account of Meursault's last days, which, because of the impact the book was to have, now seems almost prealienation, a precursor of Camus. By the time "The Stranger" or a book by D. H. Lawrence is *filmed*, the book has already changed our lives, and the movie is just a famous story. Only if you know the book and what it meant, only if you have a sense of history, does the movie version suggest more, and help to bring back to you what the book represents. To be "important," a movie must deal with characters and situations, whether historical or modern, in terms of the greatest honesty possible in its time—what Lawrence and Camus did in their novels, and Carson McCullers did, on her own scale.

February 10, 1968

Apes Must be Remembered, Charlie

"Planet of the Apes" is a very entertaining movie, and you'd better go see it quickly, before your friends take the edge off it by telling you all about it. They will, because it has the ingenious kind of plotting that people love to talk about. If it were a great picture, it wouldn't need this kind of protection; it's just good enough to be worth the rush. Adapted from a novel by Pierre Boulle, "Planet of the Apes" most closely resembles George Pal's 1960 version of H. G. Wells' 1895 novel "The Time Machine." It's also a little like "Forbidden Planet," the 1956 science-fiction adaptation of "The Tempest," though it's perhaps more cleverly sustained than either of those movies. At times, it has the primitive force of old "King Kong." It isn't a difficult or subtle movie; you can just sit back and enjoy it. That should place the genre closely enough, without spoiling the theme or the plot. The writing, by Michael Wilson and Rod Serling, though occasionally bright, is often fancy-ironic in the old school of poetic disillusion. Even more often, it is crude. But the construction is really extraordinary. What seem to be weaknesses or holes in the idea turn out to be perfectly consistent, and sequences that work only at a simple level of parody while you're watching them turn out to be really funny when the total structure is revealed. You're too busy for much disbelief anyway; the timing of each action or revelation is right on the button. The audience is rushed along with the hero, who keeps going as fast as possible to avoid being castrated or lobotomized. The picture is an enormous, many-layered black joke on the hero and the audience, and part of the joke is the use of Charlton Heston as the hero. I don't think the movie could have been so forceful or so funny with anyone else. Physically, Heston, with his perfect, lean-hipped, powerful body, is a god-like hero; built for strength, he's an archetype of what makes Americans win. He doesn't play a nice guy; he's harsh and hostile, self-centered and hot-tempered. Yet we don't hate him, because he's so magnetically strong; he represents American power—the physical attraction and admiration one feels toward the beauty of strength as well as the moral revulsion one feels toward the ugliness of violence. And he has the profile of an eagle. Franklin Schaffner, who directed "Planet of the Apes," uses the Heston of the preposterous but enjoyable "The Naked Jungle"—the man who is so absurdly a movie-star myth. He is the perfect American Adam to work off some American guilt feelings or self-hatred on, and this is part of what makes this new violent fantasy so successful as comedy.

"Planet of the Apes" is one of the best science-fiction fantasies ever to come out of Hollywood. That doesn't mean it's art. It is not conceived in terms of vision or mystery or beauty. Science-fiction fantasy is a peculiar genre; it doesn't seem to result in much literary art, either. This movie is efficient and craftsmanlike; it's conceived and carried out for maximum popular appeal, though with a cautionary message, and with some attempts to score little points against various forms of Establishment thinking. These swifties are not Swift, and the movie's posture of moral superiority is somewhat embarrassing. Brechtian pedagogy doesn't work in Brecht, and it doesn't work here, either. At best, this is a slick commercial picture, with its elements carefully engineered—pretty girl (who unfortunately doesn't seem to have had acting training), comic relief, thrills, chases—but when expensive Hollywood engineering works, as it rarely does anymore, the results can be impressive. Schaffner has thought out the action in terms of the wide screen, and he uses space and distance dramatically. Leon Shamroy's excellent color photography helps to make the vast exteriors (shot in Utah and Arizona) an integral part of the meaning. The editing, though, is somewhat distracting; several times there is a cut and then a view of what we have already seen now seen from a different angle or from much higher up. The effect is both static (we don't seem to be getting anywhere) and overemphatic (we are conscious of being told to look at the same thing another way). The makeup (there is said to be a million dollars worth) and the costuming of the actors playing the apes are rather witty, and the apes have a wonderful nervous, hopping walk. The best little hopper is Kim Hunter, as an ape lady doctor; she somehow manages to give a better performance in this makeup than she has ever given on the screen before.

Sandy Dennis, the hapless heroine of "Sweet November," is wasting away. Queried about the nameless disease, her friend Theodore Bikel explains, "It's quite rare, but it's incurable." The movie is also afflicted with an incurable disease. "Sweet November" is the kind of squishy whimsey that is always referred to as "a woman's picture." This means not that it was written or directed by a woman but that, as the trade press says, it will "undoubtedly appeal to femme audiences." Doubt might give us hope. It's a story about a kook who is also a "doomed" girl—a synthesis of the "smart," Broadway-style repartee of "Barefoot in the Park" and "Any Wednesday" and "A Thousand Clowns," with the worst of Robert Nathan and Margaret ("The Constant Nymph") Kennedy. Each month, our gallant, forlorn heroine takes into her life and her bed a different man with a problem, for therapeutic purposes—his, not hers. Impotents presumably need not apply. The nature of the therapy is not disclosed, but the man seems to be considered cured when he falls in love with her. Jennifer Jones was the forties specialist in this kind of swill, and before that, in the thirties, the genre had already become so depleted that only a superlatively gifted technician like Elisabeth Bergner had the otherworldly grace to make these frail child-women halfway tolerable. Here we are in the sixties, and box manufacturer Anthony Newley is liberated by love; he releases the poet in himself with this breakthrough composition (which also serves as the advertising copy for the movie):

47

A girl I know,
she is partly mad.

Yet beyond that smile,
she is partly sad.

She is partly calm,
she is partly wild.

But she is mostly woman—

No.

She is mostly child.

This movie, like so many others lately, assumes that characters are liberated and healthy when they behave like kids—flying model airplanes, and so on. There seems to be almost no way for a sixties movie to suggest that adults might take pride and pleasure in their work, or might need to find work in which they can take pride and pleasure. The gamine characters in early movies were often pathetically unable to survive. Now they have become innocent kooks who triumph. "Sweet November" plays it both ways. A doomed kook. It's the kind of terrible idea that just might make money. Sandy Dennis, however, has exhausted her bag of tics. Yes, her beautiful, rabbity smile is still touching, and she looks sweet in her little pinafores that might have been designed by Beatrix Potter. As a crazy lady, junior division, she has a certain authenticity, and she could be very amusing in small parts. But she doesn't have the range and variety for starring roles.

The direction, by Robert Ellis Miller, is flat—as if neither he nor anyone else had any confidence in the material. He and the rest were right, of course. Let's suppose that Sandy Dennis had little choice and that Miller was stuck with the assignment—that still doesn't explain how Michel Legrand could have composed and conducted the maudlin score, which could be self-parody if it had any wit. Newley's poem is called "Enigma," but the only enigma posed by "Sweet Novermber" is: Who is responsible? That is to say: Who is guilty? The producers, Jerry Gershwin and Elliott Kastner? Did they encourage Herman Raucher, the author of this "original"? There still seems to be an attraction for movie audiences in a kind of subnormal philosophizing issuing from the smiling mouths of unfortunates—Irene Dunne, paralyzed in a wheelchair, singing "Wishing will make it so," or Sidney Poitier, in "To Sir, with Love," hiding his sorrow at the racial discrimination he suffers while encouraging the young to go out and conquer the world with good manners. This is the miserable tradition in which dying Sandy Dennis spews out such wisdom as "People must be remembered, Charlie. Otherwise, they were never here at all. All we are are the people who remember us." She's an icky little rabbit Babbitt. If you're wondering why "Sweet November" opened in February, the answer is that it's Radio City Music Hall's valentine to the public. I'm sure pictures like this give people pimples.

Sickly "Sweet November," with its sex therapy, should provide Carol Burnett with great material for parody, and Jonathan Winters might be advised to take a look at Richard Burton in "Doctor Faustus."

Others are advised to wait for Winters' version. Perhaps by the time an actor is in a position to make a movie of Marlowe's "Doctor Faustus," further dealing with the Devil is anticlimactic. "Doctor Faustus" might at least have been the record of a good performance. Then it would be easy to overlook the misguided attempts at cinematic effect—the visual redundancies (if Faustus says "gold" or "pearls," the screen shows gold or pearls), the ominous, funereal music, the Technicolored beauties parading like the Goldwyn Girls. But Burton gives a dead, muffled reading. And so, despite an imposing young Mephistopheles (Andreas Teuber), "Doctor Faustus" becomes the dullest episode yet in the great-lovers-of-history series that started with "Cleopatra." Eventually, Burton gets to the speech that begins "Was this the face that launched a thousand ships" and ends "And none but thou shalt be my paramour!," and it is clear that Faustus and Helen of Troy are not characters from Marlowe or actors playing them; they are Liz and Dick, Dick and Liz—the King and Queen of a porny comic strip.

February 17, 1968

A Great Folly,
and a Small One

"She is madonna in an art as wild and young as her sweet eyes," Vachel Lindsay wrote of Mae Marsh, who died on Tuesday of last week. She is the heroine of D. W. Griffith's "Intolerance," which came out in 1916 and which will soon have its annual showing at the Museum of Modern Art. "Intolerance" is one of the two or three most influential movies ever made, and I think it is also the greatest. Yet many of those who are interested in movies have never seen it. "The Birth of a Nation," which Griffith brought out in 1915 (with Mae Marsh as the little sister who throws herself off a cliff through "the opal gates of death"), still draws audiences, because of its scandalous success. But those who see it projected at the wrong speed, so that it becomes a "flick," and in mutilated form—cut and in black-and-white or faded color—are not likely to develop enough interest in Griffith's art to go to see his other films. "Intolerance" was a commercial failure in 1916, and it has never had much popular reputation. After the reactions to "The Birth of a Nation," Griffith was so shocked that people could think he was anti-Negro that he decided to expand some material he had been working on and make it an attack on bigotry throughout the ages. "Intolerance" was intended to be virtuous and uplifting. It turned out to be a great, desperate, innovative, ruinous film—perhaps the classic example of what later came to be known as *cinéma maudit*. Griffith had already, in the over four hundred movies he had made—from the one-reelers on up to "The Birth of a Nation"—founded the art of screen narrative; now he wanted to try something more than simply telling the story of bigotry in historical sequence. He had developed cross-cutting in his earlier films, using discontinuity as Dickens did in his novels. In "Intolerance," he attempted to tell four stories taking place in different historical periods, crosscutting back and forth to ancient Babylon, sixteenth-century France, the modern American slums, and Calvary. He was living in an era of experiments with time in the other arts, and although he worked in a popular medium, the old dramatic concepts of time and unity seemed too limiting; in his own way he attempted what Pound and Eliot, Proust and Virginia Woolf and Joyce were also attempting, and what he did in movies may have influenced literary form as much as they did. He certainly influenced them. The events of "Intolerance" were, he said, set forth "as they might flash across a mind seeking to parallel the life of the different ages." It doesn't work. "Intolerance" almost becomes a film symphony, but four stories intercut and rushing toward simultaneous climaxes is, at a basic level, too naïve a conception to be anything more than four melodramas told at once. The titles of "Intolerance" state the theme more than the action shows it, and the four parallel stories were probably just too much and too bewildering for audiences. Also, the idealistic attack on hypocrisy, cruelty, and persecution may have seemed uncomfortably pacifistic in 1916.

No simple framework could contain the richness of what Griffith tried to do in this movie. He tried to force his stories together, and pushed them into ridiculous patterns to illustrate his theme. But his excitement—his madness—binds together what his arbitrarily imposed theme does not. "Intolerance" is like an enormous, extravagantly printed collection of fairy tales. The book is too thick to handle, too richly imaginative to take in, yet a child who loves stories will know that this is the treasure of treasures. The movie is the greatest extravaganza and the greatest folly in movie history, an epic celebration of the potentialities of the new medium— lyrical, passionate, and grandiose. No one will ever again be able to make last-minute rescues so suspenseful, so beautiful, or so absurd. In movies, a masterpiece is of course a folly. "Intolerance" is charged with visionary excitement about the power of movies to combine music, dance, narrative, drama, painting, and photography—to do alone what all the other arts together had done. And to do what they had failed to. Griffith's dream was not only to reach the vast audience but to express it, to make of the young movie art a true democratic art.

Griffith's movies are great not because he developed the whole range of film techniques—the editing, the moving camera, the closeup, the flexible use of the frame so that it becomes a pinpoint of light or a CinemaScope shape at will—but because he invented or pioneered those techniques out of an expressive need for them. When Griffith is at his best, you are hardly aware of how short the shots are, how brilliantly they are edited, how varied the camera angles are. Reaching for color, he not only had the prints of his movies dyed in different hues selected to convey the mood of the sequences but had crews of girls adding extra color by hand, frame by frame. Still dissatisfied, he had the projectionists throw beams of red or blue light to intensify the effects. Reaching for sound, he had scores specially prepared and orchestras playing in the pit. In "Intolerance," he overstretched. There is hardly anything that has been attempted in movies since (except for sound effects, of course) that was not tried in "Intolerance." "The Birth of a Nation," the longest American film up to that date, was rehearsed for six weeks, shot in nine weeks, and edited in three months; it cost a hundred thousand dollars— a record-breaking budget in those days. "Intolerance" cost several times as much. The huge statue-cluttered Babylonian set, which is the most famous of all movie sets, is big in the way DeMille's sets were to be big later on—a picture-postcard set—and neither the camera nor any of the players seems to know what to do with it. The steps on this set undoubtedly inspired Eisenstein's Odessa Steps sequence, but the action that Griffith staged on them looks mechanical and confused. The movie had got too big, and even Griffith was crushed by the weight of it. Yet the enormous project released his imagination, and there are incomparable images—for example, the death of the young mountain girl, with the toy chariot drawn by doves at her feet—and miraculously successful sequences: the prison scenes, later imitated in the Warner Brothers social-protest films of the thirties, and almost reproduced in "I Am a Fugitive from a Chain Gang"; the strike scenes, which influenced the Russians; the great night-fighting scenes, originally in red, which are imitated in practically every spectacle.

One can trace almost every major tradition and most of the genres, and even many of the metaphors, in movies to their sources of Griffith. The Ku Klux Klan rides of "The Birth of a Nation" became the knights of Eisenstein's "Alexander Nevsky"; the battle scenes, derived from Mathew Brady, influenced almost all subsequent war films, and especially "Gone with the Wind." A history of Russian movies could be based on the ice breaking up in Griffith's "Way Down East," taking that ice through Pudovkin's epic "Mother" up to Chukhrai's "Clear Skies," where the thaw after Stalin's death is represented literally by the breaking up of ice. One can also trace the acting styles. Mae Marsh returned to us via the young Garbo and other Scandinavian actresses, and Lillian Gish returned to us via Brigitte Helm of "Metropolis," Dorothea Wieck of "Mädchen in Uniform," and *most* of the European actresses of the twenties. Griffith's stylized lyric tragedy "Broken Blossoms" (which will also be shown at the Museum of Modern Art), though smaller in scope than "The Birth" or "Intolerance," is, I think, the third of a trio of great works. It is the source of much of the poignancy of Fellini's "La Strada." Donald Crisp's brutal prizefighter became Anthony Quinn's Zampano, and Lillian Gish's childish waif must have strongly influenced the conception of Giulietta Masina's role as well as her performance.

Griffith used Lillian Gish and Mae Marsh contrastingly. In his films, Lillian Gish is a frail, floating heroine from romantic novels and poems—a maiden. She is the least coarse of American screen actresses; her grace is pure and fluid and lilylike. She is idealized femininity, and her purity can seem rather neurotic and frightening. Mae Marsh is less ethereal, somehow less actressy, more solid and "normal," and yet, in her own way, as exquisite and intuitive. She is our dream not of heavenly beauty, like Gish, but of earthly beauty, and sunlight makes her youth more entrancing. She looks as if she could be a happy, sensual, ordinary woman. The tragedies that befall her are accidents that could happen to any of us, for she has never wanted more than common pleasures. There is a passage in "Intolerance" in which Mae Marsh, as a young mother who has had her baby taken away from her, grows so distraught that she becomes a voyeur, peeping in at windows to simper and smile at other people's babies. It's horrible to watch, because she has always seemed such a sane sort of girl. When Lillian Gish, trapped in the closet in "Broken Blossoms," spins around in terror, we feel terror for all helpless, delicate beauty, but when Mae Marsh is buffeted by fate every ordinary person is in danger. Mae Marsh died at seventy-two, but the girl who twists her hands in the courtroom scene of "Intolerance" is the image of youth-in-trouble forever.

It took Griffith years to pay off the disaster of "Intolerance," and though he later made box-office successes, like "Way Down East," he wasn't financially strong enough to keep his independence. By 1925, he was forced to go to work for Paramount as a contract director, which meant doing the scripts they handed him, and doing them *their* way. By the thirties, he had sunk even further; he was called in to fix films that other directors had messed up, and he didn't receive screen credits anymore. There was so much emphasis in Hollywood on the newest product that it was feared his name would make people think a picture old-fashioned. Eventually, alcoholic and embittered, he could get no work at all. Until his death, in 1948, Griffith lived in a hotel room in near obscurity in the Hollywood he had created— which was filled with famous directors he had trained and famous stars he had discovered. They could not really help him. Motion pictures had become too big a business for sentiment, or for art.

Albert Finney directed "Charlie Bubbles," in which he appears in the persona of a rich, famous writer. Though Charlie is a success, life has no romance or passion or excitement for him. He feels cut off from everything, and he'd just as soon drift away from it all. The details are well written (by Shelagh Delaney), and the movie is photographed by Peter Suschitsky in an extremely complicated style that attempts to produce for us the artificiality and flat unreality of how things look to Charlie—the world with some vital dimension omitted. The movie is glum Charlie's life seen through his eyes, and since he sees people joylessly, with apathy and distaste, much of it consists of closeups of semi-repulsive faces that look cold and dead. The entire pain-fully monotonous movie is based on this single small, unoriginal idea—the kind of idea that could be one element, or good for a short sequence. This unfertile ground was already plowed to dust in "La Notte" (and Antonioni managed to do a few other things besides); Finney takes a little handful of leftover ashes and holds it on his tongue. A pretty girl, or even the sound of a beautiful voice would disrupt the whole movie, because then we would have to ask, "Why doesn't Charlie care enough to reach out for anyone or anything? Did he ever feel any differ-ent? Has success changed him? Is he a *good* writer? And if so, why is he alienated?" We glumly watch glum Charlie's life, finding no development or varia-tion from the static mood set at the beginning, and these questions are never dealt with. There are some felicitous lines, and there is a good dramatic scene when Charlie comes back to his ex-wife's house after looking for his son, whom he had borrowed for the day and lost: he and his ex-wife quarrel, and we can see that both are right, both are wrong. But most of the movie is filled with unconvincing details —hostile servants who could easily be fired, an adoring fan-secretary whom no sensible writer would keep on. Surely these trivia—the servant problems that go with success—can't be what makes Charlie feel empty? Does Finney provide these false grounds for Charlie's desolation because he, too, doesn't know what Charlie's problem is?

February 24, 1968

That Clean Old Peasant Again

"The Two of Us" is a simple, decent story, told in a simple, direct, unaffected way. The late James Agee might perhaps have brought out his full panoply of loving terms for it, because it is bare and plain and true and honest and, of course, tender and disciplined, and it isn't artificial or corrupt, and it doesn't exploit or overdramatize its subject, and I suppose one could even say it is vigorous and healthy and masculine. It is a film that one can—indeed, must—respect, and I wish I liked it better, because not liking such an unspoiled film lays one open to the charge of not being good enough, not being pure in heart. But this was a side of Agee's criticism I never could fully accept; I always wondered if he really liked "Farrebique" (the life cycle on a French farm) as much as he said, or if he only thought he *should*. I come from a farm, and even "Sunset Boulevard" is closer to my experience than "Farrebique." Cocteau's magnificent Beast with the smoking claws seems closer than the cattle of "Farrebique," because it's exciting in a way that those cattle will never be. Was Agee's moviegoing so virtuous, or did he, perhaps, now and then, like the rest of us, enjoy decadent, sleazy, slick commercial pictures? We ought to be able to see a reasonably lousy picture without feeling we've been violated. Agee always seemed to feel personally betrayed by synthetic elements in a movie, by "sophistication."

Because Agee was so great a critic, there is a tendency to take over his terms, but his excessive virtue may have been his worst critical vice. Agee's demands were, in some ways, both impossibly high for the movie medium and peculiarly childlike. As a result, we may need to be liberated from guilt both for enjoying irresponsible movies and for failing to respond to works of such impeccable moral character as "The Two of Us," but a movie that, to use Agee's language, is tender and full of "reverence for reality" and all can still seem pretty thin, and there's so little going on in "The Two of Us" that one has to begin thinking of it as an idyll-fable, which has never been my idea of a good time. I don't think we would be expected to respond to this sort of thing in literature, but, possibly because of Agee's influence, we are expected to have very simple tastes when it comes to movies. Yet simple people in simple stories made some of us yawn even as children—which is probably why we started going to movies. The place for goodness is in life, not on the screen. I realize that Agee used words like "love" and "purity" in order to get away from clever language and professional jargon—that he wanted language as well as movies cleansed—but though movies need cleansing more than ever, we mustn't throw the whore out with the bath water. Do we want to be left with the "gentle irony" of a galumphingly lovable old anti-Semitic peasant romping around with a child in Vichy France and never realizing that the child is

Jewish? The child thus becomes a living O. Henry twist, like Sidney Poitier in "The Slender Thread."

To be half chaste is an abomination. For the kind of movie it is, "The Two of Us" should be *more* chaste; its simple artlessness is clean and good, but its director, Claude Berri, may be getting credit for purity because he doesn't (yet) know how to be corrupt. When he tries for comic situations, he's a clumsy amateur. When I saw the old man (Michel Simon) play ball with the boy and break a window, I closed my eyes in remembrance of all the movie generations of infantile adults who had done the same; the first time the Georges Delerue music commented on the simple joys of life, I forced a smile, but the same music kept coming back with the same comment. There was that arch stuff between the old man and his wife about vegetarianism, and then there was that damned dog. I believe that my own dogs are prescient, but I can't stand prescience in other people's dogs, and Simon's spoon-fed mutt who wears a bib at table is a bit much. The big problem is, of course, Simon. If ever there was an actor qualified by appearance and style to be the essence of dirty old man, it is Michel Simon (and that is how Jean Vigo and Jean Renoir used him, even when he was young). As a mischievous, dear old peasant, he's a fraudulent old actor, and he gives an impure and unconvincing performance.

There are some beautiful moments in "The Two of Us," but they don't involve the adult actors, whose roles are as one-dimensional as the grownups in a second-grade reader. But Berri, who has probably drawn much of the character of the child,

Claude, played by Alain Cohen, from himself, has endowed the child with a wonderfully complex nature, so that he is both baby and shrewd adult, lovingly dependent and resourcefully tough. And Alain Cohen is marvellous-*looking* for the role; there is a moment when this plump and happy child has his head shaved, and suddenly the horrors of the concentration camps and what happened to children just like him open before us. That, I think, is the one moment of great artistry in the movie—though there is also, for a few seconds, a memorable image of a little girl holding a goose. This is quite a lot to get from a movie, but I don't think that in order to take this away with us we should have to pretend about the quality of the rest. There's no point in over-valuing one's lost innocence, artistically speaking. Once it's lost, it's lost. Pretending it isn't is sentimentality.

In his novel "To an Early Grave," Wallace Markfield made Jewish intellectuals more "Jewish" than they are. When I moved to New York from the West a couple of years ago, friends handed me Markfield's book—for orientation, I assume, because Jewish intellectuals are indigenous to New York. Exported to the University of Minnesota or San Francisco State, they are no longer "intellectuals"; they are just writers or professors. The book was said to be funny, but I hated it; it was too petty and meanspirited for satire. In Sidney Lumet's film version, "Bye Bye Braverman," the characters could hardly pass for intellectuals, but they have become even *more* "Jewish." Now, however, they're Jewish comics. Though the movie isn't meanspirited, it isn't very satirical, either; it's crudely affectionate, and often rather gross. Jewish actors playing Jews have a tendency to overdo it, as if they thought they would be taken for Gentiles if they behaved normally, and Lumet appears to have encouraged this. One keeps wishing the camera would back away a bit. But the Jewish rhetoric has some juice in it, and there's some vitality in the movie, as there almost always is in Lumet's work. No one is ever likely to say that he was put to sleep by Sidney Lumet's good taste. Nevertheless, the milieu is so special that parts of the movie may be almost incomprehensible to those who don't know the Markfield novel or the rather small group of people it is based on—particularly since the movie is so sloppily made and thrown together (with coy musical bridges) that there is no exposition or development of who they are and what it all means. Only a careless director or an extraordinarily chauvinistic New Yorker (Lumet may be both) would think that quick shots showing the characters assembling from different parts of the city would "place" them for us. Despite the importance of verbal comedy to the whole conception, the dialogue is often wrecked by clumsy, imprecise readings, and though the sound is in sync, the voices seem disembodied (especially Zohra Lampert's). If the movie had been better constructed, the long speech made by Alan King as the rabbi might be very good indeed. Jack Warden is badly miscast as a poet, and Sorrell Booke's role—that of a fussy little book reviewer—is such obvious low comedy that he doesn't get much of a chance (though he has some mad movements of his head that are reminiscent of Oscar Levant at his best). George Segal may try a little too hard, but it's good to see him in a role that gives him a chance to stretch himself; as usual, he seems too likable—and potentially too funny—for the role he's playing. Joseph Wiseman's cold, bitter characterization of an older-style "cultured" literary figure is remarkably effective in the midst of so much emotional wallowing, and Godfrey Cambridge, who picks up the pace, brings the movie a welcome contrast.

The scale of the Italian-made Western "The Good, the Bad and the Ugly" is what most differentiates it from American-made Westerns. My guess is that everything is made vast because Europeans love the wide-open spaces in our Westerns and because Sergio Leone, the director, wanted to outdo the scenic effects in American Westerns. If a man crosses a street in Leone's Santa Fe, the street looks half a mile wide; a farmer's hut has rooms opening into rooms into the distance, like the Metropolitan Museum; the hotel in a cowtown has a plush lobby big enough for a political convention. The movie is like "High Noon" and "The Ox Bow Incident" and a dozen others all scrambled together and playing in a giant echo chamber. The bad men must then be enormously, preposterously evil—larger-than-life parodies, as in a Kurosawa film—and each wound inflicted is insanely garish. Yet, stupid as it all is, and gruesome, the change of scale is rather fascinating. This Italian Western, set in our Civil War period, looks more foreign to us than an ordinary

Italian film—which gives rise to speculation about how we alter the scale, and hence the meaning, in our movie versions of foreign stories. Because, although this huge Italian Western (shot in Spain) imitates the externals of American Westerns, it makes those externals so much bigger that what the American Western hero stands for—everything that audiences are supposed to identify with—would look too small, and so it has simply been omitted. The result seems to be popular with American men, who go to relax and enjoy the action; they probably hardly notice—and wouldn't care anyway—that the Western theme is missing.

On paper, "A Matter of Innocence" probably looked like a winner. On a cruise with her rich aunt, levelheaded Polly seizes the opportunity to be seduced by an Indian gigolo in Singapore, because in London men don't make many passes at a plain girl who works behind the counter of her mother's bakeshop. The script, by Keith Waterhouse and Willis Hall, from a Noël Coward story, is full of once-naughty "worldly" characters and situations that are now pleasantly antiquated: the blondined hairdresser and his German-sailor boyfriend who doesn't speak a word of English; the bitchy Oriental dragon lady out of an old Anna May Wong movie; the rich Englishwoman who stuffs herself at lunch, delicately lowers herself into a swimming pool, and sinks. "A Matter of Innocence" should have been a charming romantic trifle, with some wicked little touches—the kind of thing that used to be called "delicious." But it's a mess. No one could accuse the director, Guy Green, of being a Camp; he plods through this amusing script as if he were back in "A Patch of Blue." And this movie, which needed to be carried by directorial style and to be visually graceful and witty, has been poorly photographed in Universal's hideous, cheap-looking color. (The shots hardly ever match, the faces have a greenish tinge in one shot and are yellow in the next, and the time of day keeps wobbling.) Does Michel Legrand's music get worse every week, or is it just that the most recent offense always seems the worst? But Hayley Mills is surprisingly good (especially considering some of her recent performances), and, as the gigolo, Shashi Kapoor reads his parodistic lines with lovely comic inflections.

March 2, 1968

Business as Usual

There is a moment of frustration in "We Still Kill the Old Way" in which the hero, Gian Maria Volonte, presses his clenched fingers against Irene Papas's leg, just above the knee. He doesn't get any further, but that moment has more desire and passion and sex in it than several recent pictures full of beds. "We Still Kill the Old Way" is a unusual thriller, for it's not about a big heist or a cute gang of thieves and it doesn't ingratiate itself by making things easy for the hero or the audience. Based on Leonardo Sciascia's "A Man's Blessing," it's a thriller with a theme—as, in a sense, "The Trial" and "The Castle" are, and though the movie isn't pretentious about it, it has probably been influenced by Kafka. The professor hero—a man who has always been an outsider—finds himself involved in a crime in his own Mafia-ridden Sicilian home town, and this familiar region becomes as terrifying and incomprehensible as the desert in a Paul Bowles story. One can experience all philosophical systems' collapsing at home and it turns home into a desert. His life begins to resemble paranoid fantasy—which, the movie suggests, is what life is for people who live in a corrupt society. In the usual thriller, the man trying to solve the crime gets caught in a larger network of crime until he tracks down Mr. Big and exposes him. In this movie, there is no one to expose Mr. Big *to* because Mr. Big is all there is. The very concept of justice doesn't exist here, so the innocent professor becomes a fool.

It's easy to present fantasy on the screen, but to show a man's life in completely realistic terms as this film does and make us experience it as fantasy is difficult. The director, Elio Petri, tightens the hold on us as the hero becomes more desperately helpless and we begin to realize that there is no way out. It's not an "important" movie or an innovative one, and Petri does not seem to be a strikingly original talent, but he's a solidly professional young movie-maker, and one never feels superior to this picture, as so often happens with thrillers. Petri keeps one tense and uneasy, wary, expecting the worst at each moment. His method is indirect, and he exposes entangled social relations without comment. The island looks hot and barbaric, ominous and yet teeming with life in the way movie locations look only when the director and the cinematographer really know what they're doing. Volonte is one of those rare actors who are so believable on camera that one is caught up in the character rather than in the performance. As the politician who knows how to get along, Gabriele Ferzetti (the hero of "L'Avventura") is more actorish, but he, too, is smoothly convincing—perfectly weak, perfectly worldly. Irene Papas is perhaps rather too inscrutable, but she is powerful and effective in her role; one never doubts that she will survive in this society. At the end, in her white wedding dress, her black eyes shining, she seems as strong as corruption.

What is Paul Newman doing in "The Secret War of Harry Frigg"? Lately, Newman and some of our other best actors have been saying they want to direct, because acting doesn't give them enough opportunity to express and extend themselves creatively. Just when they are in a position to test themselves as actors, to take the risks that count, to prove that it has all been worth it, they want to play a different game, in which, of course, they begin at the top, so they never have to learn how to play it—and in which, because they know so much less about it than they do about acting, they don't know when they're bad or how bad they are. If only, instead of trying the director's trade, they respected acting more—and learned which directors to work with. Paul Newman, at just the time in his life when his face is ready for roles with some depth—a time when he is physically right for a great role, like Tommy Wilhelm in Saul Bellow's "Seize the Day"— is playing stupid, loutish Harry Frigg, as if in preparation for a TV series. How can an actor who is interested in becoming a director choose to work with Jack Smight *twice?* Smight directed Newman in "Harper," and if I were asked to pick the director one should emulate least, I would probably give him strong consideration; after watching the embarrassed faces of some of the actors in "The Secret War of Harry Frigg" I think he might be a popular choice. And the script, by Peter Stone and Frank Tarloff, does not seem superior to the direction.

Is Universal Pictures one of the "Majors" or is it just the biggest B-picture factory, producing more cheap films than Monogram or Republic ever did? I've never walked out on a Paul Newman picture before, but then he hasn't appeared in B pictures before, either. "The Secret War of Harry Frigg" is a stillborn service comedy photographed in a process called Techniscope, which produces a wide-screen image at minimum expense; the effect, in cavernous Radio City Music Hall, is of watching a blown-up 16-millimetre movie. The dim images, never in clear focus, are flat and ugly. Paul Newman seems to keep hiding his face from the camera (as indeed he should), but when he faces front he can't be seen clearly anyway. Perhaps the calculation behind this sort of penny-pinching is that people will come to a Paul Newman picture and that it hardly matters how they see him as long as they know he's there. Now that the old studio heads are gone and businessmen from other fields have taken their places, will economies of this sort become common in the industry? Since the businessmen have links to television that are at least as strong as their links to movies, it may not disturb them that a picture like "The Secret War of Harry Frigg" doesn't compete qualitatively with the best entertainment on television. A television show like the Rowan and Martin "Laugh-In" I saw on February 26th or almost any Carol Burnett show is better acted, better written, infinitely better directed, and even superior technically.

March 9, 1968

The Freedom
to Make Product

"I make films the way I make love," says Claude
Lelouch. "I think it is a mistake for a director to
trust someone else with the camerawork. It's as
though Van Gogh might have given his brush to
someone else." And then, just in case we thought,
Ah, yes, the fervor of youth, filmmakers often don't
know what they're saying, he polishes himself off
with "My films are for a world in which the concept
of 'alienation' has all but replaced that of 'love.' If
the audience can experience joy—though vicarious—
in response to them, then I will feel that I have been
a success." When a man has made the greatest
curtain speech since Jean Hagen's in "Singin' in the
Rain," it seems almost gratuitously analytical to
point out that if his films were good we could experience joy and it wouldn't have to be vicarious. I
don't trust the American directors who talk about
the new creative freedom, either. A director who has
had a box-office hit regards his success as proof that
Hollywood now offers artists freedom. Most of the
new "free" filmmakers want only to be successful at
"moving" us anyway; that's their definition of art.
There's a little specially equipped movie theatre in
Los Angeles with each seat wired to test audience
responses to a film. Maybe we can't help responding

the way the film companies want us to—with excitement and fear and laughter—but we sure ought to think about it afterward.

Try analyzing the appeal of a film in the presence of a person who was moved by it and you'll find that no matter how knowledgeable he is about the techniques of emotional manipulation developed in the mass media, he considers a film that moves him to be a good film and, if he was *deeply* moved by it, a work of art. He may be appalled by the propaganda power of the films he disapproves of and he may be disgusted by the way that films he considers vulgar or stupid affect others, but if *he* is moved he somehow considers this the final word on the subject. Yet a competent, cunning hack director can almost always touch our soft spots by certain scenes of deprivation or loss, or by developing audience identification with a good, sensitive hero and then showing him being beaten. The tears of the kids sitting near me in "Cool Hand Luke" were as shrewdly forced out of them as the moisture squeezed out at each showing of "The Sound of Music." The techniques of excitation are much the same, though the content is shaped differently to manipulate a different audience; "Cool Hand Luke" is a tearjerker for hip high-school students, the other a tearjerker for all squares everywhere, even the vestigial square in most of us. This has as little to do with art as the sales appeal of a television commercial or what makes a wisecracking Broadway show click (and, of course, many of us resist or remain unmoved). A lot of skills are involved in all these, however, and there are so many practitioners in these fields who are

THE FREEDOM TO MAKE PRODUCT

inept that a smart practitioner is soon acclaimed a
genius, though his method may resemble cattle
prods.

What is the difference between being moved by an
artist in ways that are aesthetically valid and being
moved by a shrewd operator? Not only do movies
combine many of the tricks of the other media but
there are many genres in which the operators' tricks
seem perfectly legitimate. In a Hitchcock thriller, it's
fun to be in the position of the mouse nibbling at
the cheese, to experience danger—yes, in this case,
vicariously. We know we're being teased and played
with, and that's just what we wanted. And there are
great melodramatic films, like "The Birth of a Nation" and "Citizen Kane," in which the directors use
both ways of moving us, and it's almost impossible
to sort them out. But, in general, perhaps we can
make the distinction by comparing the films of an
artist—say, those of Jean Renoir, who opens up a
subject for us, or the Antonioni of "L'Avventura,"
or Godard, who holds his cards face up to the
audience, or even a movie that is an artistic failure,
like Irvin Kershner's "The Luck of Ginger Coffey,"
but nevertheless is an artistic attempt—with, say,
the films of Edward ("The Carpetbaggers")
Dmytryk or Stanley Kramer (the latest, "Guess
Who's Coming to Dinner") or Robert Aldrich (the
latest, "The Dirty Dozen") or Mark Robson (the
latest, "Valley of the Dolls"), who, even though we
may enjoy some of their movies, depend for their
effects on touching a place where we're already vulnerable, rousing us or shocking us or making us
chortle. They hit us as if we were "prepared" pi-

anos—they hit and we twang. What makes it so easy for them is that they don't even have to do the preparation. An artist has to win our consent to his vision so that we can see as he does. But the piano player just strikes the keys that circumstances, current attitudes and conventions, and various forms of ignorance and fear prepare. In wartime, he hits the patriotic notes, in a period of apathy the violent ones, and he knows which are the constants— titillation, or the eyes welling with tears that will make our eyes well with tears, and so on. The new acclaimed artist may succeed because he is a more up-to-date piano player, who grasps that audiences are already prepared for a different tune. When audiences tire of his tune, they complain, as of Frank Capra, or, more recently, Elia Kazan, that he's lost his touch.

Once the question of how we are moved and the quality of the emotions we feel is raised, another question comes up: If audiences like being worked over—if they enjoy the exhausting emotional workout they get from a picture like "The Dirty Dozen," and they seem to—will many (or any) of them still care for the subtler, not so immediate or so easy, less violent pleasures of movie art? The emotional shorthand of television—climaxes with a minimum of preparation—has been developed so that the audience won't get away. Like the flip-page sex that authors of pulps now put in, so that the man in the drugstore can open the book anywhere and reach within a few pages a passage that makes him want to buy, the television director learns to keep socking the viewers so they won't get bored, so he won't lose them. They may have just tuned in, and he's got to hold them for the commercial. Similarly, the man who directs the commercial has to hook them fast with the speeded-up visual accoutrements of romance or a fast bit of comedy to keep them for the sell, which, in this new form of theatre, is the revelation. The men who have learned these lessons graduate to movies, where they try to keep up the same mechanical pace irrespective of subject or meaning, and where, increasingly, they're working with the flip-page-sex authors, who have mastered the knack of turning out a book in ten days and can produce a TV script or a movie script with the practiced indifference to quality of a short order cook. And as this kind of material floods the market and gives audiences immediate sensations (audiences that may very possibly be interested only in excitation and be indifferent to theme anyway), the very notion of movie art, or even craftsmanship, begins to seem old-fashioned, "classical"—too slow in development perhaps, or too painstaking, or too "personal." There's no doubt that the craftsmanship of the early John Ford ("The Whole Town's Talking," "Stagecoach") or of William Wyler ("The Letter") doesn't look as smart as Lelouch's. And I think it's doubtful that audiences who enjoyed a Western like "The Professionals"—and it is, in some basically mechanical but astute way, enjoyable—would react as much to the qualities of a fine, quiet example of the genre like "Ride the High Country." It's possible that audiences in general care much less even for the visual qualities of motion pictures than has been supposed. It's possible, for example, that most movies could abandon the whole concept of matching shots (with the expense that it entails of arranging lights and waiting for the weather conditions to be right to match the rest of the sequence) and audiences (by now familiar with a TV show like "The Monkees" that doesn't bother about matching shots) would hardly notice or could even be persuaded that this was a modern advance. And the product would flow faster.

A number of the new movies are full of the less familiar forms of theatre, with a frosting of "visuals." Columbia's "30 Is a Dangerous Age, Cynthia" was made in London and Dublin, and the whole damned thing looks like a televison commercial. Dudley Moore, one of the "Beyond the Fringe" group, had seemed to be a funny man—at least, he was talented at musical parody—and in "Bedazzled," with the dry delivery of Peter Cook as counterpoint, and with Stanley Donen's direction to keep the timing right, he *was* funny. Now he has become one of those awful "multiple talents"—a ghastly, puckish, dear little fellow going through skit after skit, cavorting like crazy, with lots of wig changes and jokey dreams. Not only does he star (and he really eats up the camera, which holds him in closeup for unconscionably long periods) but he helped write the script and he did the score. Joseph McGrath's direction leaves almost every actor in the movie stranded on the screen, exposed in the desperate, failed attempt to be hilarious; still, even a better director would have needed a better script to pull this movie together. Some of the jokes aren't bad, but they don't further the plot, which has to keep chugging along trying to carry all this comic freight.

"Here We Go Round the Mulberry Bush" comes from England via a United Artist subsidiary; it's an odd little movie to open at an art house, because it's a variation on the American International beach-party movies. The A.I.P. movies for teen-age audiences are loaded with morality; they're exploitation films disguised as cautionary films—a traditional movie-business masquerade. In the A.I.P. "Riot on Sunset Strip," the teen-age good girl (poor and virtuous) is drugged and raped by a pack of kids led by a movie star's no-good son who skulks around like a villian in a DeMille epic; she then gets up from her hospital bed and lectures her police-officer father on how it's all his fault because the home was a broken home and he didn't give her the love and guidance she needed, and he promises to mend his ways. "Mulberry Bush," which sends the A.I.P. ingredients spinning, is like an extended orgy based on the two little teen-agers rattling around on the lavender paper with the hero of "Blow-Up." There seem to be infinite numbers of little girls popping in and out of intercourse with little boys. It's all quite impersonal; they lie down on roads, they stand in closets, they climb on top of wardrobes for variety, they change partners at a party in a bed store—with maybe more beds with something presumably going on in them than have ever been on the screen before. The teen-age hero and his girl friend have a rather lengthy nude bathing scene, of the kind that

77

once made Swedish films famous. But the sex has no more character than the mating of penguins or titmice—less, because that might have a certain authenticity. One hardly notices the absence of moral considerations, because the parents are as giddy as the rest. The absence of human qualities makes it all tedious, though. So now Andy Hardy fornicates, but he still isn't a person. When you come out, you want to go to see a movie with somebody in it. Is the dehumanization deliberate? Did the director, Clive Donner, and the writers want to make free youthful sex seem antiseptic, or was that an unforeseen result of trying to come on with so much cute sex? Banal when it's tender and when it focusses on the hero (a smiley, supposedly "winning" young actor named Barry Evans), who is looking for an emotional attachment, the movie is rather charming when it's absurd and farcical, and there are several amusing little girls, especially a blank-eyed kewpie named Adrienne Posta. Donner directed this musical-comedy fantasy in a tricky, pseudo-lyrical, choreographic style. My hunch is that many adults will take it almost straight, as the way teen-agers really are now, and that some teen-agers will be rather depressed—feeling they're out of it because they aren't living in a state of permanent carefree orgy. Still, there's one remnant of the older morality: the girl who spends a weekend with the hero and refuses to date him for the next, because she prefers variety, flunks a course and can't get into college.

March 16, 1968

O Pioneer!

Although nothing could be more harmless than satire of the theatre, the theatre people who are satirizing themselves—making their in-group jokes public—always seem to think they're doing something incredibly audacious and that each joke is a killer. When "Sunset Boulevard" was first unveiled at private screenings in Hollywood, I remember an executive's coming away from it talking as if he'd just been to a wife-swapping session with his father. It's this self-shocking insularity of show-business people—like kids at school giggling wildly as they talk dirty about the teacher—that probably accounts for how simpleminded much of "The Producers," which was written and directed by Mel Brooks, seems, and why it is acted and directed as if each bit of horseplay were earthshaking. "The Producers" isn't basically unconventional; it only seems so because it's so amateurishly crude, and because it revels in the kind of show-business Jewish humor that used to be considered too specialized for movies. Screenwriters used to take the Jewish out, but now that television comedians exploit themselves as stereotypes, screenwriters are putting the Jewish in, pushing it for laughs—and getting them.

Mel Brooks, one of the pioneers in this all too

fertile field, is a talented man, and as a comedy writer for Sid Caesar and others he has given us all some happy moments. But he has never written a movie before and he has never directed a movie (or probably anything else) before, and he has given himself an additional handicap, a camera hurdle that has broken the back of every movie director—Zero Mostel, a one-man obstacle course. Playing the producer Max Bialystock, a role not unlike John Barrymore's Oscar Jaffe in Howard-Hawks' version of "Twentieth Century," he is grotesque where Barrymore was funny. There are no firm rules in movie business; still, to the question can a man who insists on combing long, damp hair over a bald spot become a movie star I would give a provisional no. When Mostel tries to con money out of rich, senile ladies by making love to them, he obviously constitutes a physical danger rather than a romantic attraction. An experienced director, working with a script that has so much that is good in it, could have toned down what is gross and brought out the wit. Brooks has almost no idea where to put the camera, and since the easiest way to get a powerful effect is with closeups, he keeps almost everything (including Zero Mostel) on top of us; and since he doesn't know how or why or when to move the camera, he can't really utilize the screen as a frame for expressive compositions. He just tries to get some acting going on in it, and in this he's limited by his script. The actors say their lines and do their schtik, and they use their schtik up fast, before the plot even gets under way, because the characters have only one dimension—"Nazi" or "fag" or "sexy girl." Early on, Gene Wilder does his whining, strangled-voice bit, and he's fantastic at it—it's almost a schtik of genius—but then he has to coast on hysteria for the rest of the picture. Dick Shawn is a very funny performer, but for his role as L.S.D., who has blown his mind, to be funny the others should have kept theirs. This, however, isn't a script with contrasts or changes of tone. Brooks as writer relies upon "wild" ideas, but he doesn't yet know how to join them and make them grow into a comic structure. As conceived, the sequence consisting of tryouts for the role of Hitler in a play to be called "Springtime for Hitler" is potentially a great sequence. With beautiful directorial timing, each bit could be memorable and the sequence could still build, but Brooks as director destroys his own best ideas.

There is a plot: Bialystock sells twenty-five thousand per cent of a play, intending to produce a flop so that he won't have to pay the backers anything, but his "Springtime for Hitler" is a success. The fluke success was one of the elements of the first Kaufman and Hart play, "Once in a Lifetime," and it has been a standard ingredient of many—perhaps most—farces about Broadway and Hollywood, which are full of serious plays so bad that they succeed as comedies, performers so corny that they are taken for comedians. This comic idea is perfectly sound; it all depends on what you do with it. "The Producers" treats the idea as if it were in itself so unusually wicked that it didn't have to go anywhere. Brooks has no dénouement; when the play succeeds and he needs to show us the repercussions and to get his characters disentangled, he folds up. He hasn't prepared the elements that are needed to complete the farce, so the picture dies when the play succeeds. That's not screenwriting; it's gagwriting. But one learns to take one's pleasures where one can. Terrible as this picture is, I enjoyed parts of it, because I love satire of the theatre. And for satire of the theatre as good as Brooks' gags at their best, one can endure even the rank incompetence and stupidity of most of "The Producers."

With almost every other film around so overdramatized that it beats the audience over the head, "Up the Junction" is underdramatized. It's so uninvolving that it is almost finished before the central situation begins to take form. The material is based on the writer Nell Dunn's experiences: the upper-class heroine takes a factory job and goes to live among the working class, seeking the vitality that is missing in her own inhibited, hypocritical, repressed group. There's no precise American equivalent, but up until fairly recently an educated American woman would sometimes go to live with an uneducated Negro man, only to find as the heroine of "Up the Junction" does, that she is prized for exactly what she is trying to get away from—her "whiteness," or the kind of controlled, well-bred, expensive "class" she embodies. The movie is, however, a long time getting to this, and it barely emerges, because the girl, as she is written and as she is played by Suzy Kendall, with her high, mewling little voice, is so emotionally thin, so sweetly refined and ladylike that there's nothing vital enough in her to make her break away from her own background. And since in the movie the girl is *not* a writer-observer (probably so that the movie wouldn't suggest the classic artist-as-a-young-woman autobiographical novel), she seems unmotivated—a lifeless girl with an *idée fixe*. The girls who take Harlem lovers are a lot gutsier and are full of theories and ideas, and they know their motives aren't so pure. This girl discovers things we already know, so the whole point of view of the movie is unclear and unsatisfying. To the readers of the *New Statesman,* in which Miss Dunn's accounts appeared, her observations about working-class life may have seemed like dispatches from another country, but to a movie audience the observations, filtered through a different writer and the director, Peter Collinson, may seem merely sentimentalized and sensationalized. The "colorful" factory girls, with their taste for cheap furniture and coarse romance, are movie-ish, just as the pallid heroine is a movie-ish representative of the upper class. What seems accurate in the observation is that the working-class boy the heroine is drawn to is the most sensitive boy she meets, just as the white woman finds a lover in Harlem who is "not like the others." Women have a way of looking for refinement in the act of abandoning it; they may want the rough stuff, but they always seem to convince themselves they've found a diamond in the rough. I wish the movie had dealt with some of these ambivalences in the girl's quest instead of serving us another slice of juicy life as if workers on the job and in the pub were a treat for us, like taking kids on a visit to the zoo.

Actually, the movie states what the heroine is after in terms considerably more naïve than those I have used here. She believes that in the working class, where you can yell and vent your emotions, you're "free to be yourself." You are "real," whereas "being rich makes you false and useless." But if we can forget this drool and project into the picture, we can make it a little more interesting—and "Up the Junction" needs all the help we can give it. The boy's role is well written and is exceedingly well played by Dennis Waterman; as a little factory girl who gets pregnant, Adrienne Posta has a hackneyed role, but she's as lively as a baby Bette Davis.

The problem in recording on film dancing that has been choreographed for the stage is how to get camera movement without destroying the integrity of the dance. The usual fake solutions are to jettison the dance and substitute "cinematic" effects—overhead shots of geometric patterns, and underskirts shots, and tricky camera angles, and closeups of faces or details. The Balanchine production of "A Midsummer Night's Dream" that Dan Eriksen has directed for the screen is remarkably modest and unpretentious. Instead of fighting the dance to show off other skills, it preserves the production as best it can by photographing the dances fluidly within the limited space, with unobtrusive camera shifts cut to the musical beat. The result is lovely: the movie has a fairy-tale, calendar-art prettiness that is totally inoffensive and seems appropriate to the slender, long-stemmed American ballerinas. The dancers, fortunately for the camera, are extraordinarily beautiful—especially the principals (Arthur Mitchell as Puck, Suzanne Farrell as Titania, and Edward Villella as Oberon). Movie directors who interrupt dance movement by putting in pantomime and swirling effects that they can take credit for have often made reputations with their flashy destructiveness. In this movie, the camera almost always seems to be in the right place; Eriksen, who serves the dance, is little known.

March 23, 1968

The Old Wave

The cleansing young New Wave from France was never popular the way those old "Gallic romps" and "saucy frolics" used to be, and now the old wave is back with "Benjamin," the kind of movie that will enable audiences to say once again, "The French know so much about love. They're so civilized." It's a clear demonstration of what the young directors were trying to break away from. "Benjamin" has its enticing, bawdy side for men, and it has the suggestions of sadness and "depth" that make it a kind of high-class sudser for women, who can identify with Michele Morgan's suffering and her refusal to conceal her humiliation when she can no longer hold "her man." They can say, "It's so true. What women really want is marriage."

The period is the eighteenth century, and Benjamin (Pierre Clémenti) is a seventeen-year-old virgin who has come to the château of his countess aunt (Michèle Morgan) to be educated. We learn what that means a lot faster than he does, as an assortment of ladies and ladies' maids chase him and fling him down on couches and beds and hay, and are always interrupted before completing the lesson. This harmless, rather pretty little nothing of a movie might be charming and witty if the interruptions were entertaining, if they were designed to comment on each other or to make an intricate pattern. But they are just mechanical and repetitive delaying tactics. It is not the genre itself that is objectionable, or the fact that it is an original screenplay (by Nina Companeez and the director, Michel Deville) in the manner of an earlier style—the *conte galant*. Ingmar Bergman worked in this genre in "Smiles of a Summer Night" and wrote an original screenplay that also suggested an adaptation, but Bergman used the conventions of an earlier form to achieve a formal style. "Benjamin" is merely conventional, using the libertinage of the period as an excuse to bring in that tedious French fake expertise—ironies and aphorisms about the relations of the sexes—and only in a few scenes attaining anything formal. "Benjamin" *is* a "Gallic romp," "risqué but artistic." It's the kind of movie in which the dashing, devastating Don Juan (Michel Piccoli, glowering romantically) is—oldest cliché in the sophisticated-sex business—conquered by the girl who pretends to be indifferent to him (Catherine Deneuve, who is given stupid, stilted lines, though one assumes she is meant to be as intelligent as she is, indeed, beautiful). Everyone is engaged in games of love and yet the only characters who are allowed to have any dignity are those who "truly" love only one person.

Ghislain Cloquet's color photography provides an ambiance, and we know we're supposed to breathe the atmosphere of Fragonard and Watteau, but the fragrance has evaporated. Though Deville, whose earlier films have not been imported, is only in his thirties, his flaccid, undistinguished direction could easily be mistaken for that of one of the second-string French directors now in their fifties or sixties. If he had been more fortunate in his casting of the lead, the script might have played better. Gérard Philipe used to give similar roles (like Fanfan the Tulip) a kind of spiritual elegance. But Pierre Clémenti is strangely unappealing, and he moves badly. Just as Natalie Wood in "Inside Daisy Clover" tried to be a teen-ager by moving like a tough little boy, Clémenti indicates adolescent innocence by being loose-limbed and girlish. It is essential for the boy to suggest the kind of man he will become once he has learned what everyone is so eager to teach him, but Clémenti looks as if he would become a lesbian.

"No Way to Treat a Lady" opens with a sequence in which Rod Steiger dressed as a priest turns to look at a pretty girl in the street, and the audience laughs at the tipoff that he isn't really a priest. It takes only a minute to discover that this bogus priest is a mad pervert, a strangler of middle-aged women. Apparently, the movie-makers couldn't resist getting a laugh, even though the strangler, when he's dressed in civvies, would never dream of looking at a girl. In a later sequence, Steiger is disguised as a woman and is picked up by a hustling female impersonator. But why would a female impersonator pick up a woman? Everywhere along the line, this "black" comedy by murder sacrifices consistency and point for a laugh or a shock, and why not? Because it has no consistency or point anyway. Though Jack Smight's direction has risen to banal competence this time around, though this picture is glossier and more expensive-looking than most recent films made in New York (and has been photographed considerably better than most, by Jack Priestley), it's basically crummy stuff, entertaining at some degraded level—maybe because it isn't as bad as it might be. It's bad enough; it gets most of its laughs out of Jewish-mother jokes and a screaming-queen hairdresser. Since the police detective (a generally agreeable, often charming performance by George Segal) has the comic, emasculating mother, and Eileen Heckart's performance in the role makes her a candidate for murder, we wait for the mother-hating strangler, who marks his victims with a lipstick simulation of a mother's kisses, to get to her. But the plot lines never even meet; the mothers are just there for Pop effect.

When an actor dies, he does impersonations; when an actor has poor material to work with, that's often all he can do—and it's a form of death, though he can go on working and perhaps become a bigger star. Rod Steiger is playing not multiple roles in this picture but a psychopath who employs various disguises. Yet the masquerades are played as comic turns, and we are invited by the script and the director to enjoy them as if they were night-club impersonations. They don't tell us anything about the murderer; they just give Steiger a chance to show off his comic accents. And, considering how good he was in roles like the Irish psychiatrist in "The Mark" and the Southern chief of police in "In the Heat of the Night," he's surprisingly crude—no better than his material. The miracle is that in the past he often *has* been. He's done amazing things in pictures like "The Big Knife" and "Across the Bridge" and "The Pawnbroker," and his astonishing introduction of a character out of Dostoevski into David Lean's Russo-Anglican "Doctor Zhivago" almost pumped blood into those historical facsimiles. Rod Steiger's presence is so strong that he often seems to take over a picture even when he isn't the lead. This is true of George C. Scott, too, and actors this powerful just don't fit into ordinary roles. The answer, of course, is that they need extraordinary ones—great roles. Hollywood's answer is to offer them star turns—an old codger for Scott in "The Flim-Flam Man," this fag phantom of the opera for Steiger. Except for the flashback scenes in "The Pawnbroker," I've never seen Steiger so bad, so uninventively, ordinary bad as he is in his undisguised role in this movie, and he's only a little better in his disguises, acting high on the hog.

March 30, 1968

A Minority Movie

A few weeks ago, I was startled to see a big Pop poster of Che Guevara—startled not because students of earlier generations didn't have comparable martyrs and heroes but because they didn't consider their heroes part of popular culture, though their little brothers and sisters might have been expected to conceive of them in comic-strip terms. Jean-Luc Godard, who said on the sound track of a recent film, "One might almost say that to live in society today is something like living inside an enormous comic strip," has already made a movie about the incorporation of revolutionary heroes and ideas into Pop—"La Chinoise." In the narration of an earlier movie, Godard defined his field as "the present, where the future is more present than the present." In "Masculine Feminine," which was about "the children of Marx and Coca-Cola," a man about to burn himself up needed to borrow a match, and many people were irritated by the levity and absurdity of it—but the *Times* reported just such an incident this month. In the further adventures of those children, in "La Chinoise," the heroine wants to blow up the Louvre; someone threw a stink bomb into a party at the Museum of Modern Art last week. We don't have time to catch up with the future that is here, and Godard is already making movie critiques of it—documentaries of the future in the present. His movies have become a volatile mixture of fictional narrative, reporting, essay, and absurdist interludes. His tempo is so fast that it is often difficult to keep up with the dialogue, let alone the punctuation of advertising art and allusions to history, literature, movies, and current events. There is little doubt that many of us react to movies in terms of how the tempo suits our own tempo (as a child, I could never sit still through a Laurel-and-Hardy feature, and I have something of the same problem with most of Antonioni's recent work). Since Godard's tempo is too fast for many people—perhaps most people—they have some ground for anger and confusion. But I think he is driven to ignore the difficulties that audiences may experience—not because he wants to assault them or to be deliberately "uncommercial," not out of pretentiousness or arrogance, but out of the nature of his material and his talent.

Though Godard is a social critic, using largely documentary material, he does not work in the expository manner of television documentaries but intuitively seizes new, rapidly changing elements and dramatizes them as directly as possible, projecting his feelings and interpretations into the material. He assumes in his audience an Americanized sensibility—that is, a quick comprehension of devices and conventions derived from American film style—and his temperamental affinity with American popular art probably seems particularly disreputable and trivial to those educated Americans who go to art-film

houses for the European cultural ambiance. Antonioni's ponderously serious manner serves as a
guarantee of quality; Godard is so restless and in-
quiring that he hardly develops his ideas at all. In a
new picture he may leap back to rework a theme
when he sees how to develop what was only partly
clear before. His style is a form of shorthand and
this irritates even some people who one might assume are perfectly able to read it. We all know that
an artist can't discover anything for himself—can't
function as an *artist*—if he must make everything
explicit in terms accessible to the widest possible
audience. This is one of the big hurdles that defeat
artists in Hollywood: they aren't allowed to assume
that anybody knows anything, and they become
discouraged and corrupt when they discover that
studio thinking is not necessarily wrong in its esti-
mate of the mass audience. Godard, like many
American novelists, works in terms of an audience
that is assumed to have the same background he
has. And, of course, many people do—perhaps a
majority of the people in the art-house audiences,
though they're not used to making connections
among fast references at the movies. No one complains about the quotation from Kafka's "Metamorphosis" in "The Producers," or about Gene Wilder's
being named Leo Bloom in the same film, or even
about another character's being called Carmen
Giya; this is considered cute "inside humor" when
it's obviously done just for a laugh. But if, as in "La
Chinoise," some of the names are used as a shortcut
to the characters' roles—Kirilov, for example, for
the most desperately confused of the revolutionaries

—people are sure to object, though this is done in novels all the time. There are many references that may be incomprehensible to some in the audience, but should Godard stop to explain who Rosa Luxembourg was or what Malraux stands for or why he brings in Sartre and Aragon or Artaud or Theatre Year Zero or Daniel and Sinyavsky? Can't he assume that those who care about the kind of film he is making—those who are involved with the issues of his art—already share most of his frame of reference and are prepared to respond to someone's using it in movies, that they are no longer much involved with movies in the same old frame of reference, which doesn't permit dealing with the attitudes of, as in this case, radical youth? This is minority art not by desire but by necessity. Most innovative artists working in movies have tried to reach the mass audience and failed—failed to reach it as artists. Godard, who is perhaps a symptom of the abandonment of hope for a great popular art, works as artists do in less popular media—at his own highest level.

Inventive and visually gifted, Godard is also, and perhaps even primarily, literary in his approach, and his verbal humor presupposes an educated audience. In "La Chinoise" he uses words in more ways than any other filmmaker: they're in the dialogue and on the walls, on book jackets and in headlines; they're recited, chanted, shouted, written, broken down; they're in commentaries, quotations, interviews, narration; they're in slogans and emblems and signs. Those who dislike verbal allusions will be irritated constantly, and those who want only

94

straightforward action on the screen may be driven wild by his neo-Brechtian displacement devices (his voice on the sound track, a cut to Raoul Coutard at the camera) and by his almost novelistic love of digression—his inclusion of anecdotes and of speculations about movie art and of direct-to-the-camera interviews. And his doubts can be irritating in a medium that is customarily used for banal certainties. Not many movie directors regard their movies as a place to raise the questions that are troubling them. Sometimes Godard's questioning essays come apart like hasty puddings, and then his whole method falls open to question. He is also prone to the use of the *acte gratuit,* so common in philosophical French fiction of this century but rather maddening in films because such acts violate the basic premise of dramatic construction—that the author will show us what led to the crimes or deaths. Godard gives us quick finishes that are not resolutions of what has gone before.

Some of these factors are genuine deterrents to moviegoing, but Godard is, at the moment, the most important single force keeping the art of the film alive—that is to say, responsive to the modern world, moving, reaching out for new themes. The last year has been a relatively good year for American movies—there have been more pictures fit to look at than there were in the preceding few years, when Hollywood seemed to have become a desert, but, with the exception of "Bonnie and Clyde," if you missed any or all of them you would hardly have missed a thing, because they are merely genre pieces brought up to date: thrillers, Westerns, or

"strikingly new" films, which is to say films about
adolescent rebellion that take over material, attitudes, and sensibility already commonplace to anybody who reads books or goes to plays. We can go
to foreign films, and a romantic tragedy set in another period and culture, like "Elvira Madigan,"
may be highly satisfying when we want to dream
away and weep a little and look at lovely pictures—
as we did at "Mayerling" in the thirties. And a slick
thriller or a Western may still be entertaining
enough and basically, crudely satisfying when we
are tired and just want to go sit and see some action.
But what these late-sixties versions of standard movies don't have is the excitement of contemporaneity,
of using movies in new ways. Going to the movies,
we sometimes forget—because it so rarely happens—
that when movies are used in new ways there's an
excitement about them much sharper than there is
about the limited-entertainment genres. Godard's
films—the good ones, that is—are funny, and
they're funny in a new way: "La Chinoise" is a
comic elegy on a group of modern revolutionary
youth—naïve, forlorn little ideologues who live out
a Pop version of "The Possessed."

Godard once wrote, "I want to be able sometimes
to make you feel far from the person when I do a
closeup." We feel far from Véronique, the teen-age
philosophy student of "La Chinoise," all the time,
and it's a scary sensation, because she is so much
like every other girl on campus these days. As em-
bodied by Anne Wiazemsky, the granddaughter of
Mauriac who made her début in Bresson's "Baltha-
zar" and is now married to Godard, Véronique

96

may be more of a representative of the new radical youth than any other movie has come up with. She is an engaged nihilist, an activist who wants to close the universities by acts of terrorism; she thinks that this will open the way for a new educational system, and that a few deaths don't matter. She is politically engaged, and yet this condition seems to go hand in hand with a peculiar, and possibly new, kind of detachment. She and the four other members of her Maoist group who share the apartment where most of the movie takes place seem detached from the life around them, from how they live, from feelings of any kind. In her soft, small voice, and with the unself-conscious, frightened, yet assured face of so many American college girls, Véronique makes rigid formulations about morals and philosophy; she has no resonance. The group live in a political wonderland of slogans lifted out of historical continuity; they prattle about correct programs and objective conditions and just, progressive wars and the Treaty of Brest Litovsk. They have none of the strength or the doubts that come from experience. They are disparately together in their communal life; they could just as easily recombine in another grouping. Véronique is a new version of Godard's unreachable, perfidious girl, but this unreachable ideologue, though as blankly affectless as the heroines of "Breathless" and "Masculine Feminine," is not treacherous, nor is there any deep enough emotional involvement between the boys and the girls for deceit to be necessary or for betrayal or victimization to be possible. Sex is taken for granted, is so divorced from emotion that the members of the group seem almost post-sexual, which may be just about the same as pre-sexual. They study Marxism-Leninism, and chant Chairman Mao's sayings from the little red book like nursery rhymes; they play with lethal toys, and—in that bizarre parroting of the Red Guard which is so common here, too—they attack not the economic system and the advertising culture that has produced them but the culture of the past and its institutions, and bourgeois "Compromisers," and Russian-style Communists. Véronique wants to bomb the Sorbonne, the Louvre, the Comédie-Française; she murders a Soviet cultural emissary visiting Paris, a representative of the culture stifling the universities, who is selected almost at random to be the first in a series. The group's political life in the flat is a contained universe that almost seems to dematerialize the more familiar world, because it is such a separate, paper-thin universe. Their conspiratorial plots seem like games; they are too open and naïve to hide anything. They expel a member for "revisionism," and the little bespectacled boy goes to the foot of the table and consoles himself with bread and jam. Yet from the flat where they play-act revolution they go out and commit terrorist acts with the same affectless determination. Véronique kills the wrong man and is not fazed by it; she goes back and gets "the right one" as unemotionally as she might correct a mistake in an examination. Godard shows the horror, the beauty, and the absurdity of their thinking and their living, all at the same time.

"La Chinoise" is a satire of new political youth, but a satire from within, based on observation, and a satire that loves its targets more than it loves anything else—that, perhaps, can see beauty and hope only in its targets. But not much hope. In a section toward the end, the movie goes outside comedy. Godard introduces Francis Jeanson, an older man with political experience, a humane radical who *connects*. Jeanson tries to explain to Véronique that her terrorist actions will not have the consequences she envisions. She describes her tactics for closing the universities, and, gently but persistently, he raises the question "What next?" There is no question whose side Godard is on—that of the revolutionary children—but in showing their styles of action and of thought he has used his doubts, and his fears for them. Though his purpose is didactic, the movie is so playful and quick-witted and affectionate that it's possible—indeed, likely— that audiences will be confused about Godard's "attitude."

How can the modern "possessed" be *funny?* The fusion of attitudes—seeing characters as charming and poetic and, at the same time, preposterous and absurd—is one of Godard's contributions to modern film. (Truffaut worked in almost the same mode in "Shoot the Piano Player"—the mode that in America led to "Bonnie and Clyde.") Godard's attitude toward his characters is similar to Scott Fitzgerald's in that he loves beautiful, doomed youth, but his style is late-sixties. If one examines books on modern movies, the stills generally look terrible— shlocky, dated, cluttered, and artificially lighted. Stills from Godard's films provide such a contrast that they can be spotted at once. In natural light, his figures are isolated and clearly defined in space against impersonal modern buildings with advertising posters or in rooms against white walls with unframed pictures from magazines. The look is of modern graphics, and that, of course, is why the stills reproduce so well. The ironic elegance of his hard-edge photographic compositions on screen is derived from graphics, comic strips, modern décor, and the two-dimensional television image. The frames in a Godard film are perfectly suited to fast comprehension—one can see everything in them at a glance—and to quick cutting. They can move with the speed of a comic strip, in which we also read the whole picture and the words at once. This visual style, which enables him to make a comedy out of politics and despair, has, however, often been misinterpreted as an attempt to achieve "pure form" on screen. Godard is not trying to create a separate world of abstract film that might be analogous to the arts of music and abstract painting, and it is a way not of explaining his movies but of explaining them away to say that they are works of art because they are going in the same direction as painting—as if every art reached its culmination when it was emptied of verbal meaning and references to this world. Godard uses abstract design because he responds to the future in the present and because he is trying to show how human relationships are changing in this new world of advertising art, dehumanized housing, multiple forms of prostitution. He does not work in a studio; he selects locations that reveal how abstract modern urban living already is. He fills the screen with a picture of Brecht and the definition

"Theatre is a commentary on reality." He uses words as words—for what they mean (and he satirizes the characters in "La Chinoise" for using words abstractly). He is no more an abstractionist than the comic-strip artist, who also uses simplified compositions and bright primary colors as a visual-verbal shorthand technique. If the meaning is conveyed by a balloon containing the word "Splat!" you don't need to paint in the leaves on the branches of the trees or the herringbone design on the pants. And if modern life is seen in terms of the future, the leaves and the weave are already gone. It's folly to view Godard's stripped-down-for-speed-and-wit visual style as if he were moving away from the impurities of meaning; that's a way of cancelling out everything that goes on in a movie like "La Chinoise"—of "appreciating" everything the "artist" does and not reacting to or understanding anything the person says.

For a movie-maker, Godard is almost incredibly intransigent. At this point, it would be easy for him to court popularity with the young audience (which is the only audience he has ever had, and he has had little of that one) by making his revolutionaries romantic, like the gangster in "Breathless." Romantic revolutionaries could act out political plots instead of robberies. But he does not invest the political activists of "La Chinoise" with glamour or mystery, or even passion. His romantic heroes and heroines were old-fashioned enough to believe in people, and hence to be victimized; the members of Véronique's group believe love is impossible, and for them it is. Godard does just what will be hardest to take:

101

he makes them infantile and funny—victims of Pop culture. And though he likes them because they are ready to convert their slogans into action, because they want to do something, the movie asks, "And after you've closed the universities, what next?"

April 6, 1968

II

Trash,
Art,
and
the
Movies

i

Like those cynical heroes who were idealists before they discovered that the world was more rotten than they had been led to expect, we're just about all of us displaced persons, "a long way from home." When we feel defeated, when we imagine we could now perhaps settle for home and what it represents, that home no longer exists. But there are movie houses. In whatever city we find ourselves we can duck into a theatre and see on the screen our familiars—our old "ideals" aging as we are and no longer looking so ideal. Where could we better stoke the fires of our masochism than at rotten movies in gaudy seedy picture palaces in cities that run together, movies and anonymity a common denominator. Movies—a tawdry corrupt art for a tawdry corrupt world—fit the way we feel. The world doesn't work the way the schoolbooks said it did and we are different from what our parents and teachers expected us to be. Movies are our cheap and easy expression, the sullen art of displaced persons. Because we feel low we sink in the boredom, relax in the irresponsibility, and maybe grin for a minute when the gunman lines up three men and kills them with a single bullet, which is no more "real" to us than the nursery-school story of the brave little tailor.

We don't have to be told those are photographs of actors impersonating characters. We know, and we often know much more about both the actors and the characters they're impersonating and about how and why the movie has been made than is consistent with theatrical illusion. Hitchcock teased us by killing off the one marquee-name star early in "Psycho," a gambit which startled us not just because of the suddenness of the murder or how it was committed but because it broke a box-office convention and so it was a joke played on what audiences have learned to expect. He broke the rules of the movie game and our response demonstrated how aware we are of commercial consideration. When movies are bad (and in the bad parts of good movies) our awareness of the mechanics and our cynicism about the aims and values is peculiarly alienating. The audience talks right back to the phony "outspoken" condescending "The Detective"; there are groans of dejection at "The Legend of Lylah Clare," with, now and then, a desperate little titter. How well we all know that cheap depression that settles on us when our hopes and expectations are disappointed *again*. Alienation is the most common state of the knowledgeable movie audience, and though it has the peculiar rewards of low connoisseurship, a miser's delight in small favors, we long to be surprised out of it—not to suspension of disbelief nor to a Brechtian kind of alienation, but to pleasure, something a man can call good without self-disgust.

A good movie can take you out of your dull funk and the hopelessness that so often goes with slipping into a theatre; a good movie can make you feel alive again, in contact, not just lost in another city. Good movies make you care, make you believe in possibilities again. If somewhere in the Hollywood-entertainment world someone has managed to break through with something that speaks to you, then it isn't *all* corruption. The movie doesn't have to be great; it can be stupid and empty and you can still have the joy of a good performance, or the joy of just a good line. An actor's scowl, a small subversive gesture, a dirty remark that someone tosses off with a mock-innocent face, and the world makes a little bit of sense. Sitting there alone or painfully alone because those with you do not react as you do, you know there must be others perhaps in this very theatre or in this city, surely in other theatres in other cities, now, in the past or future, who react as you do. And because movies are the most total and encompassing art form we have, these reactions can seem the most personal and, maybe the most important, imaginable. The romance of movies is not just in those stories and those people on the screen but in the adolescent dream of meeting others who feel as you do about what you've seen. You do meet them, of course, and you know each other at once because you talk less about good movies than about what you love in bad movies.

ii

There is so much talk now about the art of the film that we may be in danger of forgetting that most of the movies we enjoy are not works of art. "The Scalphunters," for example, was one of the few entertaining American movies this past year, but skillful though it was, one could hardly call it a work of art—if such terms are to have any useful meaning. Or, to take a really gross example, a movie that is as crudely made as "Wild in the Streets"— slammed together with spit and hysteria and opportunism—can nevertheless be enjoyable, though it is almost a classic example of an unartistic movie. What makes these movies—that are not works of art—enjoyable? "The Scalphunters" was more entertaining than most Westerns largely because Burt Lancaster and Ossie Davis were peculiarly funny together; part of the pleasure of the movie was trying to figure out what made them so funny. Burt Lancaster is an odd kind of comedian: what's distinctive about him is that his comedy seems to come out of his physicality. In serious roles an undistinguished and too obviously hard-working actor, he has an apparently effortless flair for comedy and nothing is more infectious than an actor who can relax in front of the camera as if he were having a good time. (George Segal sometimes seems to have this gift of a wonderful amiability, and Brigitte Bardot was radiant with it in "Viva Maria!") Somehow the alchemy of personality in the pairing of Lancaster and Ossie Davis—another powerfully funny actor of tremendous physical presence— worked, and the director Sydney Pollack kept tight control so that it wasn't overdone.

And "Wild in the Streets?" It's a blatantly crummy-looking picture, but that somehow works for it instead of against it because it's smart in a lot of ways that better-made pictures aren't. It looks like other recent products from American International Pictures but it's as if one were reading a comic strip that looked just like the strip of the day before, and yet on this new one there are surprising expressions on the faces and some of the balloons are really witty. There's not a trace of sensitivity in the drawing or in the ideas, and there's something rather specially funny about wit without *any* grace at all; it can be enjoyed in a particularly crude way—as Pop wit. The basic idea is corny—*It Can't Happen Here* with the freaked-out young as a new breed of fascists—but it's treated in the paranoid style of editorials about youth (it even begins by blaming everything on the parents). And a cheap idea that is this current and widespread has an almost lunatic charm, a nightmare gaiety. There's a relish that people have for the idea of drug-taking kids as monsters threatening them—the daily papers merging into "Village of the Damned." Tapping and exploiting this kind of hysteria for a satirical fantasy, the writer Robert Thom has used what is available and obvious but he's done it with just enough mockery and style to make it funny. He throws in touches of characterization and occasional lines that are not there just to further the plot, and these throwaways make odd connections so that the movie becomes almost frolicsome in its paranoia (and in its delight in its own cleverness).

If you went to "Wild in the Streets" expecting a good movie, you'd probably be appalled because the directing is unskilled and the music is banal and many of the ideas in the script are scarcely even carried out, and almost every detail is messed up (the casting director has used bit players and extras who are decades too old for their roles). It's a paste-up job of cheap movie-making, but it has genuinely funny performers who seize their opportunities and throw their good lines like boomerangs—Diane Varsi (like an even more zonked-out Geraldine Page) doing a perfectly quietly convincing freakout as if it were truly a put-on of the whole straight world; Hal Holbrook with his inexpressive actorish face that is opaque and uninteresting in long shot but in closeup reveals tiny little shifts of expression, slight tightenings of the features that are like the movement of thought; and Shelly Winters, of course, and Christopher Jones. It's not so terrible—it may even be a relief—for a movie to be without the look of art; there are much worse things aesthetically than the crude good-natured crumminess, the undisguised reach for a fast buck, of movies without art. From "I Was a Teen-Age Werewolf" through the beach parties to "Wild in the Streets" and "The Savage Seven," American International Pictures has sold a cheap commodity, which in its lack of artistry and in its blatant and sometimes funny way of delivering action serves to remind us that one of the great appeals of movies is that we don't have to take them too seriously.

"Wild in the Streets" is a fluke—a borderline, special case of a movie that is entertaining because some talented people got a chance to do something at American International that the more respectable companies were too nervous to try. But though I don't enjoy a movie so obvious and badly done as the big American International hit, "The Wild Angels," it's easy to see why kids do and why many people in other countries do. Their reasons are basically why we all started going to the movies. After a time, we may want more, but audiences who have been forced to wade through the thick middle-class padding of more expensively made movies to get to the action enjoy the nose-thumbing at "good taste" of cheap movies that stick to the raw materials. At some basic level they *like* the pictures to be cheaply done, they enjoy the crudeness; it's a breather, a vacation from proper behavior and good taste and required responses. Patrons of burlesque applaud politely for the graceful erotic dancer but go wild for the lewd lummox who bangs her big hips around. That's what they go to burlesque for. Personally, I hope for a reasonable minimum of finesse, and movies like "Planet of the Apes" or "The Scalphunters" or "The Thomas Crown Affair" seem to me minimal entertainment for a relaxed evening's pleasure. These are, to use traditional common-sense language, "good movies" or "good bad movies"—slick, reasonably inventive, well-crafted. They are not art. But they are almost the maximum of what we're now getting from American movies, and not only these but much worse movies are talked about as "art"—and are beginning to be taken seriously in our schools.

It's preposterously egocentric to call anything we enjoy art—as if we could not be entertained by it if it were not; it's just as preposterous to let prestigious, expensive advertising snow us into thinking

we're getting art for our money when we haven't
even had a good time. I did have a good time at
"Wild in the Streets," which is more than I can say
for "Petulia" or "2001" or a lot of other highly
praised pictures. "Wild in the Streets" is not a work
of art, but then I don't think "Petulia" or "2001" is
either, though "Petulia" has that kaleidoscopic hip
look and "2001" that new-techniques look which
combined with "swinging" or "serious" ideas often
pass for motion picture art.

iii

Let's clear away a few misconceptions. Movies
make hash of the schoolmarm's approach of how
well the artist fulfilled his intentions. Whatever the
original intention of the writers and director, it is
usually supplanted, as the production gets under
way, by the intention to make money—and the
industry judges the film by how well it fulfills that
intention. But if you could see the "artist's intentions" you'd probably wish you couldn't anyway.
Nothing is so deathly to enjoyment as the relentless
march of a movie to fulfill its obvious purpose. This
is, indeed, almost a defining characteristic of the
hack director, as distinguished from an artist.

The intention to make money is generally all too
obvious. One of the excruciating comedies of our
time is attending the new classes in cinema at the
high schools where the students may quite shrewdly
and accurately interpret the plot developments in a

mediocre movie in terms of manipulation for a desired response while the teacher tries to explain everything in terms of the creative artist working out his theme—as if the conditions under which a movie is made and the market for which it is designed were irrelevant, as if the latest product from Warners or Universal should be analyzed like a lyric poem.

People who are just getting "seriously interested" in film always ask a critic, "Why don't you talk about technique and 'the visuals' more?" The answer is that American movie technique is generally more like technology and it usually isn't very interesting. Hollywood movies often have the look of the studio that produced them—they have a studio style. Many current Warner films are noisy and have a bright look of cheerful ugliness, Universal films the cheap blur of money-saving processes, and so forth. Sometimes there is even a *spirit* that seems to belong to the studio. We can speak of the Paramount comedies of the Thirties or the Twentieth-Century Fox family entertainment of the Forties and CinemaScope comedies of the Fifties or the old MGM gloss, pretty much as we speak of Chevvies or Studebakers. These movies look alike, they move the same way, they have just about the same engines because of the studio policies and the *kind* of material the studio heads bought, the ideas they imposed, the way they had the films written, directed, photographed, and the labs where the prints were processed, and, of course, because of the presence of the studio stable of stars for whom the material was often purchased and shaped and who dominated the output of the studio. In some cases, as at Paramount in the Thirties, studio style was plain and rather tacky and the output—those comedies with Mary Boland and Mae West and Alison Skipworth and W. C. Fields—looks the better for it now. Those economical comedies weren't slowed down by a lot of fancy lighting or the adornments of "production values." Simply to be enjoyable, movies don't need a very high level of craftsmanship: wit, imagination, fresh subject matter, skillful performers, a good idea—either alone or in any combination—can more than compensate for lack of technical knowledge or a big budget.

The craftsmanship that Hollywood has always used as a selling point not only doesn't have much to do with art—the expressive use of techniques—it probably doesn't have very much to do with actual box-office appeal, either. A dull movie like Sidney Furie's "The Naked Runner" is technically competent. The appalling "Half a Sixpence" is technically astonishing. Though the large popular audience has generally been respectful of expenditure (so much so that a critic who wasn't impressed by the money and effort that went into a "Dr. Zhivago" might be sharply reprimanded by readers), people who like "The President's Analyst" or "The Producers" or "The Odd Couple" don't seem to be bothered by their technical ineptitude and visual ugliness. And on the other hand, the expensive slick techniques of ornately empty movies like "A Dandy in Aspic" can actually work against one's enjoyment, because such extravagance and waste are morally ugly. If one compares movies one likes to movies one doesn't like, craftsmanship of the big-studio variety is hardly a decisive factor. And if one compares a movie one likes by a competent director such as John Sturges or Franklin Schaffner or John Frankenheimer to a movie one doesn't much like by the same director, his technique is probably not the decisive factor. After directing "The Manchurian Candidate" Frankenheimer directed another political thriller, "Seven Days in May," which, considered just as a piece of direction, was considerably more confident. While seeing it, one could take pleasure in Frankenheimer's smooth showmanship. But the material (Rod Serling out of Fletcher Knebel and Charles W. Bailey II) was like a stràight (i.e., square) version of "The Manchurian Candidate." I have to chase around the corridors of memory to summon up images from "Seven Days in May"; despite the brilliant technique, all that is clear to mind is the touchingly, desperately anxious face of Ava Gardner—how when she smiled you couldn't be sure if you were seeing dimples or tics. But "The Manchurian Candidate," despite Frankenheimer's uneven, often barely adequate, staging, is still vivid because of the script. It took off from a political double entendre that everybody had been thinking of ("Why, if Joe McCarthy were working for the Communists, he couldn't be doing them more good!") and carried it to startling absurdity, and the extravagances and conceits and conversational non sequiturs (by George Axelrod out of Richard Condon) were ambivalent and funny in a way that was trashy yet liberating.

Technique is hardly worth talking about unless

115

it's used for something worth doing: that's why most of the theorizing about the new art of television commercials is such nonsense. The effects are impersonal—dexterous, sometimes clever, but empty of art. It's because of their emptiness that commercials call so much attention to their camera angles and quick cutting—which is why people get impressed by "the art" of it. Movies are now often made in terms of what television viewers have learned to settle for. Despite a great deal that is spoken and written about young people responding visually, the influence of TV is to make movies visually less imaginative and complex. Television is a very noisy medium and viewers listen, while getting used to a poor quality of visual reproduction, to the absence of visual detail, to visual obviousness and overemphasis on simple compositions, and to atrociously simplified and distorted color systems. The shifting camera styles, the movement, and the fast cutting of a film like "Finian's Rainbow"—one of the better big productions—are like the "visuals" of TV commercials, a disguise for static material, expressive of nothing so much as the need to keep you from getting bored and leaving. Men are now beginning their careers as directors by working on commercials—which, if one cares to speculate on it, may be almost a one-sentence résumé of the future of American motion pictures.

I don't mean to suggest that there is not such a thing as movie technique or that craftsmanship doesn't contribute to the pleasures of movies, but simply that most audiences, if they enjoy the acting and the "story" or the theme or the funny lines, don't notice or care about how well or how badly the movie is made, and because they don't care, a hit makes a director a "genius" and everybody talks about his brilliant technique (i.e., the technique of grabbing an audience). In the brief history of movies there has probably never been so astonishingly gifted a large group of directors as the current Italians, and not just the famous ones or Pontecorvo ("The Battle of Algiers") or Francesco Rosi ("The Moment of Truth") or the young prodigies, Bertolucci and Bellocchio, but dozens of others, men like Elio Petri ("We Still Kill the Old Way") and Carlo Lizzani ("The Violent Four"). "The Violent Four" shows more understanding of visual movement and more talent for movie-making than anything that's been made in America this year. But could one tell people who are not crazy, dedicated moviegoers to go see it? I'm not sure, although I enjoyed the film enormously, because "The Violent Four" is a gangster genre picture. And it may be a form of aestheticism—losing sight of what people go to movies for, and particularly what they go to foreign movies for—for a critic to say, "His handling of crowds and street scenes is superb," or, "It has a great semi-documentary chase sequence." It does, but the movie is basically derived from our old gangster movies, and beautifully made as it is, one would have a hard time convincing educated people to go see a movie that features a stunning performance by Gian Maria Volonte which is based on Paul Muni and James Cagney. Presumably they want something different from movies than a genre picture that offers images of modern urban decay and is smashingly directed. If a movie is interesting primarily in terms of technique then it isn't worth talking about except to students who can learn from seeing how a good director works. And to talk about a movie like "The Graduate" in terms of movie technique is really a bad joke. Technique at this level is not of any aesthetic importance; it's not the ability to achieve what you're after but the skill to find something acceptable. One must talk about a film like this in terms of what audiences enjoy it for or one is talking gibberish—and might as well be analyzing the "art" of commercials. And for the greatest movie artists where there is a unity of technique and subject, one doesn't need to talk about technique much because it has been subsumed in the art. One doesn't want to talk about how Tolstoi got his effects but about the work itself. One doesn't want to talk about how Jean Renoir does it; one wants to talk about what he has done. One can try to separate it all out, of course, distinguish form and content for purposes of analysis. But that is a secondary, analytic function, a scholarly function, and hardly needs to be done explicitly in criticism. Taking it apart is far less important than trying to see it whole. The critic shouldn't need to tear a work apart to demonstrate that he knows how it was put together. The important thing is to convey what is new and beautiful in the work, not how it was made—which is more or less implicit.

Just as there are good actors—possibly potentially great actors—who have never become big stars because they've just never been lucky enough to get the roles they needed (Brian Keith is a striking example) there are good directors who never got the scripts and the casts that could make their reputations. The question people ask when they consider going to a movie is not "How's it made?" but "What's it about?" and that's a perfectly legitimate question. (The next question—sometimes the first—is generally, "Who's in it?" and that's a good, honest question, too.) When you're at a movie, you don't have to believe in it to enjoy it but you do have to be interested. (Just as you have to be interested in the human material, too. Why should you go see *another* picture with James Stewart?) I don't want to see another samurai epic in exactly the same way I never want to read "Kristin Lavransdatter." Though it's conceivable that a truly great movie director could make any subject interesting, there are few such artists working in movies and if they did work on unpromising subjects I'm not sure we'd really enjoy the results even if we did *admire* their artistry. (I recognize the greatness of sequences in several films by Eistenstein but it's a rather cold admiration.) The many brilliant Italian directors who are working within a commercial framework on crime and action movies are obviously not going to be of any great interest unless they get a chance to work on a subject we care about. Ironically the Czech successes here ("The Shop on Main Street," "Loves of a Blonde," "Closely Watched Trains") are acclaimed for their techniques, which are fairly simple and rather limited, when it's obviously their human concern and the basic modesty and decency of their attitudes plus a little barnyard humor which

audiences respond to. They may even respond partly because of the *simplicity* of the techniques.

iv

When we are children, though there are categories
of films we don't like—documentaries generally
(they're too much like education) and, of course,
movies especially designed for children—by the
time we can go on our own we have learned to
avoid them. Children are often put down by adults
when the children say they enjoyed a particular
movie; adults who are short on empathy are quick
to point out aspects of the plot or theme that the
child didn't understand, and it's easy to humiliate a
child in this way. But it is one of the glories of
eclectic arts like opera and movies that they include
so many possible kinds and combinations of pleasure. One may be enthralled by Leontyne Price in
"La Forza del Destino" even if one hasn't boned up
on the libretto, or entranced by "The Magic Flute"
even if one has boned up on the libretto, and a
movie may be enjoyed for many reasons that have
little to do with the story or the subtleties (if any) of
theme or character. Unlike "pure" arts which are
often defined in terms of what only they can do,
movies are open and unlimited. Probably everything
that can be done in movies can be done some other
way, but—and this is what's so miraculous and so
expedient about them—they can do almost anything
any other art can do (alone or in combination) and

they can take on some of the functions of exploration, of journalism, of anthropology, of almost any branch of knowledge as well. We go to the movies for the variety of what they can provide, and for their marvellous ability to give us easily and inexpensively (and usually painlessly) what we can get from other arts also. They are a wonderfully *convenient* art.

Movies are used by cultures where they are foreign films in a much more primitive way than in their own; they may be enjoyed as travelogues or as initiations into how others live or in ways we might not even guess. The sophisticated and knowledgeable moviegoer is likely to forget how new and how amazing the different worlds up there once seemed to him, and to forget how much a child reacts to, how many elements he is taking in, often for the first time. And even adults who have seen many movies may think a movie is "great" if it introduces them to unfamiliar subject matter; thus many moviegoers react as naïvely as children to "Portrait of Jason" or "The Queen." They think they're wonderful. The oldest plots and corniest comedy bits can be full of wonder for a child, just as the freeway traffic in a grade Z melodrama can be magical to a villager who has never seen a car. A child may enjoy even a movie like "Jules and Jim" for its sense of fun, without comprehending it as his parents do, just as we may enjoy an Italian movie as a sex comedy although in Italy it is considered social criticism or political satire. Jean-Luc Goddard liked the movie of "Pal Joey," and I suppose that a miserable American movie musical like "Pal Joey" might look good in France because I can't think of a single good dance number performed by French dancers in a French movie. The French enjoy what they're unable to do and we enjoy the French studies of the pangs of adolescent love that would be corny if made in Hollywood. A movie like "The Young Girls of Rochefort" demonstrates how even a gifted Frenchman who adores American musicals misunderstands their conventions. Yet it would be as stupid to say that the director Jacques Demy couldn't love American musicals because he doesn't understand their conventions as to tell a child he couldn't have liked "Planet of the Apes" because he didn't get the jokey references to the Scopes trial.

Every once in a while I see an anthropologist's report on how some preliterate tribe reacts to movies; they may, for example, be disturbed about where the actor has gone when he leaves the movie frame, or they may respond with enthusiasm to the noise and congestion of big-city life which in the film story are meant to show the depths of depersonalization to which we are sinking, but which they find funny or very jolly indeed. Different cultures have their own ways of enjoying movies. A few years ago the new "tribalists" here responded to the gaudy fantasies of "Juliet of the Spirits" by using the movie to turn on. A few had already made a trip of "8½," but "Juliet," which was, conveniently and perhaps not entirely accidentally, in electric, psychedelic color, caught on because of it. (The color was awful, like in bad MGM musicals—so one may wonder about the quality of the trips.)

The new tribalism in the age of the media is not

necessarily the enemy of commercialism; it is a direct outgrowth of commercialism and its ally, perhaps even its instrument. If a movie has enough clout, reviewers and columnists who were bored are likely to give it another chance, until on the second or third viewing, they discover that it affects them "viscerally"—and a big expensive movie is likely to do just that. "2001" is said to have caught on with youth (which can make it happen); and it's said that the movie will stone you—which is meant to be a recommendation. Despite a few dissident voices— I've heard it said, for example, that "2001" "gives you a bad trip because the visuals don't go with the music"—the promotion has been remarkably effective with students. "The tribes" tune in so fast that college students thousands of miles apart "have heard" what a great trip "2001" is before it has even reached their city.

Using movies to go on a trip has about as much connection with the art of film as using one of those Doris Day-Rock Hudson jobs for ideas on how to redecorate your home—an earlier way of stoning yourself. But it is relevant to an understanding of movies to try to separate out, for purposes of discussion at least, how we may personally *use* a film—to learn how to dress or how to speak more elegantly or how to make a grand entrance or even what kind of coffee maker we wish to purchase, or to take off from the movie into a romantic fantasy or a trip— from what makes it a good movie or a poor one, because, of course, we can *use* poor films as easily as good ones, perhaps *more* easily for such non-

123

aesthetic purposes as shopping guides or aids to tripping.

V

We generally become interested in movies because we *enjoy* them and what we enjoy them for has little to do with what we think of as art. The movies we respond to, even in childhood, don't have the same values as the official culture supported at school and in the middle-class home. At the movies we get low life and high life, while David Susskind and the moralistic reviewers chastise us for not patronizing what they think we should, "realistic" movies that would be good for us—like "A Raisin in the Sun," where we could learn the lesson that a Negro family can be as dreary as a white family. Movie audiences will take a lot of garbage, but it's pretty hard to make us queue up for pedagogy. At the movies we want a different kind of truth, something that surprises us and registers with us as funny or accurate or maybe amazing, maybe even amazingly beautiful. We get little things even in mediocre and terrible movies—José Ferrer sipping his booze through a straw in "Enter Laughing," Scott Wilson's hard scary all-American-boy-you-can't-reach face cutting through the pretensions of "In Cold Blood" with all its fancy bleak cinematography. We got, and still have embedded in memory, Tony Randall's surprising depth of feeling in "The Seven Faces of Dr. Lao," Keenan Wynn and Moyna Macgill in the lunch-counter sequence of "The Clock," John W. Bubbles on the dance floor in "Cabin in the Sky," the inflection Gene Kelly gave to the line, "I'm a rising young man" in "DuBarry Was a Lady," Tony Curtis saying "avidly" in "Sweet Smell of Success." Though the director may have been responsible for releasing it, it's the human material we react to most and remember longest. The art of the performers stays fresh for us, their beauty as beautiful as ever. There are so many kinds of things we get—the hangover sequence wittily designed for the CinemaScope screen in "The Tender Trap," the atmosphere of the newspaper offices in "The Luck of Ginger Coffey," the automat gone mad in "Easy Living." Do we need to lie and shift things to false terms—like those who have to say Sophia Loren is a great actress as if her *acting* had made her a star? Wouldn't we rather watch her than better actresses because she's so incredibly charming and because she's probably the greatest model the world has ever known? There are great moments—Angela Lansbury singing "Little Yellow Bird" in "Dorian Gray." (I don't think I've ever had a friend who didn't also treasure that girl and that song.) And there are absurdly right little moments—in "Saratoga Trunk" when Curt Bois says to Ingrid Bergman, "You're very beautiful," and she says, "Yes, isn't it lucky?" And those things have closer relationships to art than what the schoolteachers told us was true and beautiful. Not that the works we studied in school weren't often great (as we discovered *later*) but that what the teachers told us to admire them for (and if current texts are any indication, are still telling students to admire them for) was generally so false and prettified and moralistic that what might have been moments of pleasure in them, and what might have been cleansing in them, and subversive, too, had been coated over.

Because of the photographic nature of the medium and the cheap admission prices, movies took their impetus not from the desiccated imitation European high culture, but from the peep show, the Wild West show, the music hall, the comic strip—from what was coarse and common. The early Chaplin two-reelers still look surprisingly lewd, with bathroom jokes and drunkenness and hatred of work and proprieties. And the Western shoot-'em-ups certainly weren't the schoolteachers' notions of art—which in my school days, ran more to didactic poetry and "perfectly proportioned" statues and which over the years have progressed through nice stories to "good taste" and "excellence"—which may be more poisonous than homilies and dainty figurines because then you had a clearer idea of what you were up against and it was easier to fight. And this, of course, is what we were running away from when we went to the movies. All week we longed for Saturday afternoon and sanctuary—the anonymity and impersonality of sitting in a theatre, just enjoying ourselves, not having to be responsible, not having to be "good." Maybe you just want to look at people on the screen and know they're not looking back at you, that they're not going to turn on you and criticize you.

Perhaps the single most intense pleasure of movie-going is this non-aesthetic one of escaping from the

responsibilities of having the proper responses required of us in our official (school) culture. And yet
this is probably the best and most common basis for
developing an aesthetic sense because responsibility
to pay attention and to appreciate is anti-art, it
makes us too anxious for pleasure, too bored for
response. Far from supervision and official culture,
in the darkness at the movies where nothing is
asked of us and we are left alone, the liberation
from duty and constraint allows us to develop our
own aesthetic responses. Unsupervised enjoyment is
probably not the only kind there is but it may feel
like the only kind. Irresponsibility is part of the
pleasure of all art; it is the part the schools cannot
recognize. I don't like to buy "hard tickets" for a
"road show" movie because I hate treating a movie
as an occasion. I don't want to be pinned down
days in advance; I enjoy the casualness of moviegoing—of going in when I feel like it, when I'm in
the mood for a movie. It's the feeling of freedom
from respectability we have always enjoyed at the
movies that is carried to an extreme by American
International Pictures and the Clint Eastwood Italian Westerns; they are stripped of cultural values.
We may want more from movies than this negative
virtue but we know the feeling from childhood moviegoing when we loved the gamblers and pimps and
the cons' suggestions of muttered obscenities as the
guards walked by. The appeal of movies was in the
details of crime and high living and wicked cities
and in the language of toughs and urchins; it was in
the dirty smile of the city girl who lured the hero
away from Janet Gaynor. What draws us to movies

in the first place, the opening into other, forbidden or surprising, kinds of experience, and the vitality and corruption and irreverence of that experience are so direct and immediate and have so little connection with what we have been taught is art that many people feel more secure, feel that their tastes are becoming more cultivated when they begin to *appreciate* foreign films. One foundation executive told me that he was quite upset that his teen-agers had chosen to go to "Bonnie and Clyde" rather than with him to "Closely Watched Trains." He took it as a sign of lack of maturity. I think his kids made an honest choice, and not only because "Bonnie and Clyde" is the better movie, but because it is closer to us, it has some of the qualities of direct involvement that make us care about movies. But it's understandable that it's easier for us, as Americans, to see *art* in foreign films than in our own, because of how we, as Americans, think of art. Art is still what teachers and ladies and foundations believe in, it's civilized and refined, cultivated and serious, cultural, beautiful, European, Oriental: it's what America isn't, and it's especially what American movies are not. Still, if those kids had chosen "Wild in the Streets" over "Closely Watched Trains" I would think that was a sound and honest choice, too, even though "Wild in the Streets" is in most ways a terrible picture. It connects with their lives in an immediate even if a grossly frivolous way, and if we don't go to movies for excitement, if, even as children, we accept the cultural standards of refined adults, if we have so little drive that we accept "good taste," then we will probably never really

128

begin to care about movies at all. We will become like those people who "may go to American movies sometimes to relax" but when they want "a little more" from a movie, are delighted by how colorful and artistic Franco Zeffirelli's "The Taming of the Shrew" is, just as a couple of decades ago they were impressed by "The Red Shoes," made by Powell and Pressburger, the Zeffirellis of their day. Or, if they like the cozy feeling of uplift to be had from mildly whimsical movies about timid people, there's generally a "Hot Millions" or something musty and faintly boring from Eastern Europe—one of those movies set in World War II but so remote from our ways of thinking that it seems to be set in World War I. Afterward, the moviegoer can feel as decent and virtuous as if he'd spent an evening visiting a deaf old friend of the family. It's a way of taking movies back into the approved culture of the schoolroom—into gentility—and the voices of schoolteachers and reviewers rise up to ask why America can't make such movies.

vi

Movie art is not the opposite of what we have always enjoyed in movies, it is not to be found in a return to that official high culture, it is what we have always found good in movies only more so. It's the subversive gesture carried further, the moments of excitement sustained longer and extended into new meanings. At best, the movie is totally informed by the kind of pleasure we have been taking from bits and pieces of movies. But we are so used to reaching out to the few good bits in a movie that we don't need formal perfection to be dazzled. There are so many arts and crafts that go into movies and there are so many things that can go wrong that they're not an art for purists. We want to experience that elation we feel when a movie (or even a performer in a movie) goes farther than we had expected and makes the leap successfully. Even a film like Godard's "Les Carabiniers," hell to watch for the first hour, is exciting to think about after because its one good sequence, the long picture-postcard sequence near the end, is so incredible and so brilliantly prolonged. The picture has been crawling and stumbling along and then it climbs a high wire and walks it and keeps walking it until we're almost dizzy from admiration. The tight rope is rarely stretched so high in movies, but there must be a sense of tension somewhere in the movie, if only in a bit player's face, not just mechanical suspense, or the movie is just more hours down the drain. It's the rare movie we really *go* with, the movie that keeps us tense and attentive. We learn to dread Hollywood "realism" and all that it implies. When, in the dark, we concentrate our attention, we are driven frantic by events on the level of ordinary life that pass at the rhythm of ordinary life. That's the self-conscious striving for integrity of humorless, untalented people. When we go to a play we expect a heightened, stylized language; the dull realism of the streets is unendurably boring, though we may escape from the play to the nearest bar to listen to the same language with relief. Better life than art imitating life.

If we go back and think over the movies we've enjoyed—even the ones we knew were terrible movies while we enjoyed them—what we enjoyed in them, the little part that was good, had, in some rudimentary way, some freshness, some hint of style, some trace of beauty, some audacity, some craziness. It's there in the interplay between Burt Lancaster and Ossie Davis, or, in "Wild in the Streets," in Diane Varsi rattling her tambourine, in Hal Holbrook's faint twitch when he smells trouble, in a few of Robert Thom's lines; and they have some relation to art though they don't look like what we've been taught is "quality." They have the joy of playfulness. In a mediocre or rotten movie, the good things may give the impression that they come out of nowhere; the better the movie, the more they seem to belong to the world of the movie. Without this kind of playfulness and the pleasure we take from it, art isn't art at all, it's something punishing, as it so often is in school where even artists' little *jokes* become leaden from explanation.

Keeping in mind that simple, good distinction that all art is entertainment but not all entertainment is art, it might be a good idea to keep in mind also that if a movie is said to be a work of art and you don't enjoy it, the fault may be in you, but it's probably in the movie. Because of the money and advertising pressures involved, many reviewers discover a fresh masterpiece every week, and there's that cultural snobbery, that hunger for respectability that determines the selection of the even bigger annual masterpieces. In foreign movies what is most often mistaken for "quality" is an imitation of earlier movie art or a derivation from respectable, approved work in the other arts—like the demented, suffering painter-hero of "Hour of the Wolf" smearing his lipstick in a facsimile of expressionist anguish. Kicked in the ribs, the press says "art" when "ouch" would be more appropriate. When a director is said to be an artist (generally on the basis of earlier work which the press failed to recognize) and especially when he picks artistic subjects like the pain of creation, there is a tendency to acclaim his new bad work. This way the press, in trying to make up for its past mistakes, manages to be wrong all the time. And so a revenge-of-a-sour-virgin movie like Truffaut's "The Bride Wore Black" is treated respectfully as if it somehow revealed an artist's sensibility in every frame. Reviewers who would laugh at Lana Turner going through her *femme fatale* act in another Ross Hunter movie swoon when Jeanne Moreau casts significant blank looks for Truffaut.

In American movies what is most often mistaken for artistic quality is box-office success, especially if it's combined with a genuflection to importance; then you have "a movie the industry can be proud of" like "To Kill a Mockingbird" or such Academy Award winners as "West Side Story," "My Fair Lady," or "A Man for All Seasons." Fred Zinnemann made a fine modern variant of a Western, "The Sundowners," and hardly anybody saw it until it got on television; but "A Man for All Seasons" had the look of prestige and the press felt honored to praise it. I'm not sure most movie reviewers consider what they honestly enjoy as being central to criticism. Some at least appear to think that that would be relying too much on their own tastes, being too personal instead of being "objective"—relying on the ready-made terms of cultural respectability and on consensus judgment (which, to a rather shocking degree, can be arranged by publicists creating a climate of importance around a movie). Just as movie directors, as they age, hunger for what was meant by respectability in their youth, and aspire to prestigious cultural properties, so, too, the movie press longs to be elevated in terms of the cultural values of their old high schools. And so they, along with the industry, applaud ghastly "tour-de-force" performances, movies based on "distinguished" stage successes or prize-winning novels, or movies that are "worthwhile," that make a "contribution"—"serious" messagy movies. This often involves praise of bad movies, of dull movies, or even the praise in good movies of what was worst in them.

This last mechanism can be seen in the honors bestowed on "In the Heat of the Night." The best thing in the movie is that high comic moment when Poitier says, "I'm a police officer," because it's a reversal of audience expectations and we laugh in delighted relief that the movie is not going to be another self-righteous, self-congratulatory exercise in the gloomy old Stanley Kramer tradition. At that point the audience sparks to life. The movie is fun largely because of the amusing central idea of a black Sherlock Holmes in a Tom and Jerry cartoon of reversals. Poiter's color is used for comedy instead of for that extra dimension of irony and pathos that made movies like "To Sir, with Love" unbearably sentimental. He doesn't really play the super sleuth very well: he's much too straight even when spouting the kind of higher scientific nonsense about right-handedness and left-handedness that would have kept Basil Rathbone in an ecstasy of clipped diction, blinking eyes and raised eyebrows. Like Bogart in "Beat the Devil" Poitier doesn't seem to be in on the joke. But Rod Steiger compensated with a comic performance that was even funnier for being so unexpected—not only from Steiger's career which had been going in other directions, but after the apparently serious opening of the film. The movie was, however, praised by the press as if it had been exactly the kind of picture that the audience was so relieved to discover it wasn't going to be (except in its routine melodramatic sequences full of fake courage and the climaxes such as Poitier slapping a rich white Southerner or being attacked by white thugs; except that is, in its worst parts). When I saw it, the audience, both black and white, enjoyed the joke of the fast-witted, hyper-educated black detective explaining matters to the backward, blundering Southern-chief-of-police slob. This racial joke is far more open and inoffensive than the usual "irony" of Poitier being so good and so black. For once it's *funny* (instead of embarrassing) that he's so superior to everybody.

"In the Heat of the Night" isn't in itself a particularly important movie; amazingly alive photographically, it's an entertaining, somewhat messed-up comedy-thriller. The director Norman Jewison destroys the final joke when Steiger plays redcap to

Poitier by infusing it with tender feeling, so it comes out sickly sweet, and it's too bad that a whodunit in which the whole point is the demonstration of the Negro detective's ability to unravel what the white man can't, is never clearly unraveled. Maybe it needed a Negro super director. (The picture might have been more than just a lively whodunit if the detective had proceeded to solve the crime not by "scientific" means but by an understanding of relationships in the South that the white chief of police didn't have.) What makes it interesting for my purposes here is that the audience enjoyed the movie for the vitality of its surprising playfulness, while the industry congratulated itself because the film was "hard-hitting"—that is to say, it flirted with seriousness and spouted warm, worthwhile ideas.

Those who can accept "In the Heat of the Night" as the socially conscious movie that the industry pointed to with pride can probably also go along with the way the press attacked Jewison's subsequent film, "The Thomas Crown Affair," as trash and a failure. One could even play the same game that was played on "In the Heat of the Night" and convert the "Crown" trifle into a sub-fascist exercise because, of course, Crown, the superman, who turns to crime out of boredom, is the crooked son of "The Fountainhead," out of Raffles. But that's taking glossy summer-evening fantasies much too seriously: we haven't had a junior executive's fantasy-life movie for a long time and to attack this return of the worldly gentlemen-thieves genre of Ronald Colman and William Powell *politically* is to fail to have a sense of humor about the little romantic-adolescent fascist lurking in most of us. Part of the fun of movies is that they allow us to see how silly many of our fantasies are and how widely they're shared. A light romantic entertainment like "The Thomas Crown Affair," trash undisguised, is the kind of chic crappy movie which (one would have thought) nobody could be fooled into thinking was art. Seeing it is like lying in the sun flicking through fashion magazines and, as we used to say, feeling rich and beautiful beyond your wildest dreams.

But it isn't easy to come to terms with what one enjoys in films, and if an older generation was persuaded to *dismiss* trash, now a younger generation, with the press and the schools in hot pursuit, has begun to talk about trash as if it were really very serious art. College newspapers and the new press all across the country are full of a hilarious new form of scholasticism, with students using their education to cook up impressive reasons for enjoying very simple, traditional dishes. Here is a communication from Cambridge to a Boston paper:

To the Editor:
"The Thomas Crown Affair" is fundamentally a film about faith between people. In many ways, it reminds me of a kind of updated old fable, or tale, about an ultimate test of faith. It is a film about a love affair (note the title), with a subplot of a bank robbery, rather than the reverse. The subtlety of the film is in the way the external plot is used as a matrix to develop serious motifs, much in the same way that the "Heat of the Night" functioned.
Although Thomas Crown is an attractive and fascinating character, Vicki is the protagonist. Crown is consistent, predictable: he courts personal danger to feel superior to the system of which he is a part, and

to make his otherwise overly comfortable life more interesting. Vicki is caught between two opposing elements within her, which, for convenience, I would call masculine and feminine. In spite of her glamour, at the outset she is basically masculine, in a man's type of job, ruthless, after prestige and wealth. But Crown looses the female in her. His test is a test of her femininity. The masculine responds to the challenge. Therein lies the pathos of her final revelation. Her egocentrism had not yielded to his.

In this psychic context, the possibility of establishing faith is explored. The movement of the film is towards Vicki's final enigma. Her ambivalence is commensurate with the increasing danger to Crown. The suspense lies in how she will respond to her dilemma, rather than whether Crown will escape.

I find "The Thomas Crown Affair" to be a unique and haunting film, superb in its visual and technical design, and fascinating for the allegorical problem of human faith.

"The Thomas Crown Affair" is pretty good trash, but we shouldn't convert what we enjoy it for into false terms derived from our study of the other arts. That's being false to what we enjoy. If it was priggish for an older generation of reviewers to be ashamed of what they enjoyed and to feel they had to be contemptuous of popular entertainment, it's even more priggish for a new movie generation to be so proud of what they enjoy that they use their education to try to place trash within the acceptable academic tradition. What the Cambridge boy is doing is a more devious form of that elevating and falsifying of people who talk about Loren as a great actress instead of as a gorgeous, funny woman. Trash doesn't belong to the academic tradition, and that's part of the *fun* of trash—that you know (or

should know) that you don't have to take it seriously, that it was never meant to be anymore than
frivolous and trifling and entertaining.

It's appalling to read solemn academic studies of
Hitchcock or von Sternberg by people who seem to
have lost sight of the primary reason for seeing films
like "Notorious" or "Morocco"—which is that they
were not intended solemnly, that they were playful
and inventive and faintly (often deliberately) absurd.
And what's good in them, what relates them to art, is
that playfulness and absence of solemnity. There is
talk now about von Sternberg's technique—his use
of light and décor and detail—and he is, of course,
a kitsch master in these areas, a master of studied
artfulness and pretty excess. Unfortunately, some
students take this technique as proof that his films
are works of art, once again, I think, falsifying what
they really respond to—the satisfying romantic glamour of his very pretty trash. "Morocco" is great
trash, and movies are so rarely great art, that if we
cannot appreciate great *trash*, we have very little
reason to be interested in them. The kitsch of an
earlier era—even the best kitsch—does not become
art, though it may become camp. Von Sternberg's
movies became camp even while he was still making
them, because as the romantic feeling went out of his
trash—when he became so enamored of his own
pretty effects that he turned his human material into
blank, affectless pieces of décor—his absurd trashy
style was all there was. We are now told in respectable museum publications that in 1932 a movie like
"Shanghai Express" "was completely misunderstood
as a mindless advanture" when indeed it was com-

pletely *understood* as a mindless adventure. And enjoyed as a mindless adventure. It's a peculiar form of movie madness crossed with academicism, this lowbrowism masquerading as highbrowism, eating a candy bar and cleaning an "allegorical problem of human faith" out of your teeth. If we always wanted works of complexity and depth we wouldn't be going to movies about glamorous thieves and seductive women who sing in cheap cafés, and if we loved "Shanghai Express" it wasn't for its mind but for the glorious sinfulness of Dietrich informing Clive Brook that, "It took more than one man to change my name to Shanghai Lily" and for the villainous Oriental chieftain (Warner Oland!) delivering the classic howler, "The white woman stays with me."

If we don't deny the pleasures to be had from certain kinds of trash and accept "The Thomas Crown Affair" as a pretty fair example of entertaining trash, then we may ask if a piece of trash like this has any relationship to art. And I think it does. Steve McQueen gives probably his most glamourous, fashionable performance yet, but even enjoying him as much as I do, I wouldn't call his performance art. It's artful, though, which is exactly what is required in this kind of vehicle. If he had been luckier, if the script had provided what it so embarrassingly lacks, the kind of sophisticated dialogue—the sexy shop-talk—that such writers as Jules Furthman and William Faulkner provided for Bogart, and if the director Norman Jewison had Lubitsch's lightness of touch, McQueen might be acclaimed as a suave, "polished" artist. Even in this flawed setting, there's a self-awareness in his performance that makes his elegance funny. And Haskell Wexler, the cinematographer, lets go with a whole bag of tricks, flooding the screen with his delight in beauty, shooting all over the place, and sending up the material. And Pablo Ferro's games with the split screen at the beginning are such conscious, clever games designed to draw us in to watch intently what is of no great interest. What gives this trash a lift, what makes it entertaining is clearly that some of those involved, knowing of course that they were working on a silly shallow script and a movie that wasn't about anything of consequence, used the chance to have a good time with it. If the director, Norman Jewison, could have built a movie instead of putting together a patchwork of sequences, "Crown" might have had a chance to be considered a movie in the class and genre of Lubitsch's "Trouble in Paradise." It doesn't come near that because to transform this kind of kitsch, to make art of it, one needs that unifying grace, that formality and charm that a Lubitsch could sometimes provide. Still, even in this movie we get a few grace notes in McQueen's playfulness, and from Wexler and Ferro. Working on trash, feeling free to play, can loosen up the actors and craftsmen just as seeing trash can liberate the spectator. And as we don't get this playful quality of art much in movies except in trash, we might as well relax and enjoy it freely for what it is. I don't trust anyone who doesn't admit having at some time in his life enjoyed trashy American movies; I don't trust *any* of the tastes of people who were born with such good taste that they didn't need to find their way through trash.

There is a moment in "Children of Paradise" when the rich nobleman (Louis Salou) turns on his mistress, the pearly plebeian Garance (Arletty). He complains that in all their years together he has never had her love, and she replies, "You've got to leave something for the poor." We don't ask much from movies, just a little something that we can call our own. Who at some point hasn't set out dutifully for that fine foreign film and then ducked into the nearest piece of American trash? We're not only educated people of taste, we're also common people with common feelings. And our common feelings are not all *bad*. You hoped for some aliveness in that trash that you were pretty sure you wouldn't get from the respected "art film." You had long since discovered that you wouldn't get it from certain kinds of American movies, either. The industry now is taking a neo-Victorian tone, priding itself on its (few) "good, clean" movies—which are always its worst movies because almost nothing can break through the smug surfaces, and even performers' talents become cute and cloying. The lowest action trash is preferable to wholesome family entertainment. When you clean them up, when you make movies respectable, you kill them. The wellspring of their *art*, their greatness, is in not being respectable.

vii

Does trash corrupt? A nutty Puritanism still flourishes in the arts, not just in the schoolteachers' approach of wanting art to be "worthwhile," but in the higher reaches of the academic life with those ideologues who denounce us for enjoying trash as if this enjoyment took us away from the really disturbing, angry new art of our time and somehow destroyed us. If we had to *justify* our trivial silly pleasures, we'd have a hard time. How could we possibly *justify* the fun of getting to know some people in movie after movie, like Joan Blondell, the brassy blonde with the heart of gold, or waiting for the virtuous, tiny, tiny-featured heroine to say her line so we could hear the riposte of her tough, wise-cracking girlfriend (Iris Adrian was my favorite). Or, when the picture got too monotonous, there would be the song interlude, introduced "atmospherically" when the cops and crooks were both in the same never-neverland nightclub and everything stopped while a girl sang. Sometimes it would be the most charming thing in the movie, like Dolores Del Rio singing "You Make Me That Way" in "International Settlement"; sometimes it would drip with maudlin meaning, like "Oh Give Me Time for Tenderness" in "Dark Victory" with the dying Bette Davis singing along with the chanteuse. The pleasures of this kind of trash are not intellectually defensible. But why should pleasure need justification? Can one demonstrate that trash desensitizes us, that it prevents people from enjoying something better, that it limits our range of aesthetic response? Nobody I know of has provided such a demonstration. Do even Disney movies or Doris Day movies do us lasting harm? I've never known a person I thought had been harmed by them, though it does seem to me that they affect the tone of a culture, that perhaps—and I don't mean to be facetious—they may poison us collectively though they don't injure us individually. There are women who want to see a world in which everything is pretty and cheerful and in which romance triumphs ("Barefoot in the Park," "Any Wednesday,"); families who want movies to be an innocuous inspiration, a good example for the children ("The Sound of Music," "The Singing Nun"); couples who want the kind of folksy blue humor ("A Guide for the Married Man") that they still go to Broadway shows for. These people are the reason slick, stale, rotting pictures make money; they're the reason so few pictures are any good. And in that way, this terrible conformist culture does affect us all. It certainly cramps and limits opportunities for artists. But that isn't what generally gets attacked as trash, anyway. I've avoided using the term "harmless trash" for movies like "The Thomas Crown Affair," because that would put me on the side of the angels—against "harmful trash," and I don't honestly know what that is. It's common for the press to call cheaply made, violent action movies "brutalizing" but that tells us less about any actual demonstrable effects than about the finicky tastes of the reviewers—who are often highly appreciative of violence in more expensive and "artistic" settings such as "Petulia." It's almost a class prejudice, this assumption that crudely made movies, movies without the look of art, are bad for people.

If there's a little art in good trash and sometimes even in poor trash, there may be more trash than is generally recognized in some of the most acclaimed "art" movies. Such movies as "Petulia" and "2001" may be no more than trash in the latest, up-to-the-minute guises, using "artistic techniques" to give trash the look of art. The serious art look may be the latest fashion in *expensive* trash. All that "art" may be what prevents pictures like these from being *enjoyable* trash; they're not honestly crummy, they're very fancy and they take their crummy ideas seriously.

I have rarely seen a more disagreeable, a more dislikable (or a bloodier) movie than "Petulia" and I would guess that its commercial success represents a triumph of publicity—and not the simple kind of just taking ads. It's a very strange movie and people may, of course, like it for all sorts of reasons, but I think many may dislike it as I do and still feel they should be impressed by it; the educated and privileged may now be more susceptible to the mass media than the larger public—they're certainly easier to reach. The publicity about Richard Lester as an artist has been gaining extraordinary momentum ever since "A Hard Day's Night." A critical success that is also a hit makes the director a genius; he's a magician who made money out of art. The media are in ravenous competition for ever bigger stories, for "trend" pieces and editorial essays, because once the process starts it's considered news. If Lester is "making the scene" a magazine that hasn't helped to build him up feels it's been scooped. "Petulia" is the come-dressed-as-the-sick-soul-of-America-party and in the opening sequence the guests arrive—rich victims of highway accidents in their casts and wheel chairs, like the spirit of '76 coming to opening night at the opera. It's science-horror fiction—a garish new world with charity balls at which you're invited to "Shake for Highway Safety."

Lester picked San Francisco for his attack on America just as in "How I Won the War" he picked World War II to attack war. That is, it looks like a real frontal attack on war itself if you attack the war that many people consider a just war. But then he concentrated not on the issues of that war but on the class hatreds of British officers and men—who were not engaged in defending London or bombing Germany but in building a cricket pitch in Africa. In "Petulia," his hate letter to America, he relocates the novel, shifting the locale from Los Angeles to San Francisco, presumably, again, to face the big challenge by showing that even the best the country has to offer is rotten. But then he ducks the challenge he sets for himself by making San Francisco look like Los Angeles. And if he must put carnival barkers in Golden Gate Park and invent Sunday excursions for children to Alcatraz, if he must invent such caricatures of epicene expenditure and commercialism as bizarrely automated motels and dummy television sets, if he must provide his own ugliness and hysteria and lunacy and use filters to destroy the city's beautiful light, if, in short, he must falsify America in order to make it appear hateful, what is it he really hates? He's like a crooked cop framing a suspect with trumped-up evidence. We never find out *why:* he's too interested in making a flashy case to examine what he's doing. And reviewers seem unwilling to ask questions which might expose them to the charge that they're *still* looking for meaning instead of, in the new cant, just reacting to images—such questions as why does the movie keep juxtaposing shots of bloody surgery with shots of rock groups like the Grateful Dead or Big Brother and the Holding Company and shots of the war in Vietnam. What are these little montages supposed to do to us—make us feel that even the hero (a hardworking life-saving surgeon) is implicated in the war and that somehow contemporary popular music is also allied to destruction and death? (I thought only the moralists of the Soviet Union believed that.) The images of "Petulia" don't make valid connections, they're joined together for shock and excitement, and I don't believe in the brilliance of a method which equates hippies, war, surgery, wealth, Southern decadents, bullfights, etc. Lester's mix is almost as fraudulent as "Mondo Cane"; "Petulia" exploits any shocking material it can throw together to give false importance to a story about Holly Golightly and The Man in the Gray Flannel Suit. The jagged glittering mosaic style of "Petulia" is an armor protecting Lester from an artist's task; this kind of "style" no longer fools people so much in writing but it knocks them silly in films.

Movie directors in trouble fall back on what they love to call "personal style"—though how impersonal it often is can be illustrated by "Petulia"—which is not edited in the rhythmic, modulations-of-graphics style associated with Lester (and seen most distinctively in his best-edited, though not necessarily best film, "Help!") but in the style of the movie surgeon, Anthony Gibbs, who acted as chopper on it, and who gave it the same kind of scissoring which

146

he had used on "The Loneliness of the Long Distance Runner" and in his rescue operation on "Tom Jones." This is, in much of "Petulia," the most insanely obvious method of cutting film ever devised; keep the audience jumping with cuts, juxtapose startling images, anything for effectiveness, just make it *brilliant*—with the director taking, apparently, no responsibility for the *implied* connections. (The editing style is derived from Alain Resnais, and though it's a debatable style in his films, he uses it responsibly not just opportunistically.)

Richard Lester, the director of "Petulia," is a shrill scold in Mod clothes. Consider a sequence like the one in which the beaten-to-a-gruesome-pulp heroine is taken out to an ambulance, to the accompaniment of hippies making stupid, unfeeling remarks. It is embarrassingly reminiscent of the older people's comments about the youthful sub-pre-hippies of "The Knack." Lester has simply shifted villains. Is he saying that America is so rotten that even our hippies are malignant? I rather suspect he is, but why? Lester has taken a fashionably easy way to attack America, and because of the war in Vietnam some people are willing to accept the bloody montages that make them feel we're all guilty, we're rich, we're violent, we're spoiled, we can't relate to each other, etc. Probably the director who made three celebrations of youth and freedom ("A Hard Day's Night," "The Knack," and "Help!") is now desperate to expand his range and become a "Serious" director, and this is the new look in seriousness.

It's easy to make fun of the familiar ingredients of trash—the kook heroine who steals a tuba (that's not like the best of Carole Lombard but like the worst of Irene Dunne), the vaguely impotent, meaninglessly handsome rotter husband, Richard Chamberlain (back to the rich, spineless weaklings of David Manners), and Joseph Cotten as one more insanely vicious decadent Southerner spewing out villainous lines. (Even Victor Jory in "The Fugitive Kind" wasn't much meaner.) What's terrible is not so much this feeble conventional trash as the director's attempts to turn it all into scintillating art and burning comment; what is really awful is the trash of his ideas and artistic effects.

Is there any art in this obscenely self-important movie? Yes, but in a format like this the few good ideas don't really shine as they do in simpler trash; we have to go through so much unpleasantness and showing-off to get to them. Lester should trust himself more as a director and stop the cinemagician stuff because there's good, tense direction in a few sequences. He got a good performance from George C. Scott and a sequence of post-marital discord between Scott and Shirley Knight that, although overwrought, is not so glaringly overwrought as the rest of the picture. It begins to suggest something interesting that the picture might have been about (Shirley Knight should, however, stop fondling her hair like a miser with a golden hoard; it's time for her to get another prop.) And Julie Christie is extraordinary just to look at—lewd and anxious, expressive and empty, brilliantly faceted but with something central missing, almost as if there's no woman inside.

148

viii

"2001" is a movie that might have been made by the hero of "Blow-Up," and it's fun to think about Kubrick really doing every dumb thing he wanted to do, building enormous science-fiction sets and equipment, never even bothering to figure out what he was going to do with them. Fellini, too, had gotten carried away with the Erector Set approach to moviemaking, but his big science-fiction construction, exposed to view at the end of "8½," was abandoned. Kubrick never really made his movie either but he doesn't seem to know it. Some people like the American International Pictures stuff because it's rather idiotic and maybe some people love "2001" just because Kubrick did all that stupid stuff, acted out a kind of super sci-fi nut's fantasy. In some ways it's the biggest amateur movie of them all, complete even to the amateur-movie obligatory scene—the director's little daughter (in curls) telling daddy what kind of present she wants.

There was a little pre-title sequence in "You Only Live Twice" with an astronaut out in space that was in a looser, more free style than "2001"—a daring little moment that I think was more fun than all of "2001." It had an element of the unexpected, of the shock of finding death in space lyrical. Kubrick is carried away by the idea. The secondary title of "Dr. Strangelove," which we took to be satiric, "How I learned to stop worrying and love the bomb," was not, it now appears, altogether satiric for Kubrick. "2001" celebrates the invention of tools of death, as an evolutionary route to a higher order of *non-human* life. Kubrick literally learned to stop worrying and love the bomb; he's become his own butt —the Herman Kahn of extraterrestrial games theory. The ponderous blurry appeal of the picture may be that it takes its stoned audience out of this world to a consoling vision of a graceful world of space, controlled by superior godlike minds, where the hero is reborn as an angelic baby. It has the dreamy somewhere-over-the-rainbow appeal of a new vision of heaven. "2001" is a celebration of cop-out. It says man is just a tiny nothing on the stairway to paradise, something better is coming, and it's all out of your hands anyway. There's an intelligence out there in space controlling your destiny from ape to angel, so just follow the slab. Drop up.

It's a bad, bad sign when a movie director begins to think of himself as a myth-maker, and this limp myth of a grand plan that justifies slaughter and ends with resurrection has been around before. Kubrick's story line—accounting for evolution by an extraterrestrial intelligence—is probably the most gloriously redundant plot of all time. And although his intentions may have been different, "2001" celebrates the *end of man;* those beautiful mushroom clouds at the end of "Strangelove" were no accident. In "2001, A Space Odyssey," death and life are all the same: no point is made in the movie of Gary Lockwood's death—the moment isn't even defined—and the hero doesn't discover that the hibernating scientists have become corpses. That's unimportant in a movie about the beauties of resurrection. Trip off to join the cosmic intelligence and come back a better mind. And as the trip in the movie is the usual psychedelic light show, the audience doesn't even have to worry about getting to Jupiter. They can go to heaven in Cinerama.

It isn't accidental that we don't care if the characters live or die; if Kubrick has made his people so uninteresting, it is partly because characters and individual fates just aren't big enough for certain kinds of big movie directors. Big movie directors become generals in the arts; and they want subjects to match their new importance. Kubrick has announced that his next project is "Napoleon"—which, for a movie director, is the equivalent of Joan of Arc for an actress. Lester's "savage" comments about affluence and malaise, Kubrick's inspirational banality about how we will become as gods through machinery, are big-shot show-business deep thinking. This isn't a new show-business phenomenon; it belongs to the genius tradition of the theatre. Big entrepreneurs, producers, and directors who stage big spectacular shows, even designers of large sets have traditionally begun to play the role of visionaries and thinkers and men with answers. They get too big for art. Is a work of art possible if pseudoscience and the technology of movie-making become more important to the "artist" than man? This is central to the failure of "2001." It's a monumentally unimaginative movie: Kubrick, with his $750,000 centrifuge, and in love with gigantic hardware and control panels, is the Belasco of science fiction. The special effects—though straight from the drawing board—are good

151

and big and awesomely, expensively detailed. There's a little more that's good in the movie, when Kubrick doesn't take himself too seriously—like the comic moment when the gliding space vehicles begin their Johann Strauss waltz; that is to say, when the director shows a bit of sense of proportion about what he's doing, and sees things momentarily as comic—when the movie doesn't take itself with such idiot solemnity. The light-show trip is of no great distinction; compared to the work of experimental filmmakers like Jordan Belson, it's third-rate. If big film directors are to get credit for doing badly what others have been doing brilliantly for years with no money, just because they've put it on a big screen, then businessmen are greater than poets and theft is art.

ix

Part of the fun of movies is in seeing "what everybody's talking about," and if people are flocking to a movie, or if the press can con us into thinking that they are, then ironically, there is a sense in which we want to see it, even if we suspect we won't enjoy it, because we want to know what's going on. Even if it's the worst inflated pompous trash that is the most talked about (and it usually is) and even if that talk is manufactured, we want to see the movies because so many people fall for whatever is talked about that they make the advertisers' lies true. Movies absorb material from the culture and the other arts so fast that some films that have been widely *sold* become culturally and sociologically important whether they are good movies or not. Movies like "Morgan!" or "Georgy Girl" or the "The Graduate"—aesthetically trivial movies which, however, because of the ways some people react to them, enter into the national bloodstream—become cultural and psychological equivalents of watching a political convention—to observe what's going on. And though this has little to do with the art of movies, it has a great deal to do with the appeal of movies.

An analyst tells me that when his patients are not talking about their personal hangups and their immediate problems they talk about the situations and characters in movies like "The Graduate" or "Belle de Jour" and they talk about them with as much personal involvement as about their immediate problems. I have elsewhere suggested that this way of reacting to movies as psychodrama used to be considered a pre-literate way of reacting but that now those considered "post-literate" are reacting like pre-literates. The high school and college students identifying with Georgy Girl or Dustin Hoffman's Benjamin are not that different from the stenographer who used to live and breathe with the Joan Crawford-working girl and worry about whether that rich boy would really make her happy—and considered her pictures "great." They don't see the movie as a movie but as part of the soap opera of their lives. The fan magazines used to encourage this kind of identification; now the *advanced* mass media encourage it, and those who want to sell to youth use the language of "just let it flow over you." The person who responds this way does not respond more freely but less freely and less fully than the person who is aware of what is well done and what badly done in a movie, who can accept some things in it and reject others, who uses all his senses in reacting, not just his emotional vulnerabilities.

Still, we care about what other people care about —sometimes because we want to know how far we've gotten from common responses—and if a movie is important to other people we're interested in it because of what it means to them, even if it doesn't mean much to us. The small triumph of "The Graduate" was to have domesticated alienation and the difficulty of communication, by making what Benjamin is alienated from a middle-class comic strip and making it absurdly evident that he has nothing to communicate—which is just what makes him an acceptable hero for the large movie audience. If he said anything or had any ideas, the audience would probably hate him. "The Graduate" isn't a *bad* movie, it's entertaining, though in a fairly slick way (the audience is just about programmed for laughs). What's surprising is that so many people take it so seriously. What's funny about the movie are the laughs on that dumb sincere boy who wants to talk about art in bed when the woman just wants to fornicate. But then the movie begins to pander to youthful narcissism, glorifying his innocence, and making the predatory (and now crazy) woman the villainess. Commercially this works: the inarticulate dull boy becomes a romantic hero for the audience to project into with all those squishy and now conventional feelings of look, his parents don't communicate with him; look, he wants truth not sham, and so on. But the movie betrays itself and its own expertise, sells out its comic moments that click along with the rhythm of a hit Broadway show, to make the oldest movie pitch of them all—asking the audience to identify with the simpleton who is the latest version of the misunderstood teen-ager and the pure-in-heart boy next door. It's almost painful to tell kids who have gone to see "The Graduate" eight times that once was enough for you because you've already seen it eighty times with Charles Ray and Robert Harron and Richard Barthelmess and Richard Cromwell and Charles Farrell. How could you convince them that a movie that sells innocence is a very commercial piece of work when they're so clearly in the market to buy innocence? When "The Graduate" shifts to the tender awakenings of love, it's just the latest version of "David and Lisa." "The Graduate" only wants to succeed and that's fundamentally what's the matter with it. There is a pause for a laugh after the mention of "Berkeley" that is an unmistakable sign of hunger for success; this kind of movie-making shifts values, shifts focus, shifts emphasis, shifts everything for a sure-fire response. Mike Nichols' "gift" is that he lets the audience direct him; this is demagoguery in the arts.

Even the cross-generation fornication is standard for the genre. It goes back to Pauline Frederick in "Smouldering Fires," and Clara Bow was at it with mama Alice Joyce's boyfriend in "Our Dancing Mothers," and in the Forties it was "Mildred Pierce." Even the terms are not different: in these movies the seducing adults are customarily sophisticated, worldly, and corrupt, the kids basically innocent, though not so humorless and blank as Benjamin. In its basic attitudes "The Graduate" is corny American; it takes us back to before "The Game of Love" and Edwige Feuillère as the sympathetic older woman and "A Cold Wind in August" with the sympathetic Lola Albright performance.

What's interesting about the success of "The Graduate" is sociological: the revelation of how emotionally accessible modern youth is to the same old manipulation. The recurrence of certain themes in movies suggests that each generation wants romance restated in slightly new terms, and of course it's one of the pleasures of movies as a popular art that they can answer this need. And yet, and yet—one doesn't expect an *educated* generation to be so soft on itself, much softer than the factory workers of the past who didn't go back over and over to the same movies, mooning away in fixation on themselves and thinking this fixation meant movies had suddenly become an art, and *their* art.

X

When you're young the odds are very good that you'll find something to enjoy in almost any movie. But as you grow more experienced, the odds change. I saw a picture a few years ago that was the sixth version of material that wasn't much to start with. Unless you're feebleminded, the odds get worse and worse. We don't go on reading the same kind of manufactured novels—pulp Westerns or detective thrillers, say—all of our lives, and we don't want to go on and on looking at movies about cute heists by comically assorted gangs. The problem with a popular art form is that those who want something more are in a hopeless minority compared with the millions who are always seeing it for the first time, or for the reassurance and gratification of seeing the conventions fulfilled again. Probably a large part of the older audience gives up movies for this reason—simply that they've seen it before. And probably this is why so many of the best movie critics quit. They're wrong when they blame it on the movies going bad; it's the odds becoming so bad, and they can no longer bear the many tedious movies for the few good moments and the tiny shocks of recognition. Some become too tired, too frozen in fatigue, to respond to what *is* new. Others who *do* stay awake may become too demanding for the young who are seeing it all for the first hundred times. The critical task is necessarily comparative, and younger people do not truly know what is new. And despite all the chatter about the media and how smart the young are, they're incredibly naïve about mass culture—perhaps *more* naïve than earlier generations (though I don't know why). Maybe watching all that television hasn't done so much for them as they seem to think; and when I read a young intellectual's appreciation of "Rachel, Rachel" and come to "the mother's passion for chocolate bars is a superb symbol for the second coming of childhood" I know the writer is still in his first childhood, and I wonder if he's going to come out of it.

157

One's moviegoing tastes and habits change—I still like in movies what I always liked but now, for example, I really want documentaries. After all the years of stale stupid acted-out stories, with less and less for me in them, I am desperate to know something, desperate for facts, for information, for faces of nonactors and for knowledge of how people live—for revelations, not for the little bits of show-business detail worked up for us by show-business minds who got them from the same movies we're tired of.

But the big change is in our *habits*. If we make any kind of decent, useful life for ourselves we have less need to run from it to those diminishing pleasures of the movies. When we go to the movies we want something good, something sustained, we don't want to settle for just a bit of something, because we have other things to do. If life at home is more interesting, why go to the movies? And the theatres frequented by true moviegoers—those perennial displaced persons in each city, the loners and the losers—depress us. Listening to them—and they are often more audible than the sound track—as they cheer the cons and jeer the cops, we may still share their disaffection, but it's not enough to keep us interested in cops and robbers. A little nose-thumbing isn't enough. If we've grown up at the movies we know that good work is continuous not with the academic, respectable tradition but with the glimpses of something good in trash, but we want the subversive gesture carried to the domain of discovery. Trash has given us an appetite for art.

III

Movies by the Week: Second Sequence

Bravo!

Barbra Streisand arrives on the screen, in "Funny Girl," when the movies are in desperate need of her. The timing is perfect. There's hardly a star in American movies today, and if we've got so used to the absence of stars that we no longer think about it much, we've also lost one of the great pleasures of moviegoing: watching incandescent people up there, more intense and dazzling than people we ordinarily encounter in life, and far more charming than the extraordinary people we encounter, because the ones on the screen are objects of pure contemplation—like athletes all wound up in the stress of competition—and we don't have to undergo the frenzy or the risks of being involved with them. In life, fantastically gifted people, people who are driven, can be too much to handle; they can be a pain. In plays, in opera, they're divine, and on the screen, where they can be seen in their perfection, and where we're even safer from them, they're *more* divine.

Let's dispose at once of the ugly-duckling myth. It has been commonly said that the musical "Funny Girl" was a comfort to people because it carried the message that you do not need to be pretty to succeed. That is nonsense; the "message" of Barbra Streisand in "Funny Girl" is that talent is beauty.

And this isn't some comforting message for plain people; it's what show business is all about. Barbra Streisand is much more beautiful than "pretty" people. This has not always been as true for the movies as for the stage; not handled carefully, some stage stars looked awful on the screen, so the legend developed that movie actors and actresses had to have "perfect" little features, and studio practices kept the legend going. But the banality of mere prettiness is a blight on American movies: Who can tell those faces apart? The Italian actresses, with their big, irregular features, became so popular here because we were starved for a trace of life after all those (usually fake) Wasp stereotypes. It's unfortunate that in this case the (I assume unintentional) demonstration of how uninteresting prettiness is should be at the expense of Omar Sharif, who goes as far as to demonstrate that good looks can be nothing.

Most Broadway musicals are dead before they reach the movies—the routines are so worked out they're stiff, and the jokes are embalmed in old applause. But Streisand has the gift of making old written dialogue sound like inspired improvisation; almost every line she says seems to have just sprung to mind and out. Her inflections are witty and surprising, and, more surprisingly, delicate; she can probably do more for a line than any screen comedienne since Jean Arthur, in the thirties. There hasn't been a funny girl on the screen for so long now that moviegoers have probably also got used to doing without one of the minor, once staple pleasures of moviegoing: the wisecracking heroines, the clever funny girls—Jean Arthur, of course, and Claudette

Colbert, and Carole Lombard, and Ginger Rogers, and Rosalind Russell, and Myrna Loy, and all the others who could be counted on to be sassy and sane. They performed a basic comic function—they weren't taken in by sham; they had the restorative good sense of impudence—and in the pre-bunny period they made American women distinctive and marvellous. The story and the situations of "Funny Girl" are even drearier than those of most big musicals, but we know the form is corrupt and we're used to the conventions of rags-to-riches-to-price-of-fame, and it's easy to take all that for granted and ignore it when a performer knows how to deliver a line. The form is corrupt but the spirit of the performer isn't— that's why a big, heavy, silly musical like this can still have some brute force in it. The comedy is the comedy of cutting through the bull, of saying what's really on your mind. Such comedy was usually derived from urban Jewish humor, even in the thirties; now the Midwestern mask has been removed. Though this comedy is often self-deprecating (not hostile or paranoid), it's *lightly* self-mocking, in a way that seems admirably suited to the genre. Here one can see the experience and tact of a good, solid director like William Wyler. Younger, less capable, more anxious directors will permit anything for a laugh, and material like this could easily become raucous and embarrassing; we're never in danger in Wyler's hands, and that sense of security puts us in the right mood for laughter.

It is Streisand's peculiar triumph that in the second half, when the routine heartbreak comes, as it apparently must in all musical biographies, she shows an aptitude for suffering that those clever actresses didn't. Where they became sanctimonious and noble, thereby violating everything we had loved them for, she simply drips as unself-consciously and impersonally as a true tragic muse. And the tears belong to her face; they seem to complete it, as Garbo's suffering in "Camille" seemed to complete her beauty. Much stronger and more dominating than the earlier comediennes, she skirts pathos because her emotions are so openly expressed. She doesn't "touch" us for sympathy in the Chaplinesque way by trying to conceal her hurt. She conceals nothing; she's fiercely, almost frighteningly direct.

Whenever Streisand is not on the screen, the movie is stodgy, advancing the plot and telegraphing information in tedious little scenes of Sharif with servants, Sharif gambling, etc. We know that he's playing Nicky Arnstein, Fanny Brice's husband, but we can't make any sense of him. If shady gamblers are not going to be flashy and entertaining, what good are they as musical-comedy heroes? This Arnstein is too phlegmatic for a playboy and too proper for a gambler, and he seems not only devoid of humor but almost unaware of it. So what is supposed to draw him and a funny girl together? Sharif appears to be some sort of visiting royalty, with a pained professional smile to put the common people at their ease. The result is that no one seems to know how to talk to him. But then there's no one in the movie but Streisand anyway; the world of the movie is a stage full of stooges (with Walter Pidgeon stuck playing Ziegfeld like Mr. Miniver). In all these ways it's a terrible movie, and though Streisand's makeup and costumes are beautiful and sumptuous (she sometimes resembles Monica Vitti), the other girls are not well served—partly, it appears, through a failure to decide whether the Ziegfeld girls should be glorified or parodied. (No definite tone is taken.) And the sets are not elegant and stylized; they're just bad period reconstructions. Sometimes all this gets in the way of enjoyment: the visual affront of square photography and a studio "alley" help to kill the "People" number (it's also strategically ill placed), and the shipboard sequences are damaged by their unappealing look. But one can fault everything else in the movie, too, and it doesn't really matter—not even the fact that the second half has to coast on the good will built up in the first. The crucial thing is that Wyler never makes the kind of mistake that Tony Richardson made in "The Entertainer" when he cut away from Laurence Olivier's great number to give us backstage business. We do not ask of a musical like "Funny Girl" that it give us the life story of Fanny Brice; we know that her story is simply the pretext for a show, a convention of our realistically rooted musical theatre, which seeks protection in great names or big properties from the past. What we do ask is that an actress who plays a star like Fanny Brice be able to live up to the image of a great star; if she isn't, we cannot accept the pretext, and the show is exposed as just an attempt to cash in on past glories. There is no such difficulty with "Funny Girl." The end of the movie, in a long single take, is a bravura stroke, a gorgeous piece of showing off, that makes one intensely, brilliantly aware of the star as a performer and of the star's pride in herself as performer. The pride is justified.

September 28, 1968

Weekend in Hell

Only the title of Jean-Luc Godard's new film is casual and innocent; "Weekend" is the most powerful mystical movie since "The Seventh Seal" and "Fires on the Plain" and passages of Kurosawa. We are hardly aware of the magnitude of the author-director's conception until after we are caught up in the comedy of horror, which keeps going further and becoming more nearly inescapable, like "Journey to the End of the Night." The danger for satirists (and perhaps especially for visionary satirists) is that they don't always trust their art. They don't know how brilliantly they're making their points; they become mad with impatience and disgust, and throw off their art as if it were a hindrance to direct communication, and they begin to preach. When Godard is viciously funny, he's on top of things, and he scores and scores, and illuminates as he scores. When he becomes didactic, we can see that he really doesn't know anymore about what should be done than the rest of us. But then he goes beyond didacticism into areas where, though he is as confused and divided as we are, his fervor and rage are so imaginatively justified that they are truly apocalyptic. It is in the further reaches—in the appalling, ambivalent revolutionary vision—that "Weekend" is a great, original work.

"Weekend" begins with a callous disrespect for life which is just a slight stylization of civilized living now; it's as if the consumers of "The Married Woman" had become more adulterous, more nakedly mercenary, and touchier. The people in "Weekend" have weapons and use them at the slightest provocation, and it seems perfectly logical that they should get into their cars and bang into each other and start piling up on the roads. By the time the bourgeois couple (Mireille Darc and Jean Yanne) start off on their weekend trip—to get money out of her mother —we have been prepared for almost anything by the wife's description of a sex orgy that moved from bedroom to kitchen and went so far she doesn't know for sure if it really happened, and by a couple of car collisions and the violence with which people responded to having their cars injured. And then the large orgy begins, with a traffic jam that is a prelude to highways littered with burning cars and corpses. As long as Godard stays with cars as the symbol of bourgeois materialism, the movie is superbly controlled; the barbarousness of these bourgeois—their greed and the self-love they project onto their possessions—is exact and funny. But the movie goes much further—sometimes majestically, sometimes with brilliantly surreal details that suggest a closer affinity between Godard (who is of Swiss Protestant background) and Buñuel than might have been expected, sometimes with methods and ideas that miss, even though the intentions are interesting. The couple wreck their car, and as they wander the highways, lost among battered cars and bleeding dead, they have a series of picaresque adventures, encountering figures from literature and from films, until they meet a new race of hippie guerrillas— revolutionary cannibals raping and feeding on the bourgeoisie. It is both the next step and a new beginning.

The movie has extraordinary sections: the sequence of the wife's erotic confession, with only very small camera adjustments slightly changing what we see; a long virtuoso sequence that is all one or two tracking shots of the cars stalled on the highway and the activities of the motorists, with the car horns sounding triumphantly, like trumpets in Purcell—a masterly demonstration of how film technique can itself become the source of wit—until we get to the accident that is the start of the congestion, and the principals drive by and out of frame; a discussion seen through the windshield of a moving car when the couple are grilled by an "exterminating angel" who promises them miracles but refuses to give them anything when he finds out what they want (a big sports Mercedes, naturally blond hair, a weekend with James Bond).

But not all the big scenes work. There is respite in the story, a musicale sequence (which might be one of the cultural programs outlined in "La Chinoise") in which a pianist plays Mozart in a farmyard while a few peasants and farm laborers listen or walk by. We are so alerted to the technical feat of this sequence (another long single shot, this one a three-hundred-and-sixty-degree tracking pan around the pianist, taking in the action in the area, and then

returning to the pianist and circling *again*, catching
the same actions at their next stage) that the actions
caught seem too mechanical. And the meaning of
the sequence is too ideological and too ambiguous
(like much of "Les Carabiniers"); Godard may possibly believe in that musicale—that is to say, Godard
may believe that art must be taken to the peasants—
but more likely he's satirizing the function and the
place of art, of himself along with Mozart. This
might be clearer if it were not for another, and
worse, ideological sequence—a big symbolic garbage
truck manned by a Negro and an Algerian, who
empty the refuse of our civilization and make
speeches directly at us. The more "direct" Godard
is, the more fuzzy and obscure he is. Who can
assimilate and evaluate this chunk of theory thrown
at us in the middle of a movie? Probably most of us
blank out on it. And there is the embarrassment of
the thirties again because artists are not as well
equipped to instruct us in political decisions as, in
the intensity of their concern, they may suppose.
Though the movie slackens during this agitprop, the
horrors soon begin to rise again, and they get higher
and higher. Some of this doesn't work, either: Godard
has been showing us life going wild and depraved
into nightmare, beyond totem and taboo, but his
method has been comic and Brechtian. Characters
become corpses and the actors reappear as new characters. We are reminded that the two principals are
moving through the landscape of a movie; the fields
are unrealistically green, and the blood on faces and
bodies is thinly painted and patterned (like the blood
on the peasant-prostitute's face in "La Chinoise"),

and when the heroine kills her mother, the mother's blood splashes over a skinned rabbit like cans of paint being spilled. But then Godard shoves at our unwilling eyes the throat-cutting of a pig and the decapitation of a goose. Now, when people are killed in a movie, even when the killing is *not* stylized, it's generally O.K., because we know it's a fake, but when animals are slaughtered we are watching life being taken away. No doubt Godard intends this to shock us out of "aesthetic" responses, just as his agitprop preaching is intended to affect us directly, but I think he miscalculates. I look away from scenes like this, as I assume many others do. Is he forcing us to confront the knowledge that there are things we don't want to look at? But we knew that. Instead of drawing us into his conception, he throws us out of the movie. And, because we know how movies are made, we instinctively recognize that his method of jolting us is fraudulent; he, the movie director, has ordered that slaughter to get a reaction from us, and so we have a right to be angry with him. Whatever our civilization is responsible for, that sow up there is his, not ours.

The excellent score, by Antoine Duhamel, is ominous and dramatic; the pulse of the music helps to carry us through some of the weaker passages (such as the witless movie jokes, and the prattling of the figures from literature, who are feeble and seem fairly arch—rather like the book people in Truffaut's "Fahrenheit 451"—though Emily Brontë has a good, flaming finish). The astonishing thing is that, with all these weaknesses, the nightmarish anger that seems to cry out for a revolution of total destruction and the visionary lyricism are so strong they hold the movie together; they transcend the perfectly achieved satire. The most hideously flawed of all Godard's movies, it has more depth than anything he's done before. Although by the end his conscious meanings and attitudes are not at all clear, the vision that rises in the course of the film is so surreally powerful that one accepts it, as one accepts a lunar landscape by Bosch or a torment by Grünewald. "Weekend" is Godard's vision of Hell, and it ranks with the visions of the greatest.

"Weekend" is the fifteenth of Godard's feature films, which began with "Breathless" in 1959, and he has also made sections of several omnibus films. At thirty-seven, he is in something of the position in the world of film that James Joyce was at a considerably later age in the world of literature; that is, he has paralyzed other filmmakers by shaking their confidence (as Joyce did to writers), without ever reaching a large public. He will probably never have a popular, international success; he packs film-festival halls, but there is hardly enough audience left over to fill small theatres for a few weeks. His experimentation irritates casual moviegoers, but those who are more than casual can see that what may have appeared to be experimentation for its own sake in a movie like "Contempt" is validated by the way he uses the techniques in "Weekend." It's possible to hate half or two-thirds of what Godard does—or find it incomprehensible—and still be shattered by his brilliance.

Again like Joyce, Godard seems to be a great but

172

terminal figure. The most gifted younger directors and student filmmakers all over the world recognize his liberation of the movies; they know that he has opened up a new kind of movie-making, that he has brought a new sensibility into film, that, like Joyce, he is both kinds of master—both innovator and artist. But when they try to follow him they can't beat him at his own game, and they can't (it appears) take what he has done into something else; he's so incredibly fast he always gets there first. He has obviously opened doors, but when others try to go through they're trapped. He has already made the best use of his innovations, which come out of his need for them and may be integral only to his material. It's the strength of his own sensibility that gives his techniques excitement. In other hands, his techniques are just mannerisms; other directors who try them resemble a schoolboy walking like his father. Godard has already imposed his way of seeing on us—we look at cities, at billboards and brand names, at a girl's hair differently because of him. And when others pick up the artifacts of his way of seeing, we murmur "Godard" and they are sunk. At each new film festival, one can see the different things that are lifted from him; sometimes one can almost hear the directors saying to themselves, "I know I shouldn't do that, it's too much like Godard, but I've just got to try it." They can't resist, and so they do what Godard himself has already gone past, and the young filmmakers look out-of-date before they've got started; and their corpses are beginning to litter the festivals. For if Godard can't save himself how can he save them? If he is driven, like his self-destructive heroes, to go to the limits and beyond, to pursue a non-reflective art as though fearful of a pause, to take all risks and burn himself out, it's partly because his imitators are without this drive—this monomaniac's logic that carries him beyond logic to mysticism—that his liberation of film technique and content becomes mere facility when they attempt to follow him. Michelangelo is said to have observed, "He who walks behind others will never advance." Jean Renoir has been a different kind of movie influence; with his masterly simplicity and unobtrusive visual style, he has helped people to find their own way. You don't have to walk behind Renoir, because he opens an infinite number of ways to go. But when it comes to Godard you can only follow and be destroyed. Other filmmakers see the rashness and speed and flamboyance of his complexity; they're conscious of it all the time, and they love it, and, of course, they're right to love it. But they can't walk behind him. They've got to find other ways, because he's burned up the ground.

October 5, 1968

War as Vaudeville

Tony Richardson's movies often look as if he had shot bits and sequences without any conception of the final structure, and Charles Wood's scripts (for Richard Lester's "The Knack" and "How I Won the War") are like the captions a bright kid might put on photographs. With these two disjointed but in some ways brilliant talents combined, the rather spectacular snafu of "The Charge of the Light Brigade" was predictable. It's a strange epic: a quasi-absurdist, theatre-of-cruelty epic with modern revue humor. It's composed of fearfully expensive Victorian vignettes, with fragments of dialogue, mostly a few lines leading to a snapper. There's a dissociation between what we see and what we hear that is only partly intentional; the other part comes from poor post-synchronization, plus lines that one suspects *were* afterthoughts thrown onto the sound track like captions. Most of it is extravagantly pretty (David Watkin shot it); some of it is very funny (especially John Gielgud as the whimsical, doddering supreme commander of the British forces, and an undressing sequence with Trevor Howard and Jill Bennett). But the sequences don't grow out of each other; they hardly appear related to each other at all. As the pieces could be shuffled around without making much difference, it all seems on the same level—like "The Knack," and from moment to moment just as forgettable. The many intended epiphanies cancel each other out. The movie is about class distinctions and about oppressors and oppressed in the military, much like the script Wood did for "How I Won the War," but here set back a century. This distancing helps to make it considerably funnier—at times the satire of patriotic platitudes is excruciatingly entertaining. But while the generals and other officers are being introduced as imbecilic snobs and amateurs we develop expectations of seeing how their characters are related to what happens in the actual charge. We wait for the bits—all those fanciful, satirical, and "realistic" incidents preceeding and during the Crimean War that seem to be establishing the background—to come together in the military debacle. But, as it turns out, Richardson is hardly in a position to satirize the blunders of the military strategists; after preparing us with characters and actions and charts and maps and explanations for a couple of hours, he stages the climax so confusingly that we can't figure out what went wrong or who was responsible. Richardson's charge is an epic debacle of staging.

It's an ambitious, desperate, flashy movie that can't seem to find an appropriate emotional tone. Trying for Goyalike scenes of the miseries of the poor and the floggings and humiliations of the common soldiers, Richardson achieves careful clichés—the illustrated suffering of that age. In his own way, he keeps the poor in their place. The rulers and military leaders are the caricatures of authority of a pam-

phleteer's cartoons, and they actually blend into in-
terpolated animation (by Richard Williams) that is
remarkably witty and effective. The animation provides the only clear exposition of what's going on in
the movie; it's too bad Richardson didn't leave the
Charge itself to Williams. From the beginning, we
are tipped off that this is to be a sophisticated modern view of the stupidity and inhumanity of the past;
it turns out to be a rather smug and narrow view.
David Hemmings as the "humane" officer Nolan is
also the softly romantic voice of youth, and he has
an Indian manservant whom he can defend against
the racist. (But Hemmings, miscast, and looking
like a tiny Mod popinjay, is more absurd than the
rest, only unintentionally so.) The older characters
are amusing grotesques out of Lewis Carroll, but the
young ones are just sticks programmed to represent
conventional ideas and conflicts, and the author and
director can apparently think of no way to make a
Victorian lady (Vanessa Redgrave) interesting except to present her as a picturesque pre-Raphaelite
adulteress.

Though the specific error that led to the massacre
of the British troops seems, in the literature on the
film, to have been made by Nolan, this fact is so
obscure in the movie itself that one would think only
stupidity in high places was responsible. Richardson
and Wood miss out on the marvellous complexity of
history, that history in which "humane" men make
rash mistakes; Nolan was a Wrong-Way Corrigan on
a tragic scale, while Lord Cardigan (Trevor
Howard), who was indeed the arrogant monster they
make him, was so much *more* than their monster—a

man so vain that, as the program for the film informs us, he paid "his men a shilling each to line the London streets on Sundays and salute him as he passed." Yet vanity can be carried to grandeur: "He was to display one of the most futile gestures of bravery in the history of the British Army—after being first over the Russian line, he turned and rode back across the bloody field to celebrate with a bottle of champagne aboard his private yacht." What a great mock-hero he could have been—almost a Victorian Ubu—if this movie had taken a more generous interest in English character.

Richardson has the idea of compassion for the poor and suffering, without the emotion. And his and Wood's ridicule of the rich and powerful comes too easy, is too superior and smallminded for an epic. Compared to most movies, "The Charge of the Light Brigade" is remarkably intelligent, yet it's a cold film that seems to shrink everything it touches. It really is rather degrading to the audience for Richardson and Wood to show the commanders quarrelling like giggly schoolboys while horses and men are falling around them. They hit too many sour, insulting notes. This epic has so little feeling for the glory that went with the idiocies of the past that it diminishes itself along with its targets.

Claude Chabrol's "Les Biches" is set in St. Tropez in December, and it's about a sexually ambiguous idle-class threesome: a mope (Jacqueline Sassard), a dope (Jean-Louis Trintignant), and a chic lesbian (Stéphane Audran). One knows at once that she's supposed to be a lesbian, because she slinks around like the daughter of Fu Manchu—the only amusement in this empty attempt at classy eroticism. It's all languor, with almost no dialogue (and what there is is poor), though the score, by Pierre Jansen, helps to build up a little tension. The three characters are so ambiguous and idle that they're opaque; they have no spirit, they just seem sleepy and tired, and although that can be explained as somehow being the meaning of it all, how can one explain the sex designed in decorator colors? The movie looks like those imitation Marie Laurencins in hotel powder rooms. This vulgarly "exquisite" style gives the show away: the intentions of the movie are as vacuous and enervated as the characters. That doesn't necessarily bother audiences, though. Early in the movie, there's a fancy shot of the lesbian making a pass at the other girl's wet body, and one could hear people drawing in their breath. The theatre was unusually, almost embarrassingly quiet throughout the film—as if the audience were so hopeful that there would be something sexy coming on that they didn't allow themselves to get bored and restless.

"You Are What You Eat" is a big, fake, hysterical, put-on orgy, with people jumping up and down and yelling. Distorting lenses frequently make them look like pinheads, and the shots are thrown together from nowhere to nowhere to make everything look frenzied and freaky. Though it was produced by Barry Feinstein and Peter Yarrow (of Peter, Paul, and Mary), this is the kind of movie about youth that one might expect Spiro Agnew or George Wallace to make. It's edited on the same irresponsible

basis as "Operation Abolition": Tiny Tim may be
singing to an audience lifted from the Beatles. It
observes the worst of the new conventions of bad
student films: random footage, shaky zoom shots, the
inevitable girl with a bubble-gum bubble, and people
eating flowers and cutting up for the camera. Up
until the end, except for the footage of a cooch
dance, there's almost no relation between shots. And
the strobe sequence at the end, which develops some
editing rhythm, captures none of the charm that
looking at dancers under strobes can have. This kind
of thing has been done infinitely better by Robert
Nelson in the short "The Grateful Dead," and in
Peter Whitehead's feature "Tonite Let's All Make
Love in London," which showed extraordinary, if
rather contemptible, facility. "You Are What You
Eat" is insensitive and not even facile; it's an ugly,
stupid instant movie made by people who substitute
promotion for talent and technique. It's the aesthetic
equivalent of mugging the audience.

Is there anything more despicable than the incompetence of those who want only to sell and haven't
enough talent to do even that? The day after I went
to see "Duffy," I couldn't remember whether I'd sat
through it or walked out on it. "Duffy" is about a
heist, and in this one the comic robbers wear long
hair and flowered shirts, talk of meditation, and use
terms like "hipster" and "uptight," and there are
crude double-entendres emphasized by pauses so
long that you wait for the baggy pants to drop.
James Coburn the actor has disappeared, and his
body is now inhabited by a dimpled, grinning star—

a spastic zombie. The movie isn't even technically first-rate; it's a cheat at every level. The foreground action is clear, but the backgrounds and the long shots are blurry. This is the businessman's approach to moviemaking; "Duffy," in one form or another, comes out every week. (At the screening, the press was handed a brochure that said, "Like man, DUFFY is *in*, a gas, it's *with* it, it's like groovy.") As an individual movie, "Duffy" is unimportantly bad, because there are so many others like it. Not even others, really—just so much *of* it. The big, undifferentiated mass of this kind of mediocrity *is* important, because it weighs us all down.

Probably nobody really responds to a "Duffy," but a "Charly" can get to people. Sometimes mawkish pictures catch on with the public and are taken seriously (like "David and Lisa" and "To Sir, with Love"); such pictures are, characteristically, naïve, "sincere," and pitifully clumsy in execution, and are usually based on material of a kind that competent moviemakers are too knowing to attempt. Yet somehow they hit the movie audience smack in its softheaded heart. I suppose one should try to understand what appeals to others, but willful gullibility appears to be its own reward—the audience gets such a big emotional profit from so little investment. I find some quick way to end a conversation as soon as someone asks "What sign were you born under?" and I duck away from people who get the gleam of excitement as they ask "What did you *really* think about 'Rosemary's Baby'?" (Imagine anyone thinking "Rosemary's Baby" gave you anything to think about!) And now there's "Charly," with that primitive, garbagey appeal that seems to reach through sophistication and education right to the primordial jerk. College students study Ionesco and Beckett and Artaud and then respond to—"Charly." A surprising number of people seem to be educated beyond their own tastes; despite education and literacy, they still want this guck.

"Charly," which has already been a heavily anthologized short story, a TV play, and a novel, has that kind of terrible idea that makes what is often called "a classic"—really a stunted perennial. In the movie version, adapted by Stirling Silliphant, Charly (Cliff Robertson), the mentally retarded adult whose teacher (Claire Bloom) helps him get brain surgery, tries to rape his teacher as soon as he gets some book learning. Rejected, he becomes a hippie and a Hell's Angel, but he soon goes back to his books and becomes a fantastic, computer-sharp supergenius, and he and the teacher have an affair. But those scheming scientists didn't tell him: his genius is only temporary—he must go back to being a dummy.

There's a possible dramatic idea here. A man who, after great effort, achieves his manhood as an intelligent human being and faces losing it is a man we might all respond to, because his story is a quickening of the processes of life that we all fear. Such a story could be a metaphor for the transciency of our fully conscious lives. Explored that way, "Charly" might conceivably be the theme of an honest piece of work, but it probably wouldn't provide the immediate gratifications of this "Charly," this cheap fantasy with its built-in sobs—from "Marty" to "The

Fountainhead" and back again. And this "Charly" provides a popular target, to boot: Charly tells off "the scientific community" with Silliphant's cracker-barrel epigrams about what is wrong with the world —which, somehow, seems to be the scientists' fault. No doubt Silliphant, like so many other people in Hollywood, thinks of himself as an artist. He and the director, Ralph Nelson, are only commercially conscious.

The production does justice to the vulgarity of the script. Selmur Pictures, "a creative production subsidiary of the American Broadcasting Companies," is helping to bring movie craftsmanship to a new low. There has been a lot of bad camera work and grainy laboratory processing since the networks and business conglomerates took over the movies, but, possibly, none worse than this. "Charly" also takes the booby prize for the worst use (yet) of the split screen. Everything in the movie is done in a slovenly way. Claire Bloom, so extraordinarily fine in "Look Back in Anger" and so beautiful in "The Outrage" and "The Chapman Report" that she seemed to be one of those rare, fortunate actresses who become more ravishing with the years, is here undone by lines that no one would say and no actress could speak, and by a bad dye job and terrible makeup, which changes from shot to shot. Even the hems on her dresses are sloppy; there seem to be boa constrictors inside them. The girls in the Run Run Shaw movies that come out of Hong Kong are better served.

And yet the shoddy craftsmanship and the howlers in this movie may work in its favor; the audience may take crudeness and awkwardness as indications of sincerity and "deep," "true" feelings. It may be that the ineptitude of a "Charly" (like the ineptitude of a "David and Lisa" or a "To Sir, with Love") is organic to its popular appeal, and that competence, technique, and polish might destroy it commercially while nothing much could really be gained aesthetically, given its kind of thinking. "Charly" may indeed represent the unity of schlock form and schlock content—true schlock art.

October 12, 1968

"She Came at Me in Sections"

"Romeo and Juliet," Franco Zeffirelli's new tale from Shakespeare, employs the latest in techniques of bowdlerization. Apparently to attract teen-agers, Zeffirelli loads on what academic bowdlerizers used to take out. His movie of "The Taming of the Shrew" seemed to be always on the edge of bursting into song; it made me wish I were seeing "Kiss Me Kate." His "Romeo and Juliet" does not make me long for "West Side Story" (what could?), but it certainly suggests it, not only in the use of un-aristocratic, teen-age gangs and a freaked-out Mercutio (John McEnery) but in the basic strategy which suggests "The Graduate" as well. Some odd readings (by Lady Capulet, and, particularly, by Friar Laurence when he says "I dare no longer stay") suggests that this teen-age tragedy is partly the result of teen-agers' betrayal by their elders. It's a bit ugly to see Shakespeare used for being with it; movie-makers drill into the "generation gap" as if it were an oil well. Zeffirelli's version is lusty and rambunctious, and busty, of course, and he provides a fashion show in codpieces—two-toned, with fringe and bows and laces. The one element he removes that the other bowdlerizers also remove is Shakespeare's language. Nobody got exercised over what he did to the language of "The Taming of the Shrew," because there's not much poetry there anyway. But "Romeo and Juliet" is another matter. It's not that there is perhaps only about half of Shakespeare's play left that is upsetting but that the quotations from Shakespeare that *are* left don't build up the rhythms of a poetic play. Heard in isolated fragments, the lines just seem a funny way of talking that is hard to understand. The movie is being sold, of course, on its "youth appeal"—on teen-agers playing teen-agers—but you can always make a movie with kids playing kids; the feat would be if the kids could read Shakespeare. The lines are unintelligible because the actors' faces and bodies aren't in tune with the words. As anyone who has ever been in a school production of Shakespeare has learned, to his shame, those great lines don't mean anything to an audience unless you have the training to make them sound as if you always talked that way. Pat Heywood playing the Nurse (as a countrywoman, and not too ancient, which is a pleasant change) is almost the only one of the principals who manages this, so in her scenes the meaning registers. Perhaps the main reason we go to Shakespeare performances in the theatre or at the movies is for the happy, square excitement of hearing those marvellous lines; here the voices and reading are so tonelessly mediocre that one hardly hears the words at all. There's not one memorable reading; the music of the great lines is missing. And without it the idiocies of the plot shine forth. Zeffirelli has not, however, left a total vacuum; he has replaced the poetry with his own "cinematic" version of poetry.

This "Romeo and Juliet" is about two young (unlucky) kids in love. They communicate with eyes and mouths and smiles (in closeup), not in words; the lines of Shakespeare that they speak are redundant as well as meaningless. Olivia Hussey (Juliet), her childish eyes wide open and her mouth open, too, and Leonard Whiting (Romeo), his hair cut like a suburban hippie's, are not really bad; they're rather sweet, and in some ways their simplicity—the simplicity of reasonably talented, blank young actors that is so familiar to us from television—is pleasing. But they're as banal in their youth and innocence as the high-school kids in "Peyton Place"; like the lovers in "West Side Story," they have been made ordinary kids in trouble. In Shakespeare's version, they played together at poetry and at love; they made love through poetry, matching each other's conceits. Here the actors seem dear little children playing at the director's notion of teen-age sex hunger, and, despite the words, they look and move like inarticulate modern kids in the latest movie cycle. Zeffirelli supplies them with nonverbal lyricism: Romeo leaps from Juliet's balcony and runs for joy through a green glade. This is recognizable as a new convention—we know we're not supposed to think about the dusty summer streets of the previous shots (which may also be a new convention; Zeffirelli is very high on dust). But if you're going to go in for the trite lyricism of running through the woods you'd better be more of a moviemaker than Zeffirelli; the scene is shot like the romantic, full-of-the-joy-of-life sequences in a dozen current second-rate movies. When he aims for exuberance, he generally settles for overacting or for images that convey common-place high spirits and coyness and puppy love.

As a movie director, Zeffirelli has a limited sense of movement, and his "cinematic" effects are forced. He goes in for strenuous knockabout stuff—for brawling, cavorting young men and for revels and roistering that have an awful way of suggesting the supers at the opera trying to keep the stage "active." For "immediacy," he plunges the camera into this busywork (which inevitably includes somebody getting kicked in the bottom). In the duel between Mercutio and Tybalt, and, particularly, in the big sword fight between Romeo and Tybalt (with Michael York's Tybalt coming on as a bullish matador), his camera-in-the-midst-of-the-horses'-hoofs technique sometimes works excitingly—perhaps because these sequences (like the scene of the baiting of the Nurse) are conceived in extravagant terms. When Zeffirelli is extravagant, he often succeeds in providing some of the flourishes and the urgency that have been lost in the cutting of the play. But the realistic locations are used like parts of a stage; we can't get our bearings. We never really know where we are in this movie; we get no sense of movement in relation to place. The interiors have no exteriors. We are at a ball without having entered the room or having got a sense of its scale. Theatricality can be effective in a movie when it is consciously used, but it's very awkward when the director is trying for realism—which Zeffirelli apparently takes horseplay and opulent clutter, and dust, to be. He brings to the screen the filler of opera—all that coarse, earthy stuff that comes on when the main singers are off.

And Zeffirelli's "robust" realistic detail is ludicrous; when he throws a closeup of the marketplace onto the screen and we see the peppers and onions, it's like the obligatory setting of the scene in the first act of an opera when the peasant girl walks on with her basket on her arm. And when Michael York enters, in a series of closeups working up from calves and thighs to torso to face, the camera is used to make an elaborate kind of stage entrance. (Among the many reasons for giggling at this is that it reminds one of Fred Astaire's description of Cyd Charisse in "The Band Wagon": "She came at me in sections.") The visual compositions are generally academic, and the camera movement and the editing, too, are often just nervous.

Zeffirelli may, however, have hit on something that could knock kids silly. Once Mercutio and Tybalt are dead, the luscious Nino Rota music (the kind of music you feel you've been hearing on car radios all your life even as you hear it for the first time—which you sure know won't be the last) is poured on in emotional torrents, and the movie is filled with weeping and lamentation and carrying-on. Romeo flings himself to the floor while Juliet, hair streaming, bangs herself against the wall. All this violence and hysteria appear to come out of nowhere, because these little child lovers, with their baby talk, hardly seem to have the sensuality or the grand passion to go mad this way. (They are so pure and sweet in bed that it is like a toy marriage.) There's nothing in Shakespeare or in the characters we have seen to prepare us for this; it's out of every wonderfully absurd operatic love-death, and kids unfamiliar with this tradition may really go for it. It's a new development, in a way—teen-agers as grand and passionate. The movie gets so theatrical, in a nineteenth-century melodramatic fashion, that it begins to be rather fascinating. (The lighting even resembles the unmodified yellowish lighting on an opera stage.) There are moments when the production is so bizarre and excessive it suggests "Throne of Blood" and Eisenstein's "Ivan the Terrible," but then it slips back into horse opera, with someone yelling "Montague!" like "Geronimo!" This movie comes at you in sections. The whole thing cries out for arias, but if it were an opera Zeffirelli might cast non-singers.

In retrospect, one may feel affection for importantly bad movies—for the unusual messes that show some talent and lots of aspiration and take themselves seriously enough to convince some people that they are works of art. (Remember "Voice in the Wind," with Francis Lederer as a deranged concert pianist, or Ben Hecht's "Spectre of the Rose," or "Mickey One," or "Privilege"? And I think a Bergman film like "Hour of the Wolf" belongs in this group. It's characteristic of these prestige-laden flops that they're so bad they often verge on self-parody, and that their champions explain their box-office failure by saying that they're "ahead of their time." Pictures like these are not mediocrities (that's the best thing to be said for them); they're awful. But they do, at least, have some kind of character. They may be hell to sit through, but you don't forget that you saw them. This crazy "Romeo and Juliet," with its bare-assed Romeo, and its shots that look like ads for "The Boy," and its Juliet leaning so far out of her dress in the balcony scene that instead of listening to her we watch her bosom as she struggles with problems of breath control, may even be a hit. There are a lot of romantic teen-agers, and a lot of other people who still have their teen-age romanticism intact. This could be a make-out movie for teen-agers the way "A Man and a Woman" was for college students.

Peter Sellers can do some things perhaps better than anyone else, and he has a scene in "I Love You, Alice B. Toklas!" in which he bends over laughing in helpless merriment that is really very beautiful. His inflections for lack of enthusiasm, however, and his look of dissatisfaction are possibly becoming too close to perfect. His general dissatisfaction, though totally in character here, is the middle-class variant of melancholy, and it begins to suggest a comment on his vehicles. Comic talents are pushed so hard in most movies that they don't have time for comedy. But Sellers, as the Italian in "After the Fox," the Spaniard in "The Bobo," the Indian in "The Party," and now the Los Angeles Jewish lawyer in "Toklas," takes that extra bit of time. He has been evolving a loose, low-keyed style that gives his characters a chance to grow, even in undistinguished pictures. "Toklas" is thin—no more than an extended television situation comedy—but it has some of the appeal of the Harold Lloyd comedies (especially one that Preston Sturges wrote for him), and it makes you laugh surprisingly often. It's the best of

his recent vehicles. Sellers' special gift is to reverse
the comedian's usual procedure: he turns stereotypes into characters; he embodies the stereotype totally, so that we see the man. The ideas and the
development here are crude, but the lines (by Paul
Mazursky and Larry Tucker) are sly, and Hy Aver-
back's directorial attitude is relaxed. The whole
thing is giddy and slapdash and entertainingly in-
consequential. And there's a charming, inventive
comedienne, Joyce Van Patten (who is a bit like
Jean Hagen); she is particularly good in her second-
wedding scene, when she stands at the altar glassy
with anxiety.

Considering what Francis Ford Coppola was
working with in "Finian's Rainbow"—a socially
conscious whimsey-fantasy operetta—he has done
pretty well, or probably as well as could be done
short of rethinking the whole thing, and then it
would hardly be "Finian's Rainbow." What a book!
For the sake of some rather pretty music, one may
be willing to swallow one's pride and put up with the
three fairy-tale wishes and the race-relations paradise, and even maybe—although it's tough—with
the appalling hypertense Tommy Steele's Puckish
leprechaun, but that Susan the Silent routine (a girl
who can't speak and, when questioned, ballet-dances
her interminable answers) is beyond sufferance.
Coppola, trying for freshness and speed and an ethereal "Midsummer Night's Dream" atmosphere,
makes a pastiche of visual styles and lyrical effects
out of what was already a pastiche. Obviously, he
can't make anything good out of it; the best he can

hope for is to keep the show moving, and he manages to do that. But the focus is so soft and there are so many filtered, gauzy shots that the occasional hard-focus closeup of the principals is really brutal—Dr. Jekyll becomes Mr. Hyde. With this kind of decaying material that reeks of old Broadway, and with performers who are—to put it as gently as possible—mature for their roles, it is surely simple tact not to let the audience get a very close look at anything. Still, compared with, say, "Doctor Dolittle" or "Half a Sixpence," this big, clean family musical isn't so bad. Al Freeman, Jr., has a good moment or two, Keenan Wynn is fine in blackface, and Petula Clark is lovely in her first big number—though the spectres of Jeanette MacDonald and Nelson Eddy hover over her duets with the stolid Don Francks.

Not having seen "The Subject Was Roses" as a play, I was inadequately prepared for the movie. Can a play that got the Pulitzer Prize, the Antoinette Perry Award, and the New York Drama Critics Circle Award really have been *this* bad? The dialogue has the insulated radio-TV-"realistic"-play sound; it nags at us with overexplicit little points, with hints and motivations drawn from the repertory of the worst domestic-crisis plays. This dialogue has been brought to the screen with such misplaced devotion that although the play concerns a family of three talking together in an apartment, the director never avails himself of the opportunities that movies provide for conversational intimacy and rapid deliv-

ery, and for throwing away lines. They should all
have been thrown away.

October 19, 1968

Cripes!

Julie Andrews could, maybe, play Beatrice Lillie, but she cannot play Gertrude Lawrence. Gertrude Lawrence wasn't much of a singer and she was an odd, limited sort of actress. What made her a star was not something that can be taught, even to as good a pupil as Julie Andrews; she was a nervy technician, with the cool technique that is so clever a projection of personality that it becomes glamour. Glamour is what Julie Andrews doesn't have. She does her duties efficiently but mechanically, like an airline stewardess; she's pert and cheerful in some professional way that is finally cheerless. She has played some of her roles with almost incredible accuracy; her dubious charm is that she makes audiences aware that she's a good girl who deserves an A. But that well-trained smile doesn't inspire confidence; one doesn't want to know what happens to the face when the curtain closes on her teeth. To do the director, Robert Wise, justice, I think that in "Star!" he was trying to use this unappealing side of Julie Andrews, who must be the least sensual young actress ever to become a movie star. One gets the feeling that he and the writer, William Fairchild, didn't really like Gertrude Lawrence very much, and that, rather than make the usual star-bio, they were trying for a dispassionate look at her. Their heroine is a hard, ruthless, self-centered, almost detestable woman, and I think this is calculated. The trouble is, it's miscalculated.

Early in his career, Robert Wise was the editor of Orson Welles' "Citizen Kane," and here he uses a much more elaborate version of the "Citizen Kane" framework. Like "Citizen Kane," "Star!" opens with sequences from a documentary film that is being made of the protagonist's life, and then, throughout the almost three-hour movie, we keep returning to it. But there's no difference in point of view between the gray, grainy, smallscreen fake documentary, with its mixture of actual and simulated newsreels, and the wide-screen, 70-mm. color movie. And although the documentary is supposed to be in production in 1940, it's not in any recognizable style of that date. It's just a linking device, to help stitch together this story that spans three decades, and as such it's reasonably efficient. However, the use of this device suggests that Wise had something much more ambitious in mind than what has been realized on the screen. I think he intended "Star!" to be a portrait of an archetypal empty rat-fink kind of star, a female Citizen Kane of the theatre and "high society." In one scene, his star "answers" a Hyde Park Corner leftist by inviting the people listening to him to come to a free show instead; in another scene, she's a narcissistic, condescending great lady giving a garden party for the children of the poor. Wise is too conscious a movie-maker for the implications of these scenes to be accidental. And surely a woman with a string of banker-lovers, a woman who coldly feigns headaches when sex is expected, a woman who neglects her only child and then feels deserted when the child grows up and neglects her, a woman without a trace of feminine softness or fluidity or grace isn't meant to be lovable. They've made her a bitch, all right, but they've failed to make her a star.

If the musical numbers were well done, and if the era were successfully epitomized by Julie Andrews as a magnetic, tough-sentimental playgirl-star, then the ambivalence toward the star might be interesting. But Robert Wise has never really directed this kind of musical before; "West Side Story" and "The Sound of Music" were not in this backstage-musical tradition. There are seventeen musical numbers here, and almost all of them are poorly staged and performed (anachronistically, too, in late-forties movie-musical style). Anyone who didn't already know the songs wouldn't be able to tell how good they are from the movie. Some of the best of Cole Porter and Noël Coward and Kurt Weill and the Gershwins is mangled while one sits there wishing Vincente Minnelli would magically take over and save it all. When the audiences inside the movie go mad with enthusiasm, cheering and applauding these cloddish performances, their acclaim has the dead sound of the canned laughter and applause on television, because it hasn't been earned.

We know in advance that Julie Andrews has a better (though a less idiosyncratic) voice than Gertrude Lawrence; we expect her to sing the twenties songs not in a twenties voice but in her own "nice" voice—clear and pure, with that rather impersonally meticulous enunciation and phrasing. But she's not even in good voice most of the time, so the songs aren't transformed and made new; they're wasted. And yet she seems to be trying hard—which just about kills everything in the conception. Hard work is the opposite of glamour. The chic of the twenties playgirl was that she was so supremely casual she appeared brittle. Her high style was the concealment of feeling—deliberate superficiality. Gertrude Lawrence had rasping sounds and expressive gestures for exasperation, and not much else except little *moues* for pleasure; she looked as if she didn't give a damn what anybody thought. She made a game of snobbery—a snobbery based on style rather than on wealth, though who but bohemian artists and the idle rich could achieve it, and would anyone of intelligence want to? She had the sort of insolent confidence that made mannerisms into a style of life. She was what drag queens want to be. If she could barely carry a tune in her thin, careless voice, she made it seem as if carrying a tune were beneath her. She wasn't even pretty. And that's what was so triumphantly witty about her: she had made herself a star and a leader of fashion and a beauty the way a great chef is supposed to be able to make a superb dinner—out of nothing. I remember her best singing "The Physician"—I think it was in "No Funny Business," her 1933 film with Laurence Olivier. She slouched around sinuously in a dress that was barely on her, and her voice wobbled as she aimed for the notes; it was a devastating demonstration of how to look so elegantly indifferent that people can't take their eyes off you. Her talent was to make it all look

198

easy, and because this no-sweat attitude of hers was the incarnation of the glamour of the era, Gertrude Lawrence is indeed a fit subject for a "Citizen Kane"-style satirical investigation. But they didn't have the actress for it, or the script, or the guts.

Julie Andrews doesn't make anything look easy; she does calisthenics while singing "The Physician," and articulates every last syllable as if Professor Higgins were standing over her. In dialogue that should be drawled, her diction is so clean and scrubbed that even vulgarisms sound hearty. Perhaps crucially, Miss Andrews and Daniel Massey, as Noël Coward, miss the point of the scene they play from Coward's "Private Lives"—a scene that might have had the essence of the elusive, magical sophistication Gertrude Lawrence stood for. As Noël Coward wrote the scene, the brittle sophistication of not allowing one's feelings to show gives way to the sentimentality of "potent cheap music," and this is, (or might be) what the whole movie is about. The "star" who lives on technique and style alone has no way to deal with war and poverty and her own emotions except at the level of potent cheap music. Miss Andrews misses not only in the bit from "Private Lives" but, along with most of the cast and the director, in the whole movie. They haven't held anything back; they've been working cheap emotion all along. Trying for the mystery of glamour, Julie Andrews merely coarsens her shining nice-girl image, becoming a nasty Girl Guide. The photography, Michael Kidd's choreography, the set designs, and the $347,000 in ugly, unflattering swell clothes that Donald Brooks put on her all contribute to the failure. Even more basic is the script: It's not evocative; it's an outline that lacks the strokes that would sum up the characters and the episodes. (It needs some of the detail of an "All About Eve" or of the original "Pal Joey" stories.) The best that William Fairchild seems able to do for the heroine is to give her a "Cripes!" to say at every turn of fortune. He gives the only entertaining lines to Noël Coward—as if only famous wits could be witty in a movie. Daniel Massey, Coward's godson, who looks like his father, Raymond Massey, but who parodies the sounds and grimaces of Coward, is charming and in period, yet his performance seems to be a sketch for an intimate revue rather than a characterization. But if his amiable impersonation appears to belong in a different kind of movie, his performance is the only one that suggests that it might work *some-where*. The movie takes the star from her cradle not to her grave but to her final marriage bed. She falls for another rich man—one who "understands" her by proclaiming psychiatric banalities and ordering her around. Apparently, she needed obedience training, and a master to love; this makes her emotionally secure. If that is your "Rosebud," Mr. Wise, cripes!

The movie suggests that those who made it wanted a big, popular project (and a pre-sold box-office star) and at the same time wanted to feel they were showing people what they really thought of Miss Lawrence. From the evidence of this movie, they don't have enough talent to know what they think. Their hostility to the subject just adds unpleasantness to the incompetence. They go rummaging around in their outworn notions of integrity, trying to find a social "statement" that they can tuck in, when the best demonstration of integrity would be to make a decent musical.

"Bullitt" is efficiently made and extremely well-edited but basically uninteresting. It's an example of commercial formalism. A competent director (Peter Yates), working with competent technicians, has given a fairly dense texture to a hackneyed script about cops and gangsters and politicians. Yates doesn't have the directorial flair that John Boorman brought to a comparable melodrama, "Point Blank," but he does an honest, brutal job in this dishonest business of making movies about nothing. With his low-key charisma, Steve McQueen plays the police-officer hero seriously and well, but I prefer the fun and romantic fantasy of his Thomas Crown. When movies are as gratuitous as this one is, it hardly seems too much to ask for the leavening of a little humor; "Bullitt" is solemn even when it is dealing with a slimy Mr. Big (Robert Vaughn) whose technique of bribery is so blatantly insulting he couldn't give away a lollipop. But Yates has a good, serviceable technique for integrating staged movie action into "documentary" city locations. San Francisco is used for the interiors as well as the exteriors, and is shown to best advantage in a spectacular chase sequence, with cars bouncing up and down those witty steep streets.

All horrors are grist for the Hollywood mill, but cheap exploitation films don't disguise their purposes, whereas an expensive, "responsible" film like

"The Boston Strangler," with real stars like Henry Fonda and Tony Curtis, deals with brutality and madness tastefully, in safe, academic terms, thus offering perversions with polite reassurances. It's money that makes a film look responsible. (In this movie, the sympathy extended to the miserable and perverted seems only a token of what they could get within clean white walls if they would just offer themselves up for treatment. Those who have seen "Titicut Follies" and observed the horrors within the dirty white walls of the institution that Albert DeSalvo, the alleged strangler, was sent to may be a little shocked by the new movie's assurances.) The good taste of "The Boston Strangler" is a form of inadequacy. The material cries out for revelations, but the movie offers no illumination of human conduct, nothing that would help us understand the nature of the crimes or the criminal—only a facile account of split personality that is not only unilluminating but unconvincing. If the movie-makers don't know any more than that, why are they making the movie? This, clearly, troubles them, too. They want to be respectable. Like "In Cold Blood," "The Boston Strangler" constantly—almost compulsively—raises the question of why it has been made. Unable to face the reasons that are all too obvious, it trumps up reasons. Since DeSalvo hasn't been executed, there is no handy issue like capital punishment for this one. At times, it rather ludicrously suggests that it's a cautionary movie made to warn women against opening their doors to strangers (though it can't resist getting easy laughs on nervous old ladies buying locks). It winds up with a fancy statement about how society should develop methods for the early detection of psychological disorders—an ending that may have made everybody working on the movie feel better but that is totally irrelevant, since the movie does not indicate that there was anything wrong with DeSalvo (Tony Curtis with a badly joined false nose bridge) that could have been detected before the murders. I know there are people of wide interests; still, I wonder what kind of revelation could have been expected from a decent, Hollywood-factory sort of director like Richard Fleischer, who goes from "The Happy Time" to "20,000 Leagues Under the Sea" to "The Girl in the Red Velvet Swing" to "The Vikings" to "Compulsion" to "Crack in the Mirror" to "The Big Gamble" to "Barabbas" to "Fantastic Voyage" to "Doctor Dolittle" to "The Boston Strangler" and is now at work on "Che," starring Omar Sharif, with Jack Palance as Fidel Castro.

October 26, 1968

A Fresh Start

When I discovered that "Pretty Poison" had opened without advance publicity or screenings, I rushed to see it, because a movie that makes the movie companies so nervous they're afraid to show it to the critics stands an awfully good chance of being an interesting movie. Mediocrity and stupidity certainly don't scare them; talent does. This is a remarkable first feature film by a gifted young American, Noel Black—a movie that should have opened in an art house—and it was playing in a vast and empty theatre, from which, no doubt, it will depart upon the week. And the losses will be so heavy that the movie companies will use this picture as another argument against backing young American directors. The television ads for "Pretty Poison" are a pitiful attempt to make it seem strident and coarse and brutal—to attract teen-agers by passing it off as a cross between "Psycho" and "Bonnie and Clyde." Those attracted this way are likely to hate the film. "Pretty Poison" simply isn't a picture for a big theatre; it doesn't have the zing to be popular with large audiences. Lorenzo Semple, Jr., has written an unobtrusively thoughtful and well-controlled script— the best script of any American movie this year. Black's subdued direction has the uncorrupted sensitivity that, given the way movies are made and sold, and what the public seems to want, doesn't last long. Although "Pretty Poison" is a psychological thriller, it is modulated and fine-drawn, and (simply because of the way it was thought out and felt out) it presupposes an attentive, intelligent audience. Whether there is an audience for an American picture of this kind is doubtful, because the audience that might respond to it expects American movies to be loud and vulgar, and escapes to quiet foreign pictures. Feeling snug in this division, they don't go to a subtle or quiet American picture when one comes along, so our movies get shriller all the time, and an American director who makes a movie on the assumption that the audience is as intelligent and sensitive as he is is a beautiful dreamer. (Yet can an artist work any other way?)

Even if "Pretty Poison" had opened in an art house, it might have had two strikes against it; art-house customers are almost certainly too snobbish to go to see Anthony Perkins and Tuesday Weld, though both are remarkably talented. Perkins' abilities *had* been recognized until his career was undermined by a lunatic piece of miscasting in Jules Dassin's preposterous but popular "Phaedra"; when Melina Mercouri swept him up in her arms, he was made to seem ludicrous. People left theatres giggling at the idea that a woman might prefer this skinny boy to her husband, when the husband was played by Raf Vallone. Perkins hasn't been a star since. Tuesday Weld has never been one, and maybe it isn't just her unlucky name. (If you talk about her ability, people think you're kidding.) Maybe it isn't because she hasn't had a big role that would catapult her to fame, either. Maybe it's because she's the kind of actress who doesn't let people know she's acting, the way Estelle Parsons or Geraldine Page lets them know. How else can one explain an actress's giving the performances Tuesday Weld has given in "Rally Round the Flag, Boys!" and "Soldier in the Rain" and "The Cincinnati Kid" and "Lord Love a Duck" and still not being taken seriously? She's not at her best in "Pretty Poison," but she's awfully good. Perkins has the better role—a character who develops from a quirky, sneaky, funny boy into a decent, sympathetic man (a loner, but not by choice), making us realize that the man was waiting there in the character all along. I think it's the most beautifully conceived and the most precise performance Perkins has ever given. John Randolph and the other performers are uniformly good. The director and his associates seem to know how to handle actors and how to edit acting. The movie was shot on location in Massachusetts (I didn't detect a single studio shot); the photography is simple and sunny, though perhaps rather too lyrical. There are a few bad plot turns (especially at the end), but they're minor. Noel Black comes from the same film school (U.C.L.A.) as Francis Ford Coppola, but his style is less commercial and less forced, if also less energetic. Some of the best students in several American film schools are beginning to work in this uncoercive, transparently honest, and unpretentious style; it may be the beginning of a clean, direct, and, if I may use the term, indigenous yet new kind of American filmmaking. One characteristic of this style is that

there's not a shot in the movie which doesn't clearly
and directly contribute to the theme. This straightforward way of working, which, among young Americans, generally distinguishes student films from
underground films, is very different from the French
New Wave. It's closer to the modest way Fred Zinnemann used to work. It's the opposite of the way
most directors from television work; there's no
fakery in it, and no shock treatment. It's a way of
using craftmanship not for flash and ingenuity and
impact (as in television commercials) but with sensibility—sticking to the subject and exploring it,
developing and opening up the material. This may
not be a completely satisfactory approach to movie-
making—we may want more immediate excitement
and more daring—but it may be one of the best
ways for young filmmakers to give American movies
a fresh start. I'm afraid almost no one will see "Pretty Poison" unless a few critics praise it excessively,
and yet excessive praise may lead to disappoint-
ment: "Pretty Poison" is a good little movie, and
I use "little" not in a pejorative sense but as a
form of protection and also a term of affection.

Elizabeth Taylor is a prostitute, whose daughter
has died, and Mia Farrow is a rich, crazy English
girl whose mother has died, and at first, as they
begin to share a very crazy mother-daughter relationship, "Secret Ceremony" seems to be a Gothic
version of *folie à deux*. But then Robert Mitchum
enters as the girl's child-molesting stepfather, and
then Pamela Brown and Peggy Ashcroft enter as her
thieving aunts, and they're all crazy, too, and by the

time it's a *folie à cinq* one knows that Joseph Losey
(the director), George Tabori (the writer), and the
producers all share in the craziness. Mia Farrow has
a peculiar voice and a strange presence (in her black
wig, she looks like a pre-Raphaelite boy); it's really
too early to tell if she is going to be an important
new star or just an oddity—a perennial green-faced,
infantile neurotic. Without Harold Pinter's dialogue
to make the overfurnished vacancy of Losey's films
ominous and oppressively interesting, Losey's work
—here and in "Boom!"—resembles the Jungian dec-
orators' dreams Albert Lewin used to produce, like
"Pandora and the Flying Dutchman" and "Saadia."
The setting is a claustrophobic Art Nouveau maus-
oleum of a house (with the best bathroom door
I've ever seen—the only thing I liked in the
movie). "Secret Ceremony" is truly terrible, but I
don't know how to fight a bowl of fudge without
getting stuck in the goo. I know that some people are
going to love it. I knew it during the movie when I
laughed inadvertently as Miss Farrow's anguished
face was cut to Christ on the Cross and my laugh
sounded very loud (and very bad) among the silent
matinée ladies in their blue minks, who gave me
pitying looks because I didn't appreciate suffering.
Sometimes it seems that the nuttier a picture is, the
more eager some people are to get caught up in it.
Folie à how many?

What would Henry James have made of Jane
Fonda, an actress so much like his heroines—an
American heiress-of-the-ages abroad, and married to
a superb example of the Jamesian villain, a sophis-

ticated European (a Frenchman of Russian origins) who is redolent of shallow morals, who is the screen's foremost celebrant of erotic trash, and who has the scandalous habit of turning each wife into a facsimile of the first and spreading her out for the camera. Yet Roger Vadim's evil is reassuringly "wicked"—it's so obvious that he tries to shock only to please. And Jane Fonda having sex on the wilted feathers and rough, scroungy furs of "Barbarella" is more charming and fresh and bouncy than ever—the American girl triumphing by her innocence over a lewd comic-strip world of the future. She's the only comedienne I can think of who is sexiest when she is funniest. (Shirley MacLaine is a sweet and sexy funny girl, but she has never quite combined her gifts as Jane Fonda does.) Jane Fonda is accomplished at a distinctive kind of double take: she registers comic disbelief that such naughty things can be happening to her, and then her disbelief changes into an even more comic delight. Her American-good-girl innocence makes her a marvellously apt heroine for pornographic comedy. She has the skittish innocence of a teen-age voluptuary; when she takes off her clothes, she is playfully and deliciously aware of the naughtiness of what she's doing, and that innocent's sense of naughtiness, of being a tarnished lady, keeps her from being just another naked actress. According to Vadim, in "Barbarella" she is supposed to be "a kind of sexual Alice in Wonderland of the future," but she's more like a saucy Dorothy in an Oz gone bad.

The sex parodies are amusing, but "Barbarella" is disappointing after the expectations that one had (I

assume I am one of many) of a film that would be
good trashy, corrupt entertainment, for a change.
"Barbarella" isn't good trash, but it's corrupt, all
right, and that's something. There hasn't been a new
Bond for over a year, and "Modesty Blaise" was two
years ago; movies have been failing even in their
comic-strip function. And after some of those worthwhile pictures from Europe we may feel we've
earned the right to sneak out to a mindless, disreputable movie. I have a hunch that everybody
(everybody I know, anyway) would go to see "Barbarella" even if it were much worse than it is. And
as our expectations were at so low a level anyway,
we can't really get worked up about the film's weaknesses. We don't go to the movies just for good
movies—not when we go to see the astronaut Barbarella on a mission from Earth to Sogo. Vadim has
always been good at seductive pictorial effects, but
here the photography is uninteresting; the designs
are not very witty, and the special effects are rather
tacky. Perhaps the project simply got away from
him; perhaps, trying for satire and the demonic lit-
tle-boy humor of Terry Southern rather than for his
usual sensuous romanticism—the camera "artistically" caressing nudes—he got lost in the clatter of
tongues and effects. What with the dubbing and the
poor writing (there were seven writers in addition to
Southern), most of the dialogue is disastrous. There
are dumb sadistic episodes, and an atrocious rock
score that mars the whole film. (Could it have been
stuck in by the businessmen? Vadim used musicians
like Thelonious Monk in his earlier movies.) The
blind angel played by John Phillip Law is a little

sickly and slightly embarrassing—not a satisfactory substitute for the Cowardly Lion—but Barbarella's other, better helpers include Ugo Tognazzi, as a hairy huntsman, and David Hemmings, who shows unexpected comic talent, as an absent-minded revolutionary. Hemmings and Jane Fonda share honors in the wittiest sequence—a futuristic copulation that, appropriately, is in the genteel-but-full-of-tics style of English comedies of the forties and fifties. As a mad wizard, Milo O'Shea is wretched, but Anita Pallenberg, as a wicked witch, is helped by a familiar purring voice, which, if my ear is to be trusted, belongs to Joan Greenwood.

November 2, 1968

Lioness in Winter

Many things can go wrong with a movie; what goes wrong with "The Lion in Winter" is so unusual that it may be some weird sort of first. The movie has been done with too much "integrity"—with inappropriate "integrity." Plays are customarily coarsened when they're filmed, but James Goldman's play has been elevated—with serious emotions, more or less authentic costumes and settings, pseudo-Stravinsky music, and historical pomp. And it just won't do to have actors carrying on as if this were a genuine, "deep" historical play, on the order of "A Man for All Seasons." What made "The Lion in Winter" entertaining on the stage was Goldman's reduction of the first Plantagenet, Henry II, and his queen, Eleanor of Aquitaine, and their three sons to a family of monsters playing Freudian games of sex and power. They were the jolliest collection of bad seeds since "The Little Foxes," and the notion that diplomatic maneuvers and historical issues were determined by *their* characters seemed no more than an elaborate theatrical conceit. On the screen, when their games are played out in a real castle, and played not for laughs and melodrama but emotionally, with impressive dramatic performances and real tears for defeats, it all seems hysterical. One begins to wonder why the actors are getting so over-wrought; the point of view is too limited and an-achronistic to justify all this howling and sobbing and carrying on. They're playing a camp historical play as if it were the real thing—delivering commercial near-poetry as if it were Shakespeare.

This melodrama for two pros and some young semi-pros to horse around in is now full of the pitiful desperation of weak, weepy people trapped by need and greed, and there are sage, important thoughts for us to take away. And the quick transitions from feigned emotion to cunning, which on the stage were so shallow and silly that they were amusing, are exhausting when the actors try to make them convincing. Goldman has a facile but not very high-grade wit, and although his screen adaptation omits some of his cheaper epigrams (it was embarrassing in the Broadway version to hear the twelfth-century rulers of England and France tossing off quips that had been popular in one's high school), what's left is still rather sophomoric. Peter O'Toole, I thought, looked a little unhappy as he disposed of the line "Well, what shall we hang? The holly or each other?" O'Toole, as Henry II, is the brightest thing in the movie. He gives the most robust performance I've seen from him; he isn't that pale-eyed O'Toole, and he keeps his pink flesh covered. He's loud and, fortunately, histrionic; underacting would *really* expose this material, by making it pretentious, whereas O'Toole, by shouting and having a good time, almost carries it off. (Not a small feat when you have to deliver lines like "The sky is pocked with stars." Goldman has the Maxwell Anderson pox.) The sons and the minor characters are good enough in their way; Anthony Hopkins as Richard the Lionhearted has urgency and weight, and Timothy Dalton as young King Philip of France is a pretty playing-card King. The sons are even fairly convincing as belonging to one family; at least, they and O'Toole all speak with some kind of English accent. Katherine Hepburn is their mother, and her accent is so peculiarly hers that we just accept it as the way she talks. And it seems proper for a queen to sound like Hepburn. I don't know what the actors *could* have done with this material that is written for clowns but would be gruesome if it were played clownishly in realistic settings; I don't know what the director, Anthony Harvey—starting with this material—could have done, either (though he might have overcome his affection for moving the camera in quickly from a great distance). The color and the photography are not especially interesting, but they're not offensive. Everybody seems to have worked hard, yet the delusion that this conception and this dialogue could bear the weight of aspirations to grandeur is crippling. Nor is that quite all that is the matter with "The Lion in Winter."

Seven years ago, in "Pocketful of Miracles," when Bette Davis became lovable and said "God bless" to Glenn Ford with heartfelt emotion in her voice, I muttered an obscenity as I slumped down in my seat. I slumped again during "Guess Who's Coming to Dinner," because Katharine Hepburn had become sweet and lovable, too. The two great heroines of American talkies, the two who dared to play smart women (who *had* to), the two most spe-

214

cifically modern of women stars—the tough, embattled Davis and the headstrong, noble Hepburn—have both gone soft on us, have become everything we admired them for not being. They had been independent enough to fight the studios, but they have given in to themselves. The public has got them at last as it always wanted them. They have become old dears—a little crotchety, maybe, but that only makes them more harmlessly lovable. And though, of course, we can't help prizing them still—because what they once meant to us is too important a part of our lives to be relinquished—there's a feeling of dismay, and even of betrayal, when we watch them now. They make us fearful that they will humiliate us by turning piteous, and they *mustn't*; we've got to have a few people who know how to age gracefully in public, who don't go flabby with the joy of being loved every time there's a fan or a reporter around.

There were occasions in the past when Hepburn had poor roles and was tremulous and affected—almost a caricature of quivering sensitivity. But at her best—in the archetypal Hepburn role as the tomboy Linda in "Holiday," in 1938—her wit and nonconformity made ordinary heroines seem mushy, and her angular beauty made the round-faced ingénues look piggy and stupid. She was hard where they were soft—in both head and body. (As Spencer Tracy said, in the Brooklyn accent he used in "Pat and Mike," "There's not much meat on her, but what's there is cherce.") Other actresses could be weak and helpless, but Davis and Hepburn had too much vitality. Unlike Davis, Hepburn was limited to mandarin roles, although some of her finest performances were as poor girls who were mandarins by nature, as in "Little Women" and "Alice Adams," rather than by birth or wealth, as in "Bringing Up Baby" and in the movie that the public liked her best in, "The Philadelphia Story" (even if her dedicated admirers, including me, tended to be less wild about it). Hepburn has always been inconceivable as a coarse-minded character; her bones are too fine, her diction is too crisp, she wears clothes too elegantly. And she has always been too individualistic, too singular, for common emotions. Other actresses who played career girls, like Crawford, could cop out in their roles by getting pregnant, or just by turning emotional—all womanly and ghastly. Hepburn was too hard for that, and so one could go to see her knowing that she wouldn't deteriorate into a conventional heroine; that didn't suit her style. As Rosemary Harris played the role on Broadway, Eleanor of Aquitaine was hard and funny—a tough cat who enjoyed scratching and fighting—and it might have been a good role for the brittle high priestess of modernism if she had still held her own. But Hepburn plays Eleanor as a gallant great lady. She's about as tough as Helen Hayes.

When an actress has been a star for a long time, we know too much about her; for years we have been hearing about her romances or heartbreaks, or whatever the case may be, and all this carries over into her presence on the screen. And if she *uses* this in a role, she's sunk. When actresses begin to use our knowledge about them and of how young and beautiful they used to be—when they offer themselves up as ruins of their former selves—they may get praise and awards (and they generally do), but it's not really for their acting, it's for capitulating and giving the public what it wants: a chance to see how the mighty have fallen. Only a few years ago, in "Long Day's Journey Into Night," the crowning achievement of her career, Katharine Hepburn kept her emotions within the role, and she was truly great—ravaged and magnificent. But in "Guess Who's Coming to Dinner" and much more in "The Lion in Winter" she draws upon our feelings for *her,* not for the character she's playing. When Hepburn, the most regal of them all, contemplates her blotches and wrinkles with tears in her anxious eyes, it's self-exploitation, and it's horrible.

November 9, 1968

Muddling Through

American educators are now concerned about making school-children "cinematically literate," but most of the new American movies aren't cinematically literate. There was a while there when well-made movies were taken for granted—so much for granted that "well-made" became a put-down, suggesting *merely* well-made, or conventional and not really interesting. Now there are so many inexplicably badly made pictures that "well-made" could be high praise. Great motion pictures are generally made by men in their twenties and thirties—before they have learned what can't be done, and while they still have the energy and heroism to do what hasn't been done before—but good, entertaining commercial movies can be made by trained, experienced "professionals." The businessmen have crushed the great talents, and they are so lacking in foresight and so indifferent to the future of their own industry that they haven't provided the conditions for the development of professionals. With the blacklisting of left-wing directors and then the breaking up of the big studios and their stables —which included directors as well as stars, and young directors getting experience on B pictures —a few generations of directors were lost. American movies may never fully recover from that discontinuity. They are exposed by competition from young movie-makers all over the world. It's as if American literature had stopped with Erskine Caldwell, Pearl Buck, John O'Hara, Thornton Wilder, John Dos Passos, and Henry Miller, still writing as they did twenty years ago, and then, when they got too tired and rich to go on, a new generation had been expected to pick up and start writing just like them (and as if the rest of the world had also paused for twenty years). Our movies are beginning to look as if people had forgotten how to make them, or had never learned how. American movies used to excel in the Western, the gangster film, and the musical. These genres developed out of a common delight in certain forms of entertainment that were not native to the screen (they had theatrical roots in the Wild West show, in melodrama, and in vaudeville, and can surely be traced much farther back) but were ideally suited to it. Popular genres gave movie people a measure of flexibility inside the commercial system. Directors knew the limits within which they had to work, and could often improvise and experiment and do something good within them (and that was true of writers, cameramen, technicians, and actors, too). Some of the best American movies have been genre movies; this had not been the case in Europe, but in recent years Europeans have been lured to the American specialties by their exotic charm and what used to be their vitality. And they are now being lured by an audience demand for American-style movies that we are no longer supplying, and may no longer be capable of supplying.

The Italians have taken over the Western, and the French and the Italians have taken over the gangster picture. Which leaves us the musical—at least, until the French learn to dance.

Unable to distinguish talent from no-talent among the French and Italians (that would require going to see some movies), and fearful of trusting young Americans, the American movie companies, with their classic acumen, are turning to England for directors. They're hiring the mediocrities and the bunglers of England—when even its best are none too good. The English can write and they can act (or, at least, *speak* beautifully, which is enough to cripple us with admiration), but they can't direct movies. They never could, but they had good scripts and so many good actors that the fundamental lack of directorial energy and distinction—of any real directorial artistry—in their movies could pass unnoticed. With the exception of Alfred Hitchcock and Carol Reed, there is scarcely an English director whose style one can discuss without giggling.

And now here are Michael Anderson with "The Shoes of the Fisherman" and Gordon Flemyng with "The Split," when we haven't yet recovered from recent joyless encounters with the work of Ken Annakin, Roy Boulting, Peter Collinson, Basil Dearden, Clive Donner, Lewis Gilbert, Peter Glenville, Guy Green, David Greene, Val Guest, Guy Hamilton, Anthony Harvey, Kenneth Loach, Joseph McGrath, Ronald Neame, Eric Till, Michael Winner, and Terence Young. Compared with the motion-picture art of Sweden or Italy or Japan or France or pre-Nazi Germany, English films have always been a sad joke; now these enervated directors may finish off what, for want of a better term, we still call the American movie.

"The Shoes of the Fisherman" is a movie made by people who don't know how. It shouldn't have taken very much talent to turn the novel into something reasonably acceptable; its idea is of an overpowering banality, but it's the kind of banality that can be amusing in a movie. I think most of us are perfectly willing to go to a movie of a book we wouldn't dream of reading. We don't turn to movies and books for the same thing, and after a while we get a sense of how movies work, and we know that second- and third-rate novels often make better movies than first-rate novels, because they're likely to be full of characters and action, while really good novels are dependent on the author's way of seeing. Movies are good at common fantasies, and "The Shoes of the Fisherman" is "If I Were Pope," combining the fantasy of becoming Pope almost overnight with the fantasy of having it in one's power to save the world. Who at some time hasn't said (if only to himself) that the Pope is hardly in a position to make humane speeches about giving to the poor? Here a Christlike Pope, played by Anthony Quinn, gives away all the riches of the Church to feed the hungry. The idea is as appealing a movie idea as going to an enchanted valley where one could live for hundreds of years, as in "Lost Horizon." It wouldn't require art to make it entertaining but only a fair amount of craftsmanship and ingenuity, and that not even on a very high level—just enough skill to turn out an old-fashioned, corny, pretentious movie (like "Lost Horizon," which, of course, was old-fashioned at the time it came out). This movie cheats even on its own fantasy level, because although the audience knows that the Pope means to feed the starving Chinese and thus prevent World War III, he doesn't mention this to the crowds who cheer his announcement about giving the wealth of the Church to the poor. One suspects that even the Italian Communists might not cheer the idea of sharing the wealth of the Church with Asia.

The fantasy of George Englund, the producer, and his crew is that they're movie-makers. They don't have the simple logic to tell a story effectively; they introduce elements that are not carried through, they load the movie with unnecessary explanations, and they forget to put in the revelations and climaxes. They reconstruct the Papal chambers and the Sistine Chapel in Cinecittà, but they don't know what to have the actors say or where to put the camera in their own specially built Vatican. (If the Church ever does divest itself of its property, who but movie-makers would want those gilded halls?) The acting, however, is not consistently bad. Quinn is too obviously trying hard for restraint and humility, but his attempt is an honest one, though his range is inadequate (particularly for the end). He manages to put on a Russian accent without too many slips; the dialogue coach is the only person on the crew who deserves a credit. The cast is what is usually called "distinguished"; it includes John Gielgud (being laid out as a corpse again), Frank Finlay, Oskar Werner (doing his doomed bit and looking

222

more like William F. Buckley, Jr., than ever), and Laurence Olivier, who seems to be having a good time, which he shares with the audience. But, oh, so briefly. MGM probably won't have to worry about giving away the profits on this picture. It hardly seems worthwhile to analyze its faults; it's cleaner work just to summarize them. "The Shoes of the Fisherman" is the worst-written, worst-directed, worst-photographed, and worst-edited *big* picture of the year. It takes movie storytelling back to before "The Great Train Robbery" of 1903. It's the coup de grâce for 1968.

Indirectly, new crime movies are begotten by old ones; the pulp novels that the movie companies buy for this kind of picture are written by fast writers, who synthesize old movies for their plots and characters. New kinds of crime rarely appear in them; the authors generally don't know anymore about crime than one can learn from old movies. Nor is it likely that the producers would take a chance on a crime script that didn't resemble earlier pictures, and so genre movies shrivel in interest. But even within the limited terrain of the straight robbery picture derived from other robbery pictures it's possible to do a workmanlike job—to present the occupational details of crime accurately (or convincingly), to assemble the gang so that we get a sense of the kinds of people engaged in crime and what their professional and nonprofessional lives are like. A good crime movie generally has a sordid, semi-documentary authenticity about criminal activities—big ones and petty, queasy ones—plus the nervous excitement of what it might be like to rob and to tangle with the law. After a run of spoof heists, robbery pictures are coming out again without self-parody. "The Split" is of the same genre (but not the same quality) as Stanley Kubrick's "The Killing"— each is about a robbery planned to coincide with a sporting event (this time it's a professional football game)—and it has some similarity to "The Asphalt Jungle" and "Rififi." But "The Split" is no more authentic than the spoofs, and no more plausible.

In a good robbery picture, the chases and the violence are integral to the story; in a poor robbery picture they're just thrown in to relieve the boredom, and you may be grateful for them because you know that's all the excitement you're going to get. Jim Brown, as the leader of the gang, selects his men in a series of brutal tests—one act of mayhem after another—that are obviously designed merely to give the picture a big opening, since they have no relationship to the skills that are later required of them. After the robbery, when the money is stolen from the men, they beat and torture Brown in another implausible sequence. They're not so stupid and unprofessional as to suppose he would have taken the money and waited around to be beaten; clearly, somebody thought it would be good for the box office to have the hero tortured. The action sequences in the James Bond films and in spoofs in general are not plausible, yet one doesn't mind, and, conceivably, action sequences in a "serious" heist film could be so well done that one wouldn't mind implausibility in them, either. But in "The

Split" the director, Gordon Flemyng, tries a lot of flashy stuff that doesn't work.

For long stretches during "The Split," I mostly listened to the Quincy Jones music; that's not so much a tribute to Quincy Jones as a comment on the action. Standard movie music is naïve program music carried to absurdity—a dramatic supplement designed to make you swoon in the romantic scenes or to shock you to attention at some brutality, but never encouraging you just to listen. It's a relief to hear the Quincy Jones music, which goes along independently, at its own rhythm, but one tends to forget about what is going on on the screen. It's like what one might see from a train window, and so some stretches of the movie are concerts.

Although "The Split" is a square comic strip, this may be enough for commercial success, because people want action so badly that they don't necessarily mind if it's stupid and patched together out of irrelevant, jarring camera angles. They want Jim Brown too. As a hood, Jim Brown is handsome and stiff—the essence of straight. He looks like an Indian, and he acts like a wooden one; he's totally unconvincing. (For a comparison, one needs to go back to Charles Starrett.) But each time he comes on the screen the kids in the theatre yell as if he had just scored a touchdown, and an actor who has the public on his side like this is almost sure to loosen up; when you're cheered for a performance like Brown's in "The Split," you have no need to be anxious and stiff. Brown may become the first Negro matinée idol of the screen. Poitier made it to the top by acting; Brown is the equivalent of the old Arrow-collar-ad idols, and he may be the new Robert Taylor or Gregory Peck. Is there a phrase along the lines of "Ontogeny repeats phylogeny" for blacks recapitulating whites' mistakes?

Only fourteen years have elapsed since "It Should Happen to You," in which Judy Holliday, as Gladys Glover, a nobody who wanted to be a somebody, thought the answer would be to have her name on a billboard—a solution that the movie presented satirically. But our notions of celebrity have changed, and John Brockman, a young mixed-media promoter who has put his face in the television and newspaper ads for "Head," has probably made himself a somebody. Brockman has made himself the star of "Head," though he doesn't even appear in the movie. The depressing possibilities that he has thus opened are sure to be seized on.

The advertising campaign for "Head" suggests some sort of turned-on movie about the drug scene, but the movie itself is designed for the subteens. The only novelty is in the selling—in convincing kids that they are visually sophisticated when they buy old jokes and blackout routines as mind-blowing, psychedelic, McLuhanite collages. "Head" is an attempt to do for the Monkees what the Richard Lester films did for the Beatles, but it borrows as much from Abbott and Costello as from Lester. (Will somebody try to sell the old Abbott and Costello films as marijuana visions, too? And "Hellzapoppin," and the Three Stooges?) This is the kind of material, taken from all over, that the Monkees have already worn out on television, only much

226

worse. The movie might have worked for bored kids at kiddie matinées, but the filmmakers got ambitious. The by now standard stuff of girls squealing as pop idols perform is not even convincing when they're squealing for the Monkees, and when this is intercut with documentary footage of the suffering and horror of war, as if to comment on the shallowness of what the filmmakers are manufacturing and packaging and desperately trying to sell, the doubling up of greed and pretensions to depth is enough to make even a pinhead walk out. So when the boys started to sing "Open your eyes, there's so much to do in the sunlight" . . .

November 23, 1968

Metamorphosis
of the Beatles

From the nursery to the boutique is now a very
short path; "Yellow Submarine" travels it with charm
and ease. The Beatles, represented by cartoons, go
to the rescue of the people of Pepperland and
save them from the Blue Meanies, their weapons
being (who'd have guessed it?) music and love—but
what is so pleasant about "Yellow Submarine" is its
lighthearted, throwaway quality, and the story seems
as disposable as the banter and the images. If the
movie tried to be significant, if it had "something to
say," it might be a disaster. One of the best characters is a gluttonous consumer with a vacuum snout,
who devours the universe, yet the movie itself sucks
up an incredible quantity of twentieth-century
graphics. If "Yellow Submarine" were not so good-
natured and—despite all the "artistic" effects—
unpretentious, one would be embarrassed; its chic
style can't support much more than the message of
"love." You could almost make a game of how many
sources you can spot, but, because of the giddy
flower-childishness of it all, this not only seems all
right but rather adds to one's pleasure. The eclecti-
cism is so open that it is in itself entertaining—we

have the fun of a series of recognitions. A little Nolde here, a bit of Klimt there, the hotel corridor from "The Blood of a Poet," with "The Mysteries of China" now become Indian, and good old Birnam Wood moving once again—it's like spotting the faces in Tchelitchew's "Cache-Cache."

The movie is extravagantly full of visual puns and transformations, but not too full (though there are places where one might wish for an extra instant to savor what is going by). The Beatles' non-singing voices are not their own, but they're good. The verbal jokes invite comparison with Edward Lear but can't sustain it. The movie seems to get its spirit back each time one of the Beatles' songs (sung by the Beatles) comes on (there are ten, three of them new), and this is not just because of the richer verbal texture but because the animation, ingenious as it is, is not much more than a shifting series of illustrations. The movie works best when the images (even though they don't quite connect with the meaning of the lyrics) are choreographed to the music.

In animation, anything can turn into anything else, and children love it for the illogic that is a visual equivalent of their nursery rhymes and jingles and word games. Recent American commercial cartoons have been so undistinguished visually and limited so much of the time to the reversibility of destruction that "Yellow Submarine," with its bright Pop flourish and inventiveness, restores the pleasure of constant surprise, which has always been the fun of good animation. Yet what will probably make "Yellow Submarine" a great success is its superlogical development: the Beatles walk by, and flowers grow out of them. They're no longer the rebellious, anarchistic Pop idols that parents were at first so outraged by; they're no longer threatening. They're hippies as folk heroes, enshrined in our mythology. The name "Beatles" no longer suits them; they have become quaint—such gentle, harmless Edwardian boys, with one foot in the nursery and the other in the boutique, nothing to frighten parents. The movie is a nostalgic fantasy—already nostalgic for the happy anarchism of "love." It finally goes a bit flat because love is no longer in bloom.

No doubt we can all do with less threat and less stress in the environment, and yet there's something depressing about seeing yesterday's outlaw idols of the teen-agers become a quartet of Pollyannas for the wholesome family trade. And if one looks at a list of the merchandise being promoted in conjunction with the movie, one may long for the simpler days of Mickey Mouse watches. That omnivorous consumer better get ready to suck up seven different "Yellow Submarine" books and a die-cast submarine and clocks and masquerade costumes and sweatshirts and stuffed dolls and inflatable swim toys and posters and lunchboxes and pillows and aprons and lamps and about fifty other products. Wasn't all this supposed to be what the Beatles were *against?* The way attacks on the consumer society become products to be consumed is, to put it delicately, discouraging. The Beatles had already become part of a comic-strip world in "Help!" By now, they have replaced Mickey Mouse as symbols of the union of art and popular success. Their loss of corporeality seems perfectly natural and right.

230

Movies are treacherous. I don't fully respect what the director, George Dunning, has done in "Yellow Submarine"; I don't truly admire much of what the chief designer, Heinz Edelmann, has done. And yet the movie is charming. They have done what hasn't been done before in animation—at least, not on anything like this scale. And if it's derivative, so was the Disney style—though not so obviously, since it was more unified. Despite all the enthusiasm registered in the press for animated features, this is one of the handful of palatable ones.

Without human characters, an animated feature is likely to be a bore, but animated human figures have never quite worked. Erwin Panofsky provided a reasonable explanation: "The very virtue of the animated cartoon is to animate; that is to say, endow lifeless things with life, or living things with a different kind of life. It effects a metamorphosis, and such a metamorphosis is wonderfully present in Disney's animals, plants, thunderclouds, and railroad trains. Whereas his dwarfs, glamourized princesses, hillbillies, baseball players, rouged centaurs, and *amigos* from South America are not transformations but caricatures at best, and fakes or vulgarities at worst." Still, this may be a little too pat. In the arts, one can never be altogether sure that the next artist who comes along won't disprove one's formulations. "Yellow Submarine" does not exactly disprove Panofsky, but one sequence, the dancing couple for "Lucy in the Sky with Diamonds," is a stunning use of stylized human figures—an apotheosis of Rogers and Astaire. Rather surprisingly, Edelmann follows the Disney and U.P.A. artists very closely in most of the human characters, making the Beatles as limply boneless and sweet as Snow White, and the Meanies grisly caricatures constantly displaying their cruel teeth. Even so, they shake Panofsky's formulations a bit, because in "Yellow Submarine" this weakness is not as crucial as in the Disney films. Where there is so much to choose from and the style is a collection of rejectable items, something bad may not matter very much. Aesthetic theories don't always allow for the variety of what we enjoy; we may like a certain amount of caricature and grisliness, and I preferred Popeye and Mr. Magoo to most animal characters in cartoons, because they were wittier. The Beatles provide a frame of reference that holds this movie together, though as cartoons they are weak facsimiles, with less character than the movie's fish, who are like windup toys, and its strange made-up monsters, or even its professorial little Boob. The single worst sequence in the movie—even worse than the addendum of filmed live Beatles—is the montage of photographed cities as the cartoon Beatles leave Liverpool; it disrupts the fantasy. But raiding the arts—shooting the works in animation—succeeds. It becomes an equivalent of the way kids dress now—cutting through the anxieties about what is appropriate and the class structure of good taste, wearing what they feel like wearing, and making life a fancy-dress ball. The movie has something of this freshness; throwing in a multiplicity of styles—even a couple of startling Op sequences—is a fluke solution to a problem that more rigorous-minded men have failed to solve.

Animation is beautifully suited to the short form—

to imaginative excursions of from four to eight minutes. Many people simply turn off after a few minutes of animation. But animators can't make a living out of shorts for theatres, because theatres pay almost nothing for shorts. Audiences come for the features, and theatre-bookers argue that they come in the same numbers when the short is an ad for travel that the theatre gets free. Few theatre men care enough about these captive audiences to give them a fair shake; many theatres provide shorts that their customers would not watch at home on television. It was because Disney couldn't make enough money on his shorts—even the Academy Award-winning ones that made his studio famous—that he turned to animated features. He made only a few, and there have been only a few from other sources. The reasons for their rarity are not only commercial; there are some peculiar artistic problems involved. This was obvious in Disney's first feature, "Snow White and the Seven Dwarfs," which rescued him financially. In order to attract audiences and to hold their interest for a full-length feature, he sacrificed the simplicity and stylization that had been so marvellous in early shorts; he employed a more naturalistic style of drawing and some semi-human characters. It's probable that if he had not done so, if he had tried to tell a full-length story with the non-realistic stick figures of early animation, he would have been wiped out. The delight that audiences took in the Disney animated features was that they were so much like "life"; the Disney artists were using animal and human models (his nature documentaries grew out of the photographic material gathered to help them), and the more naturalistic the animation became, the more complex and expensive it became. It is much cheaper and easier to photograph people in motion than to make drawings of people move smoothly and realistically; Disney took the logical step and began to make "live-action" movies. He had already tried to insert live actors in an animated feature, and, in the highly publicized "Fantasia"—which was really a package of shorts— he tried to get away from naturalism by combining several styles and tried to attract an audience by advertising Stokowski and the classical music and the abstract sequence. The attempts failed at the box office, and maybe they would have failed as badly, or even worse, if they had been more imaginative. Karel Zeman's "The Deadly Invention," which is probably the finest contemporary animated feature— and one that successfully integrates live actors—was not well received when it was released here, as "The Fabulous World of Jules Verne." Even with the live actors, the stylization seemed too much for audiences, and in neighborhood theatres they talked through it as they waited for the second half of the double bill—a routine live-action film that held their interest.

The Disney artists' animation was pre-Pop pop of a simple, consistent, and often stupid kind, and this was true, oddly, of "Animal Farm," the last animated feature to come from England. But Pop has now become a *style;* "Yellow Submarine" uses Pop heroes and Pop Art deliberately, and with sophistication. And it works. But it is merely a further development of what ads and commercials have al-

ready been doing. People who want to make animated features may now have an easier time getting
backing, but the aesthetic problems haven't been
solved. Animators can't just keep on ravaging the art
of the twentieth century; after the orgy of "Yellow
Submarine" it's going to look worn out.

November 30, 1968

The Corrupt and
the Primitive

"Why must you die?" says Joanna to languishing Lord Peter, and he replies, "It makes sense to die. Only then does it make sense to live." The surging music testifies to the rich quality of his thought, and Lord Peter, perhaps stimulated by the music to still higher cerebration, goes on, "How incredible we human beings are! . . . One thinks on how beautiful life is. . . . Oh, people are such lovely things!" Joanna learns a lot more from Lord Peter—the bums' Oscar Wilde—when he explains to her that we must "make our lives works of art."

We have to suspend disbelief that we're actually hearing and seeing this kind of gibberish. I thought I was going to need the taffy pulled out of my head. I didn't bother writing about Romain Gary's "Birds in Peru," which concerned a frigid nymphomaniac goddess luring men to their doom (and was full of such great lines as "Take me"), because the theatre was empty when I saw it. But the house was packed for "Joanna," and though I kept listening for snorts, every time I heard one I could feel the breath on my hands. I hope some of the silent people were at least thinking bad thoughts. Explicitly, the movie is about the aimlessness of a young Mod girl's life in London and the pointlessness of her sleeping

around, and the message is spelled out, and re-
peated, that one "must be committed to something."
On the other hand, it's the kind of Mod fashion-
show movie in which you expect the clothes to be
on sale in the lobby, along with picture postcards of
the parks and the fountains and the yacht. The
photography is disgustingly pretty, but the movie
attempts a fancy rationale; the baroque, we are informed in a statement within the film, represents
rebellion against classicism. (This can be translated
as: Anything in the movie can be explained away as
not meant to be taken straight.) But classicism is
scarcely the enemy of film, since it has so rarely
been even approximated in film. And the baroque
of "Joanna" is the already conventional enticement
for swinging-London movies. It's the beautiful people leading the easy life, with dabs of "The Umbrellas of Cherbourg" and Godard and "8½," with
sartorial assists from "Bonnie and Clyde," and with
posters of the usual deities—Brando, Dean, Monroe. The characters are out of Elinor Glyn via forties Hollywood. It turns out that the dying lord has
been befriending a swank black racketeer who has
"a streak of violence." Joanna gets pregnant by this
beautiful black, and though he goes to prison for ten
years, she decides to have the baby; she's learned
the lessons that the lord wheezed out to her (though
they must surely have been familiar from nursery
and classroom). I tell this appalling plot only to
make a plain point—that we are getting the howling
banalities of the past brought back in creamy Pana-
vision and fruity DeLuxe color and enough Mod
clothes to choke a clotheshorse, and they're brought

back not with irony but with moronic solemnity. There's a less publicized side of the generation gap: *we* remember this stuff from the last time around. Mod filmmakers, it appears, have just discovered the Rubáiyát and are working their way toward "The Razor's Edge." This movie has the trivial narcissism of old *Collier's* and *Cosmopolitan* stories, and the Rod McKuen songs pour on inspirational tonic. Movies are still providing what even the ladies' slick magazines have abandoned in fiction. (And now, trying to be with it, those magazines applaud the dazzling originality of these movies.) The movie is decorated with such conceits as a lament that the emancipation of women has led to nothing more than promiscuity—this in a movie that introduces the heroine in bikini panties. It's as if Hugh Hefner were to denounce Bunnies for wearing tails. Joanna (Genevieve Waite) is an odd, passionless, blank little bunny-bird with a voice out of Glynis Johns. The camera never discovers any soul in her; she's embalmed in infantilism, and we're supposed to find her adorable. And what a perfect fulfillment for a bunny—to multiply.

Michael Sarne, the spokesman for commitment who wrote and directed "Joanna," is twenty-nine years old and is said to be a former pop singer and composer, book and film critic, journalist, and photographer. This commentator on the emancipation of women is credited with the photograph of his heroine—nude with necktie—that appears in the film and in the advertising. He doesn't even have a head stuffed with old movies; his borrowings and references are already secondhand movie memories,

238

not obsessive for him and not part of the mythology
of his characters' lives but just new standard com-
mercial-movie equipment for "now-generation"
movies—the kind of movies that buy and sell and
attack "amorality." He's got the soft-edge mind to
go with his luxuriously blurred cinematography. His
facile, splashy, rotten style makes a shallow, romantic director like Claude Lelouch seem positively austere. "Facile" means in this case that Sarne can do
so many things not worth doing; "Joanna" is a
monument to cheap ambition. At the risk of being
crude, I here note the wish that Mr. Sarne would
add "writer-director" to the list of his former occu-
pations.

Although I am far from being an enthusiast of
John Cassavetes' kind of movie-making, after seeing
something like "Joanna" one may think back on the
glum, naïve realism of "Faces" with respect, if not
quite affection. When his "Shadows" came out, almost a decade ago, it was generally thought of as a
group improvisation rather than as a first film by
John Cassavetes. But from bits of his two interven-
ing, commercially produced films ("Too Late
Blues" and "A Child Is Waiting"), and now from
"Faces," in which he apparently had full control, it
is clear that either he made "Shadows" or working
on "Shadows" made his style. Cassavetes' method is
peculiar in that its triumphs and its failures are not
merely inseparable from the method but often truly
hard to separate from each other. The acting that is
so bad it's embarrassing sometimes seems also to
have revealed something, so we're forced to recon-

sider our notions of good and bad acting. In 1961, I commented on "Shadows," "As the creative effort of a group, it has the rawness and insistence of a form of psychodrama, but it has a special fascination—it reveals a good deal about what actors think is the content of drama (and what they think life is)." In "Faces," the people are older and richer, and the milieu is southern California rather than New York, yet not only is the method the same (though the technique is infinitely smoother and the *cinéma-vérité*-style photography is generally handsome and effective) but the attitudes are the same. The heroine, after a night of extramarital sex, experiences the very same pathos and guilt and disgust that the virgin in "Shadows" experienced when she was seduced. In fact, nobody seems to have got very far, except downhill. "Faces" is going to be a big success and it doesn't need critical generosity, so, still awarding Cassavetes high marks for doing something "interesting," I would like to point out some of the limitations and implications of the method.

Cassavetes' approach to making a film is not unlike Andy Warhol's in "The Chelsea Girls" and Norman Mailer's in "Wild 90" and "Beyond the Law"; by depending on the inspiration of the amateurs and professionals in their casts, they attempt to get at something more truthful than ordinary movies do. And the actors act away. The movie equivalent of primitive painters may be moviemakers like these, who expect the movie to happen when the camera is on. Their movies become the games actors play (and this can be true even when there is a conventional script, as in "Rachel, Rachel"). They are likely to go for material that they feel is being left out of commercial films, but they make their movies in terms of what impressed them in their childhood—the stars—and ignore the other elements of movies. In Warhol and in Mailer, the best moments may be when the actors have a good time performing for the camera. Cassavetes has a good, clear sense of structure; he uses a script and allows improvisation only within strict limits, and, as a result, "Faces"—which is like an upper-middle-class, straight version of "The Chelsea Girls"—has the unified style of an agonizing honesty. Many professional and non-professional actors have something they're particularly good at, and in this kind of movie they may get a chance to show it: in "Shadows," the heroine's flirtatiousness, the quarrelling of the two men in the train station; in "Faces," Lynn Carlin's comic rapport with John Marley in her first scene. And there are nuances and inventions we get from such scenes which in context seem remarkable—seem to be unlike what we get in ordinary movies. But these actors may be inadequate or awful in the rest of the film, because, working out of themselves this way, they can't create a character. Their performances don't have enough range, so one tends to tire of them before the movie is finished. It's my feeling that nothing makes one so aware of acting as this self-conscious kind of willed realism, and I think we may over-react to the occasional small victories because we sit there waiting for the actors to think up something to say and do. The actors dominate, as they do on a stage, and they can bring something like the tedium of dull people on the stage to the screen. But what actors think is true to life, and what, given the impetus to be sincere and the opportunity to improvise, they come up with, is very much like what the public thinks is true to life.

Glowering with integrity, determined not to pander to commercial tastes, Cassavetes has stumbled on a very commercial idea. His great commercial asset is that he thinks not like a director but like an actor. His deliberately raw material about affluence and apathy, loneliness and middle age, the importance of sex and the miseries of marriage may not say any more about the subject than glossy movies on the same themes, and the faces with blemishes may not be much more revealing than faces with a little makeup, but the unrelieved effort at honesty is, for some people, intensely convincing. When it's done as psychodrama rather than as entertainment, they seem to accept all this bruising-searing stuff, the sad whore and the tender hustler, and the false-laughter bit, and the-lies-people-live-by, etc. Watching the kind of drunken salesmen one would have sense enough to avoid in life can, I suppose, seem an illumination. Watching a fat, drunken old woman fall on top of a man she has just begged for a kiss can seem an epiphany. There are scenes in "Faces" so dumb, so crudely conceived, and so badly performed that the audience practically burns incense. I think embarrassment is not a quality of art but our reaction to failed art, yet many members of the audience apparently feel that embarrassment is a sign of flinching before the painful truth, and hence they accept what is going on as deeper and truer because they have been embarrassed by it. Cassavetes' people are empty, lecherous middle-aged failures, like Benjamin's parents and their friends in "The Graduate," seen not in terms of comedy but in terms of bitterness and despair—a confirmation of the audience's anxieties. The theme of "Faces" is exactly the same theme as that of many now fashionable films—sex as the last quest for meaning in this meaningless, godless, etc., life, or "We who are about to die want to try everything." But the aging people and the Los Angeles setting (which, of course, makes it all seem suburban) have the ghastliness and monotonousness of the commonplace. The heroine is the most banal of all statistical entities—"housewife." And no matter how much is written on aesthetics people think something is good because "I've known people just like that. It's so true to life."

Artists use their technique in order to express themselves more fully; the actors in "Faces" strip away technique as if it were a falsehood that stood between them and "reality." This idea has great popular appeal; it's like the theory of character in "The Boys in the Band"—that when you peel away the protective layers of personality you get to the real person inside. "Faces" has the kind of seriousness that a serious artist couldn't take seriously—the kind of seriousness that rejects art as lies and superficiality. And this lumpen-artists' anti-intellectualism, this actors' unformulated attack on art may be what much of the public also believes—that there is a real thing that "art" hides. The audi-

ence comes out shaken and in no mood for levity—
as I discovered when I attempted to cheer someone
up by remarking that if people's lives were so empty, wasn't it lucky that they had a little money to
ease the pain? I was reprimanded with "The pain is
due to America and money." (A) I don't believe it,
and (B) just about every "serious" movie lately has
been saying it. But audiences really seem to want to
hear it. I have tried to describe the audience reaction rather than just my own because that reaction
may be important to the future of movies. A movie
like "Joanna" makes one want to throw up, but
"Faces" makes a sacrament of throwing up modern
life and American society. Like a number of new
forms of theatre, "Faces" is being taken as a religious experience. It's almost a form of self-
flagellation to go to a movie like this—"to see
yourself," which, of course, means to see how awful
you are. And the hushed seriousness with which
people respond (to what is really not much more
than the routine sorrows of middle age or a bad
office party) seems almost hysterical. They come
out chanting the liberal forms of "Mea culpa."

December 7, 1968

The Concealed Art
of Carol Reed

Carol Reed has just made the kind of movie they don't make anymore, and it's as good as ever—maybe better, coming when it's more difficult to do. Maybe the most revolutionary thing that can be done in movies at the moment is to make them decently again. "Oliver!" has been made by people who know how; it's a civilized motion picture, not only emotionally satisfying but so satisfyingly crafted that we can sit back and enjoy what is going on, secure in the knowledge that the camera isn't going to attack us and the editor isn't going to give us an electric shock. It's not an innovative work or a disturbing work, it does not advance the art of the film, but if we don't admire the real thing in fine big-studio methods, then we probably can't perceive what is *new* in movie art, either. Carol Reed is in the tradition of the older movie artists who conceal their art, and don't try to dazzle us with breathtaking shots and razor-sharp cuts. They are there, all right, but we hardly notice them, because there is always a reason for the camera to be where it is; the camera and the complex, unobtrusive editing serve the story. "Oliver!" is not put together like TV commercials and it doesn't have a psychedelic look or a rock beat, but neither is it rotting on the screen,

like "My Fair Lady." Reed uses tact and skill to tell
a story that can be enjoyed by "everyone," and it's a
very great pleasure to see a movie that can be
enjoyed by everyone that one really does enjoy.
There's something restorative about a movie that is
made for a mass audience and that respects that
audience.

Though "Oliver!" is not presented realistically, we
become involved in the material—more consciously
involved than we do in realistic movies. The tone of
the picture is set in the opening sequence, in the
children's workhouse, when Oliver's "Please, sir, I
want some more" leads into a choreographed children's riot. The stylization encourages us to notice
the conventions of the story as we are enjoying the
story. It seems to put quotation marks around everything Dickensian, yet not in a cloying way—
rather, in a way that makes us more aware of some
of the qualities of Dickens' art. It's as if the movie
set out to be a tribute to Dickens and a comment on
his melodramatic art as well as to tell the story of
Oliver Twist. The set designs—a remarkable blend
of realism and stylization, by John Box—are an
enormous aid in this. Similarly, Reed has got from
little Mark Lester, as Oliver, what in an adult would
be called Brechtian acting. We can sit there and enjoy the beauty and wit of the child's performance,
because we are never pushed over into realism and
pathos. Music is the most painless of all alienating
devices; the songs provide the distancing that enables us to appreciate Dickens' pathos intellectually.
Reed sustains the tone that tells us it's all theatre,
and he's a gentleman: he doesn't urge an audience to

tears, he always leaves us our pride. He offers his gifts modestly. Typically, the best moment is a quiet one. Oliver, who has been listening to "Who Will Buy?," the lovely early-morning song of the tradespeople in Bloomsbury, walks along singing a few bars to himself, and it is probably the most delicately beautiful reprise in movie-musical history.

No one who sees this movie is likely to say, "But you should have seen 'Oliver!' on the stage!" On the stage, it was the kind of undistinguished musical that people took their children to, dutifully. Though not on a level with "The Sound of Music," it had that detestable kind of mediocre respectability; it was an English version of Broadway Americana, and I walked out on it. The material in "Oliver!" has been more than a little transformed. I hate to describe the Lionel Bart score as adequate—which always really means inadequate to one's hopes—but, at least, it's well sung. And though there is a Broadway-London sound and an awful kind of commercial thinking in numbers like "You've Got to Pick a Pocket or Two," the good voices and the playful performing spirit often suggest Gilbert and Sullivan. Ron Moody, as Fagin the fence, is a controlled singer-actor, and his performance grows and becomes very impressive. As Nancy, Shani Wallis is an unexpected pleasure—hearty (as Dickens described her), with a tough vitality that brings poignancy to the role, though her solo "As Long As He Needs Me" has that designed-to-stop-the-show vulgarity which is not redeemable when the song is as poor as this one. I never thought I'd have cause to praise Oliver Reed, but as Bill Sikes he has found the right outlet for his peculiar talents. The choreographer, Onna White, can take a banal song and a banal conception of a routine and build them up until the number becomes so effective it's just about irresistible; you can hardly help feeling elated, even though you're aware of the whole synthetic process. Her talent is not one I respect, but she succeeds where many others fail. The musical numbers emerge from the story with a grace that has been rarely seen since the musicals of René Clair. It isn't really surprising that Carol Reed, a master of planned montage, should be so adroit. Still, he was a young man when he made his last musical (thirty years ago), and we tend to think of him as the director of suspense films ("Night Train," "The Fallen Idol," "The Third Man," "The Man Between," "Our Man in Havana"), social dramas, and stories of outcasts ("The Stars Look Down," "Odd Man Out," and the brilliant commercial failure "An Outcast of the Islands"). He has always had a gift for handling children; the last example was in his generally underrated "A Kid for Two Farthings"—a realistic fantasy with a number of resemblances to "Oliver!" Like the boy in "A Kid for Two Farthings," Mark Lester and Jack Wild (the Artful Dodger) suggest that childhood is a period of fable, a period in our lives that we look back on as if we had dreamed it all. They are bemused in the midst of activity. The movie of "Oliver!" is much more than the stage production could be; it's not only a musical entertainment but a fine, imaginative version of "Oliver Twist" that treats the novel as a lyrical, macabre fable.

Dickens wrote "Oliver Twist" to counter seductive stories of criminal life—specifically, "The Beggar's Opera," with its gallant thief-hero. "To draw a knot of such associates in crime as really did exist; to paint them in all their deformity, in all their wretchedness, in all the squalid misery of their lives; to show them as they really were, forever skulking uneasily through the dirtiest paths of life, with the great black ghastly gallows closing up their prospect, turn they where they might; it appeared to me that to do this, would be to attempt a something which was needed, and which would be a service to society." And so it may seem ironic that "Oliver!" turns his book into what it was supposed to be against; Bart's libretto for "Oliver!" resembles "The Beggar's Opera," though it is much inferior to it. But perhaps it's not really so ironic; Dickens, only twenty-five when he wrote the novel, had already made low life commercially acceptable with the first of those great, silly, rhyming plots of his, and, later in life, he gave lurid public readings of the murder of Nancy. (Well pleased with one performance, he wrote, "We had a contagion of fainting. . . . I should think we had from a dozen to twenty ladies taken out stiff and rigid at various times!") And it's clear in reading "Oliver Twist" that, despite his cautionary purpose, Dickens fell in love with his scoundrels and couldn't do anything with his proper characters. (The movies have done better by them, and much better than Cruikshank, whose drawings of Oliver made him so bleakly virtuous he looked malformed.) Bart has taken the next step—

an extension not of what Dickens the pamphleteer thought he was doing but of what Dickens the emotional artist did. Bart has left only one unlovable villain—Bill Sikes. It's scarcely the first time in the history of the arts that a work written to break with a tradition has seemed in subsequent years to be much closer to that tradition than the rebel realized. This is almost a résumé of the development of any art.

"Oliver!" is much easier to take than the very fine non-musical film version of "Oliver Twist" produced in 1948, and I don't think the softening of this particular material is to be lamented. There were scenes in the David Lean film that were simply too painful, and the trumpery of the Dickensian plotting was too stylized and conventional to go with the pain of the child's suffering and the horrible murder of Nancy. (I know in my bones why those women turned rigid). In this new version, in which the whole story is stylized and the suffering and murder become conventions in themselves (as in an opera), the plot is entertainingly functional. When men sing about what rogues they are, when children sing about how hungry they are, they are domesticated. (This is probably why the villain Bill Sikes does not sing, though in an opera, as opposed to this musical-theatre form, he would doubtless have had an aria to express his anguish over his foul deeds.) One villain is enough, really; we simply cannot take the melodramatics of wickedness and virtue the way nineteenth-century readers did, and the omission of the mechanism of the mistreatment of Oliver (that whole apparatus of the half brother and the will) is a blessing—and not only because it's too much freight for a musical to carry. Closer fidelity to Dickens' text and his warnings about the perils of a sinful life would make the work not more realistic but quite absurd; it would turn into Camp.

I admire the artist who can make something good for the art-house audience, but I also applaud the commercial heroism of a director who can steer a huge production and keep his sanity and perspective and decent human feelings as beautifully intact as they are in "Oliver!" I'm not being facetious when I suggest that the quiet, concealed art of good craftsmanship may be revolutionary now. It's more difficult than ever before for a director to trust his accumulated knowledge and experience, because on big commercial projects there's so much pressure on movie-makers to imitate the techniques of the latest hit, to be "up to date," which means always to be out of date. The camera pranks and the flamboyant scissorwork that seem so creative to young filmmakers are easy, and because they express nothing much deeper than Mod alienation and fragmentation, they're consumed by TV specials—if the commercials don't get them first. Artists like Carl Dreyer and Robert Bresson have pointed the way to a pure, austere style, and Jean-Luc Godard, the major new influence, has been evolving a technique that depends on long takes. The period of the cutups may be over—among movie artists, that is; the hacks are just beginning to call for scissors and strobes. In this context of a search for new ways of *integrating* material on the screen, the unostentatious work of a man like Carol Reed may be both behind and ahead of what is now exhaustingly fashionable.

December 14, 1968

Frightening the Horses

Having just seen "The Killing of Sister George," "The Fixer," "The Girl on a Motorcycle" (half), "A Flea in Her Ear" (half), "The Magus," "The Birthday Party," and "Greetings," I have to report that the only one I *enjoyed* was "Greetings." Not that "Greetings" (a cheaply made little exploitation film for the youth market) is anything special, but it has some fresh humor—like a new-life-style college revue—while most of the others, except "Sister George," suffer from aspirations.

Robert Aldrich's "The Killing of Sister George" has low intentions, all right, but it's as fresh as Joan Crawford's smile. It isn't difficult to see the remains of Frank Marcus's play—the screen is full of stage business—and it's obvious that what the movie has done is scarcely desecration. Here's the mechanism. Start with pathos in the form of an actress who is going to be killed in her television soap-opera role; add the irony that this sanctimonious soap-opera heroine is a butch lesbian; compound the pathos by having her lose her girl-friend to a chic rival. And since all that would in itself be too much like a soap opera, add grotesque touches: the girl-friend playing with dolls, sadomasochistic rituals, etc. And, to be sporty and tolerant, make the actress (played by

Beryl Reid) an earthy, twinkling darling of an over-grown baby boy. It's hearts and flowers, sixties style, with swelling strings for fetishism. This clumpingly archaic piece of movie-making is forties emotional stuff, from the period when the ladylike emotions of movie queens became a travesty of human feelings. To convey a flicker of expression, Aldrich sends a messenger bicycling across the screen; after a while, the screen is so covered with grooves that the messengers sink in their tracks. In the guided tour through a London lesbian bar, every shot is locked in with significance, so that there is nothing we can see for ourselves; the obvious supposition is that we're going to be shocked and wowed. But the gay-bar sequence has already ranged from the response of the horrified innocent in "Advise and Consent" to the satire of "P.J.," with so many permutations that one could put together a season of it for the Museum of Modern Art Department of Film (which has been doing rather less amusing programming). This just looks like the beginning of a new cycle, with girls.

All this nonsense about how liberal the screen is getting. Doesn't anybody remember anything? A year or so ago, "Loves of a Blonde" was widely discussed as having the first nude love scene in a Czech movie, as if no one had ever heard of "Ecstasy." Such movies as "Mädchen in Uniform" (1932) and "Pit of Loneliness" (1951)—both directed by women—were sympathetic studies of lesbianism. The general opinion was that American directors—trained on action films—wouldn't have the right, "delicate" touch for the psychology of sex, and Aldrich seems determined to prove the general opinion correct. Bluntness can be liberating, but Aldrich's attitude is reactionary. His is the leering view that the others were trying to break away from; he wants us to be horrified and excited by what he shows us.

When Robert Aldrich is being overt, it's best to clear the streets, because he's enough to frighten the horses. He starts out in that overwrought style of his and keeps pounding away at us. Coral Browne plays the seducer like Basil Rathbone at his most villainous—hooded cobra eyes, cruel mouth, and all. I've always heard that there was no such thing as a happy lesbian, but I assumed that was male propaganda. Don't lesbians ever have any light moments? Not in an Aldrich movie, they don't, and neither does anybody else. In his entire repertory, I can't remember a single scene that could be described as deft or debonair. "Kiss Me Deadly," "The Big Knife," "Attack!," "Autumn Leaves," "What Ever Happened to Baby Jane?," "The Dirty Dozen," "The Legend of Lylah Clare"—his range is from nagging to screeching, from hysteria to violence, and he has the grace of a diesel. Aldrich directs like a lewd tourist (Would you *believe* it? They're all *girls!*); he tries to get his camera in as close as he can, and he comes back with pictures that reveal nothing. His big scene (Coral Browne kissing Susannah York's breast) has about as much relevance to this movie as such a scene would have to any other movie. Aldrich simply picked up the ball where Preminger dropped it in "Hurry Sundown," and ran like hell. What's ironic is that this kind of scene has reached the big screen in a lesbian movie before it has been put into a heterosexual movie—skipping a stage, as it were.

Competent, professional American directors are generally at their worst when they become serious and ambitious; when they reach for mighty themes, they fall for banalities. They become clods who think they can turn into important artists by the simple expedient of not being entertaining. John Frankenheimer's "The Fixer" crawls along on its intentions, and will no doubt be revered by those who believe that movies are being elevated when a picture is based on a prestige-laden prize-winning novel with a "universal" theme. Frankenheimer, who has demonstrated a talent for pace and pyrotechnics, for melodramatic suspense and showmanship (in "The Manchurian Candidate," and even when working with less, in "Seven Days in May"), abandons the skills he has, and trusts in his new nobility to carry him through. One would think that Frankenheimer, who was confined to a cell for "Bird Man of Alcatraz," would avoid being trapped again, but he's more heavily shackled than his hero. He forgets how to stage the simplest actions. A book that won both the Pulitzer Prize and the National Book Award, that has a pre-revolutionary Russian setting and a Jewish hero falsely accused of crime, a man who refuses to confess and becomes a symbol of human dignity—what a set of chains! Do all the directors in Hollywood long to become respectable in the eyes of their old high-school English teachers? Does each have to make his own version of "The

Life of Emile Zola"? Don't they know what a drag it was?

There is a kind of classic inevitability about Dalton Trumbo's doing the adaptation of Bernard Malamud's novel. Last year, in Hollywood, I asked a group of ten veteran screenwriters who in their opinion was the greatest living writer and who the greatest living screenwriter. To the first, *all* of them answered Arthur Miller; to the second, eight answered Dalton Trumbo (two said Carl Foreman). Miller and Trumbo, who both refused to turn informer for the House Un-American Activities Committee, have something else in common: dialogue as flat as unleavened bread. Trumbo, the screenwriters' hero, is the leading exponent of the dictates-of-conscience and the dignity-and-indomitable-spirit-of-man school of screenwriting. He rarely has to write those terrible lines—he has a knack for finding them in the novels he adapts. This is what is called "construction." In the movie of "The Fixer," some of the lines that stand out as true, vintage Trumbo come straight from Malamud; the trick is to take them out of the rhythm and context in which they sound (reasonably) alive and irrational, and even comic, and stiffen them into the banality that will make them seem important enough for a timeless movie about human agony which is supposed to make your spirit soar.

Frankenheimer is apparently so sure that exaltation will take place that he doesn't cover his bets by developing any other possible sources of interest; the movie is unrelieved suffering. Borrowed grandeur can make a movie look awfully seedy (and in Mala-

mud the grandeur was maybe already a little tat-
tered). The movie of "The Fixer" flogs you—not
because you're watching a man being beaten and
tormented but because you're seeing an incompetent
movie about a man being beaten and tormented. In
the opening pogrom sequence—a try for power and
intensity like Eisenstein's and Kurosawa's—when
Frankenheimer does go in for some pyrotechnics, he
demonstrates only that his are inadequate for "serious," "epic" material. For the rest of the movie, his
staging and his handling of the actors are almost
incomprehensibly solemn and inept, unless one re-
calls other Hollywood essays in sublimity. Scenes
like the rescue of the merchant from death in the
snow are so implausible that one simply doesn't
know how to react, and as scenes like this mount
up, one becomes a detached observer. The movie
was made in Hungary and the principal actors are
English, but it's as American as George Stevens'
version of "The Diary of Anne Frank." If the script
and the direction had given him some help, Alan
Bates, in the title role, might almost have carried the
picture by sheer intelligence and determination. Although he doesn't get a chance to take hold of the
part until late in the movie, he very nearly brings
the character to interest, if not to "life." His scenes
with Dirk Bogarde, as the decent, melancholy
magistrate, make the movie seem promising, but
then the magistrate dies (and his death is so confusingly staged it's impossible to figure out what is
supposed to be happening). I might have thought
Ian Holm impressive as the odious anti-Semitic
prosecutor if I hadn't been seeing him give that

performance too much lately. It is kinder not to speak of the ladies. And as for David Warner, playing a decadent aristocrat with a Machiavellian-Marxist point of view—well, he'd frighten the horses, too.

Marianne Faithfull, nude, zips on her Lanvin black leather jump suit, climbs onto her Harley-Davidson, and, after many miles of sub-Fascist, high-toned, literary stream of consciousness, arrives at the home of her lover (Alain Delon) and says "Skin me." That's a pretty good line, but after an hour of "The Girl on a Motorcycle" I had a strong feeling there wouldn't be another one. . . . Whenever a movie version of a French farce fails, as the new movie "A Flea in Her Ear" does, and as "Hotel Paradiso" did recently, there are always critics with neat little formulations about the incompatibility of stage farce with the screen, which are supposed to explain why farce can't be done successfully in the movies. But it has been done successfully *many* times—by René Clair ("The Italian Straw Hat"), by Claude Autant-Lara ("Occupes-Toi d'Amélie"), by Pietro Germi ("Mademoiselle Gobette"), etc.—and although Ernst Lubitsch's comedies may have derived more from Viennese operetta than from French farce, he solved similar formal problems, as, of course, Ingmar Bergman did in "Smiles of a Summer Night" and Bellocchio in "China Is Near." "A Flea in Her Ear," a first film by Jacques Charon, is an unfortunate failure, but I hope it won't discourage other attempts to bring the pleasures of this genre to the screen, or discourage Rosemary Harris,

who is charming in it, from other screen roles. . . .
As a movie, "The Magus" is an elaborate, trashy
literary conceit that should be fun but isn't. . . .
"The Birthday Party," directed by William
Friedkin, is remarkably well photographed by Denys
Coop (considering that, except for the beginning
and the ending, it's all in two rooms), and well
played, especially by Sydney Tafler, as Goldberg;
and although Patrick Magee, as McCann, seems to
be suffering from the delusion that he's Boris Kar-
loff, this seems as plausible an interpretation of the
character (who is obsessed with tearing strips off
newspapers) as any other. Despite its virtues, the
movie is an unendurably ponderous exercise in
transferring early Harold Pinter to the screen. The
trouble, I am afraid, is in the original: it looks like
drama, it sounds like drama, and the actors play it
like drama, but what has traditionally been considered the most important ingredient has been left
out, though not *completely* out, as it is in his later
plays. One can see Pinter's digestive processes at
work here. There are remnants of so many plays
about mysterious strangers that those who don't
know his later style may understandably try to follow the mystic hints and look for allegorical interpretations, and think the movie must be deep even
if they can't understand it. Pinter is the actor as
dramatist, and his plays are a kind of actor's conceit, an actor's view of what people come to see at
the theatre; that is, actors playing juicy roles and
skillfully building up scenes. Holding the stage becomes the drama; in this movie version, however, the
camera movements take over for what the actors on

stage do by force and magnetism, and these camera movements seem odd and arbitrary because they determine what is in contest on the stage. Onstage, Pinter plays so well that one can get involved in the "pure theatre" of the actors' exercises, but on the screen "The Birthday Party," with its ominous suggestions of retribution and the supernatural, is thumpingly rigid in its pauses and trivia and repetitions and pathetic revelations and nameless fears and sudden climaxes. Lacking the finesse he later developed, this early Pinter is a caricature of its author, and all too revealing. . . . The title "Greetings" is from a draft-induction notice, and the movie is fairly consistently funny when it follows three boys around New York City as two of them advise the third on how to stay out of the Army. But the director, Brian De Palma, and the producer, Charles Hirsch, who wrote this movie together (and shot it in two weeks—in color—on a budget of under forty thousand dollars), apparently didn't have enough confidence in this theme, or possibly couldn't provide enough invention, because they threw in another plot, about a computer dating service, that is very low-grade stuff. Structurally, the movie is a mess, but the actors are young and talented (especially a tall boy who tells a long, euphoric sex fantasy, his eyes glazed with the ecstasy of it), and there are charming, funny girls who keep turning up (especially one, reminiscent of Gloria Grahame, who chatters as she strips). De Palma has staged a good Village-party sequence, and though many of the scenes in the movie go on too long, and it's all fairly tawdry, it's tawdry in such a good-humored, casually obscene way that Robert Aldrich should take a look. The difference in movies between what is called "good taste" and what is called "bad taste" is often a fraction of a second in the timing, and although De Palma's timing is often bad, Aldrich's timing isn't off just by seconds. More like aeons.

December 21, 1968

A Sign of Life

"Ingmar Bergman's 'Shame,'" the screening invitation said, "is that director's ultimate personal vision of war and its effects on two people," and if there was anything I didn't want to see, it was another Ingmar Bergman picture, and Bergman on *war!* Years had passed, but I hadn't yet fully recovered from that tank creaking along on the plywood streets in the nameless country of "The Silence," and recent Bergman pictures had been organized so subconsciously that they were only partly on the screen—the rest still in his head. I have always thought it rather funny that Bergman's most famous statement is that his purpose is to be like one of the anonymous artisans involved in the collective building of the Cathedral of Chartres. Every time I hear that reverentially quoted, I marvel at the power of fancy sentiments to seduce people—because no movie-maker is less of an anonymous artisan on a collective project than Ingmar Bergman. There is teamwork—of a kind—in Hollywood, but Bergman's team is *his* team, working to express *his* vision. I have seen more than twenty of his twenty-nine feature films, and if ever there was a "personal" and "individual" movie director, it's Ingmar Bergman. Before "Shame," he had, indeed, become so personal that he was beginning to treat his own mind as a cathedral—sanctifying his ideas and obsessions. Movies like "Persona" and "Hour of the Wolf," despite brilliant passages, were so disordered and so full of associations with his earlier work that though one could respond to parts of them emotionally, trying to understand what he was getting at required exegesis and, finally, guesswork. He seemed to be dealing with material that was only semiconscious—material so close to him and so confused that he was unable to make it accessible.

In recent years, the movie audience has split into the audience for popular films—the mass audience—and the art-house audience, and movies, once heralded as the great new democratic art, have followed the route of the other arts. The advances are now made by "difficult" artists who reach a minority audience, and soon afterward, the difficult artists, or their bowdlerizers, are consumed by the mass audience. Yesterday's interesting, difficult new directors become commercial, and their work becomes part of the film industry's anonymous product, which will never be compared to Chartres. Infrequent moviegoers are likely to be irritated when they go to a highly recommended art-house picture and find it bewildering and obscure. What they may not be aware of is that in this new, divided world of film the commercial movies have become so omnivorous and so grossly corrupt that frequent moviegoers may, for the first time in movie history, be looking for traces of talent and for evidence of thought, and may care more for an "interesting" failure than for a superficially entertaining "hit."

During the last New York film festival, I, for example, was impressed by a film called "Signs of Life," written and directed by a young German, Werner Herzog, even though the film was maddeningly dull and lacked flair and facility, because Herzog was clearly highly intelligent and was struggling toward a distinctive new approach. As a casual moviegoer, I might have thought: What a bore! As a constant one, I thought: This young man, I hope, will invent the techniques he needs, and the movie itself is a sign of life. For constant moviegoers, facility is no longer very important. Television commercials and the tricks of thousands of clever technicians have devalued facility; it's like the graceful literary style of all those college writers who will never have anything to say.

Bergman was one of the few directors who had managed to stay clear of international financing and the big industry; he had worked out his own techniques and gone his own way. But his own way had become a bleak and thorny path in a landscape by Edvard Munch and he took it so often, with the same actors representing "the artist's"—i.e., *his* conflicts and anguish, that it was becoming a well-travelled psychotic freeway. By "Hour of the Wolf," released earlier this year, I no longer found him "interesting"; if a movie director isn't going to provide a joke or two and some dancing girls, if he's going to be serious, then he'd better have something serious to say. I knew a Catholic girl in college who was losing her faith and who spent a semester extracting the last dregs of drama from her spiritual crisis by going around asking everybody, "If you

265

don't believe in God, what basis do you have for going on living?" Bergman pulled that same dumb stunt for a much longer period, and when he graduated to the agony-of-the-creator theme, it really seemed about time for him to give us more creation and less agony. I wanted a sign of life from him—not just masterly passages like the great erotic monologue in "Persona" but the kind of sign I thought I had seen back in the mid-fifties when "Summer Interlude" first turned up (as an exploitation picture), followed by "Smiles of a Summer Night" and "The Seventh Seal" and his early "Törst." But then came ten years that were a regular death knell of movies, from "Wild Strawberries" to "Hour of the Wolf," though he developed an extraordinary expressive technique and an extraordinary control over actors, and though, intermittently, he produced sequences of great intensity. But what a tiresome deep thinker of second-rate thoughts he had become—the Billy Graham of the post-analytic set. And how absurdly gloomy and self-absorbed—a man living alone in the world and stewing in his own intellectual juice. When the heroine of "Persona" turned on the television and saw Vietnam atrocities, we in the audience experienced culture shock—a medievalist had crossed the time barrier. If, despite his erratic brilliance, I was fed up with Bergman, it was because of the pall of profundity that hung over his work and because so many people had come to think that that pall was art.

"Shame" is a masterpiece, and it is so thoroughly accessible that I'm afraid some members of the audience may consider it too obvious. They have had so many years now of grappling with puzzles that they may consider all that figuring out *responding* to a work of art; when they devised a theory about what was going on in a film, they took their own ingenuity as proof that the film was art. And now here is Bergman, of all people, making a direct and lucid movie; they may, in self-defense, decide it's banal. But if "Shame" is banal, it's the most powerful banal movie ever made—the obvious redeemed. Bergman has pulled himself together and objectified his material. There are no demons, no delusions. Everybody is exactly who he appears to be, so we can observe the depth and complexity of what he is. There is no character who may or may not represent Bergman; he is not lost in the work but is in control of it, and is thus more fully present than before. "Shame" is indeed a vision of the effect of war on two people, but there are a great many people in the movie—it is full of characters and incidents—and as the movie started to develop and *people* began to appear, I began to breathe easier about what Bergman was doing this time. Although he had earlier made several films I didn't like, I think I really first despaired of him in "Through a Glass Darkly," because that was when he began to empty the screen and make chamber dramas. Though limiting the cast to a girl, her brother, her husband, and her father and setting them on an island marked the beginning of a new concentration on screen technique for him, and though he began to make severe *formal* demands on himself, he also made incredible demands on the audience. One of the blessings of movies was to liberate us from the lighthouses and remote cottages of the theatre; he was taking us back to them, and not for convenience. Using few people is as difficult for a movie director as using a great many people is for a stage director. One always knows that a young movie-maker is impossibly ignorant when he says he's going to do something simple, like a monologue; that's probably even more difficult to do successfully on the screen than an epic battle of angels is to do on the stage. Bergman, of course, knew the difficulties—knew that the fewer people on the screen and the simpler the settings, the more surely the director must be in control and the more crucial every nuance becomes —but the very fact that he was determined to do something so difficult, when it is so much easier to keep a movie audience interested with a variety of faces and backgrounds, suggested that he was wrestling with material that he felt had to be worked out in isolated settings, that was "private" material. When people go off somewhere "to think," they're generally just hung up, and his austerity made one suspect the worst. In film, concentrating on a few elements gives those elements such importance that the material can easily become inflated, and the method is generally attempted by people who overvalue their few ideas and have little sense of the abundance of ideas that must go into a good movie. Bergman was not in such straitened intellectual circumstances, but he was given to inflation of "dark" and messy ideas. The order he imposed on his chamber dramas was a false order. The films looked formal and disciplined, but (as often happens in movies) that "abstract" look concealed conceptual chaos. If a movie director cannot control both his thematic material and the flux of visual material, it is far better to have inner order and outer chaos, because then there is at least a lot to look at—different people and things and places to distract one —even if it is disorganized, while if the movie looks formally strict but the ideas and emotions are disturbed, the viewer may feel that the fault is in himself for not understanding the work, or, worse, feel that this kind of artistic-looking, disturbing ambiguity is what art *is*. As Bergman went from one isolated-island or unknown-country situation to the next, with characters who spoke little and loomed large in closeup, his movies became so private that one began to wonder what he was doing by exposing this unresolved mass of anxieties and guilts and fears. In "Shame," on the contrary, he has full control of the material, and though the film, set in the chaotic last stages of war—the mopping-up operations—is a narrative of complex incidents, the outer chaos, too, is controlled. It is the chaos of life in wartime seen through an ordering intelligence.

"Shame" has an almost magical lack of surprise; it has the inevitability of a common dream. Although, in order to project us just a little beyond our current situation, it is set a tiny step into the future— 1971—we feel we have already known this time. This world of 1971 has been at war long enough for events to have become confused, and (like the characters) we are the civilians in the middle of it even though we feel out of it. It is all so exactly detailed that it seems to be war as we have always known it—a war that is so familiar from our fears that it is normal, everyday total war. Liv Ullmann and Max von Sydow become survivors—as in our dreams of war we are the survivors. Bergman's war is the imaginary war we remember at night. It's the semi-documentary war we know from "The Moon Is Down" and "Edge of Darkness" and Rossellini and "Les Carabiniers" and television coverage of Vietnam. There's nothing startling about it; even the weapons are conventional. It doesn't, after all, take a hydrogen bomb to finish us—a rifle can do the job. This is just degrading, ordinary old war, and it takes a while before we realize that Bergman has put us in the position of the Vietnamese and all those occupied peoples we have seen being interrogated and punished and frightened until they can no longer tell friend from enemy, extermination from liberation. "Shame" is too exact and too strongly simplified to be merely realistic; the details register upon us with an intensity and a consistency beyond realism. Sven Nykvist's photography is so straightforward it's like an unblinking eye on the universe—realistic photography that achieves an aesthetic effect beyond realism.

"Shame," it is true, "says" nothing new, but then neither did our great national elegy "The Birth of a Nation." "Shame" is an elegy written in advance for a civilization that seems already lost. Bergman finally took the death knell itself for his theme, and no one could say he hadn't prepared. He had already played around with so many macabre fantasies that he may have worked the fantastic out of his system. When he got to this vision of man's last days on earth, he looked at his subject with astonishing purity. The terror in "Shame" is in how prosaically awful the end can be. "Shame" is, in many ways, Bergman's equivalent of Godard's "Weekend"—also an account of what people do to survive—but artists of different temperaments see the destruction of their world very differently. There is not a trace of the surreal or the comic in "Shame"; Bergman does not have Godard's daring wit or his gift for making the contemporary fantastic. But it's a much more nearly perfect work than "Weekend." In the past, it was a weakness of Bergman as an artist that although he can do comedy and he can do tragic material, he cannot (as yet) combine them in one film. (When he tried, it was disastrous.) In "Shame," his unvarying, unchanging mood is effective in a new way; I have never been fond of "brooding" minds at work in film, but the vision here creates its own suspense. Can the picture possibly sustain this level of tension? It does. And without even the time-honored crutch of music. Bergman uses the sounds of war percussively—war becomes a monster beating and waiting. Maybe all those years of developing the technical mastery that made sketches of madness look controlled gave him the equipment to do precisely what he wanted to do. This is part of the excitement of watching a movie artist develop—seeing his new films the way one reads the new books of a contemporary writer, and finding, just when one is ready to give him up, that he has renewed himself, transformed his materials, demonstrated that what he has learned can be used in a new direction. Bergman's austerity of style—when it is applied to objectified material—is splendid. He is now a master at creating effects of dislocation without any need for the superficial apparatus of movie surrealism. And he is a master of what is perhaps most difficult of all on film—the simple domestic scene. The way a husband and wife sit together, the way a lover's body leans as he observes his mistress, white wine in a crystal glass—the pleasures and the amenities are plainly stated, without emphasis or atmospheric touches. "Shame" is a *just* elegy, without false emotion.

Liv Ullmann is superb in the demanding central role—one that calls for emotional involvements with both von Sydow and Gunnar Björnstrand. The screen uses up actors in certain roles the way television uses up political figures—and particularly in roles in which they exhibit their least attractive qualities. Von Sydow is perhaps too familiar—and therefore slightly tiresome—in this slack-faced incarnation (he isn't when he's playing magnetic roles); we already know how good he is at it, just as we know how good Dirk Bogarde is at weaklings. Björnstrand, however, is beautifully restrained as an aging man clinging to the wreckage of his life.

There is a search through a house I thought was shot too dramatically and was excessively edited, and I could have done without the explicit formulation of the theme (which diminishes it with "poetry"), and a few confusing details, but these faults are so minor one might as well go ahead and call "Shame" a flawless work and a masterly vision.

Treating the most dreaded of all subjects, the film makes one feel elated. The subject is our responses to death, but a work of art is a true sign of life.

December 28, 1968

Big Misses

The submarine commander (Rock Hudson) is given his top-secret special assignment by his superior, who asks, "Jim, just how much do you know about Ice Station Zebra?" We're in purest old Hollywood, with such exquisite locutions as "Something's gone wrong up there, that's for sure." One of my least favorite actors (Ernest Borgnine) delivers my favorite example of Douglas Heyes' screenwriting: "Aha!" I hadn't heard a real "Aha!" like that in years. "Ice Station Zebra" is one of the most expensive adventure movies ever made, because after the picture was cast—with Gregory Peck as the submarine commander—the producer, Martin Ransohoff, became dissatisfied with the Paddy Chayevsky script and shelved the film until a new one was prepared. If the dialogue I heard was the *improved* version, what could the version Ransohoff was *dissatisfied* with have been like? After a very few minutes of "Ice Station Zebra," I wanted to leave, but it was icy outside, too, so inertia kept me, and after a while I had invested so much time I thought I might as well try to figure out what the devil was supposed to be going on. It was obvious that the movie hadn't been made to exhibit the wit and wisdom of Mr. Heyes; perhaps there was a good spy-adventure story buried in the verbal muck, and the director, John Sturges, would dig it out. Eventually, the sort of plot one expects in an episode of a television series emerged, and the silliness of the whole big movie became almost satisfying, in a ritualistic, bad-movie way. After your ear is numbed, the tired old lines don't really bother you; it gets to be like living in an echo chamber, and pop music has taken the mystery out of *that*. You begin to think Hudson isn't really as ghastly as he used to be; you've got so used to his dreariness he's just colorless and inoffensive, and you begin to think he's held up pretty well—which is somehow reassuring. They may have forgotten how to make pictures in Hollywood, but they sure know how to keep people in an excellent state of preservation. And people turn up that you know from other places (Patrick McGoohan, of the "Secret Agent" television series, doing his stylish smarty-pants act— and never has a movie needed a little style and smartness more) and better times (Alf Kjellin, who was the first Ingmar Bergman hero, in the film "Torment," made from a Bergman script, and now plays a lean Russian colonel). And there is Jim Brown—so blankly beautiful he almost passes for enigmatic—and troops of actors flopping around in their pretty parkas. Sturges' direction is as dull as in "The Satan Bug," but after a while you don't expect it to be good, the way it was in "Escape from Fort Bravo" or "Bad Day at Black Rock" or "The Great Escape," and so you adjust to this, and don't mind it very much. Your expectations get scaled down in everything else, too; "Ice Station Zebra" is terrible in such a familiar way that at some level it's *pleasant*. We learn to settle for so little, we moviegoers.

You can't get adjusted to "Candy," even though it has some good bits, because, in defiance of all your expectations, it keeps getting worse than seems possible. What might have been a classic sex burlesque in the genre of "I'm No Angel" (Mae West as the lion-tamer who brought out the beast in men) is just a shambles of a sex spoof, and though it sticks fairly closely to the book, which was an erotic satire, it isn't erotic. "Candy," based on the novel by Terry Southern and Mason Hoffenberg, is late in arriving on the screen. For maximum effect, it should have been done several years ago, with a young version of Marilyn Monroe; George Axelrod did something similar in "Lord Love a Duck," with Tuesday Weld. The material—Candide as a teen-age American girl who believes what men tell her and is pleased that they *need* her—no longer holds many surprises, so it was necessary for the movie to be very cleverly directed. It's an incompetent mess, but there are Richard Burton's parody of Dylan Thomas (though it does go on), Marlon Brando's Grindl the Guru episode (especially under the covers), and the bloody hospital sequence, with James Coburn as Dr. Krankeit. This satire of surgery seems to work not just because it's well acted by Coburn and because the comic ideas build but because it's in such terrible taste that it's almost irresistible. You know that it's a bad sick joke and that you should want it to end, because it's crude and wicked, but you're laughing helplessly—which demonstrates once again that it's impossible to use "good taste" as any kind of aesthetic standard. But Charles Aznavour's Hunchback and Ringo Starr's Emmanuel don't work at any level, and although Walter Matthau acts acceptably, his part—a right-wing general—is tired. John Astin is well cast as the Daddy and Uncle Jack characters. He seems the true Terry Southern hero—and, like Southern, funny but not as funny as he seems to think. The women are *all* terrible (especially Elsa Martinelli, who is arch as Aunt Livia). Ewa Aulin, who plays Candy, looks great in stills and has the requisite lewd quality for a born dupe whose innocence serves as an aphrodisiac, but she lacks the necessary dewy *freshness*. And she isn't, and can't act, American (her vocal inflections are reminiscent of Peter Lorre's in his pussycat roles), and she's too untrained (and unassisted by the director) for her happy martyrdom to be funny. The movie looks as if the director, Christian Marquand, had been delighted to have all those stars and beautiful women around and hoped it would all come out right. I have visions of the editor holding his head—his brain slipping through his fingers—as he tried to figure out how to put this stuff together. The picture gives one total geographical confusion: you can never believe that it was shot where the action is supposed to be—you keep wondering if you're in Europe or America, or where. This absence of a sense of milieu is one of the clearest signs of the director's incompetence, and there are many others. One is a scene of two cops beating a man up: we know how to read it, but it's so badly and brutally done it's just ugly. The movie needed to be crude—and ugly in places—but deliberately, not helplessly. Treating sex as lust, the book carries things so grossly far that it brings out in us the naughty, dirty kid who carries jokes too far, until they turn stupid and ugly, and this out-in-the-open dirty kid's approach might have been entertaining if Marquand knew how to direct burlesque (as some of the stars obviously knew how to play it).

It's one of the paradoxes of movie business that the movies designed expressly for children are generally the ones that frighten them most. I have never heard children screaming in fear at any of those movies we're always told they should be protected from as they screamed at "Bambi" and "Dumbo." Bambi's mother is murdered, Dumbo's mother is goaded to madness and separated from Dumbo; these movies really hit children where it counts. And here we are again in "Chitty Chitty Bang Bang," with its climax of a child-catcher (Robert Helpmann) who lures hungry children with promises of sweets, traps them right before the eyes of helpless adults, and throws them into prison. What a sweet bit of whimsey! This musical for children is almost sadistically ill-planned: it runs a hundred and fifty-six minutes, plus intermission, and almost all the fantasy material is in the last hour. That means that the small children (and who else wants to see it?) will be restless, exhausted, overfed, sticky, and irritable long before they even get a chance to become frightened and upset. Do the men who concoct these entertainments ever consider the simple logistics of

278

what parents go through before, during, and after a three-hour movie?

This ten-million-dollar musical fantasy for children has a desperate jollity; everybody has been doing his damnedest and everything has gone hopelessly wrong. The script, by Roald Dahl and the director Ken Hughes, from Ian Fleming's volume of stories about an Edwardian motorcar which makes noises that sound like "chitty chitty bang bang"), tries to be fanciful. The writers try to appeal to kids with the kind of cheerlessly cheerful "imaginative fantasy" that falls flat between comic strip and fairy tale, and they try to appeal to adults with a jokey tone of complicity that keeps saying: Look at those precious children, and doesn't everybody love harmless eccentrics? They might as well have gone the rest of the way and put canned laughter on the sound track. The movie needs it, because the writers have failed to make the eccentrics into characters. And Ken Hughes directs in that "Isn't this humorous?" style of Ken Annakin's "Those Magnificent Men in Their Flying Machines," only much worse. I have some residual affection for Dick Van Dyke, but I don't understand why, so early in his career, when he should be fighting for good roles, he has sunk to family pictures of the sort that actors fall back on when they're finished. He *is* ingratiating; he shouldn't *act* ingratiating. He has become a daddy before he needed to.

Maybe it's just because the action in "Chitty Chitty Bang Bang" eventually shifts from England to a Bavarian kingdom called Vulgaria, where people talk in comic German accents, but the whole thing seemed to be an Aryan nightmare. Sally Ann Howes (as Truly Scrumptious) has that cold "princess" look that the movie moguls have always foisted on us as beauty. She's the female equivalent of the "handsome" Hudsons and Pecks who are cast as "the hero" because they don't project enough character or interest for anything else. She looks absolutely in place when she's pretending to be the mechanical doll on a German music box. This bland operetta of a movie is hardly in a position to satirize Vulgaria. German dialect humor has never been very witty—it's always broad and forced—but Anna Quayle manages to bring off a duet with Gert Frobe, called "Chu-Chi Face," that is the high point of the movie. Miss Quayle is getting to be a picture-redeemer, the way Angela Lansbury (whom she somewhat resembles) used to be. Other good points are the first sight of Ken Adam's two big sets for the Scrumptious Candy Cookery, and the little-girl heroine (Heather Ripley), a storybook girl who is serenely, unconscionably beautiful. The magical flying-floating car itself is elegant when seen from underneath in the air, but the technical processes are a disgrace; when children have waited so long to be carried aloft in imagination, such clumsy fakery seems cruel. The construction of the Pushmi-Pullyu and the Great Pink Sea Snail in "Doctor Dolittle" were also pathetic. "Finian's Rainbow," with fewer magical effects, had more magical feeling. Big, expensive movie fantasies used to be very proud of their technical perfection, but perhaps fantasy must always be the imaginative expression of one person, whether a storyteller or a designer or a director, and the factory methods of the big, new, overanxious productions don't work. It may be that modern movie-making methods take the magic out of magic.

January 4, 1969

Filmed Theatre

There is something about the way a character who has discharged his dramatic function exits just before the character who is now dramatically necessary enters that, though perfectly logical on the stage, seems farcical or archaic on the screen. The novel form is more readily adaptable to movies than the play, because the conventions are usually more fluidly naturalistic. A character who is left behind in an early chapter to reappear later on can come and go with ease in a movie, but that poor stage character who exits and waits in the wings for his logical, structured reappearance is likely, in a movie, to convey precisely the impression that he has been waiting in the wings. The revelations and conflicts and climaxes of stage drama present problems, too, and the dialogue is likely to seem mechanical and artificial on the screen. These problems are sometimes, though rarely, solved by the adapters and directors (for example, by Cocteau in "Les Parents Terribles" and by Howard Hawks in "His Girl Friday"—movies that retain the limited settings of the stage originals and yet are, triumphantly, movies). Usually, they're not solved. The movie breaks the back of the play by "opening it up," and then makes a halfhearted gesture toward transforming it. Because the movie lacks action or dialogue for the new locales, the characters merely take walks or go to discotheques or do something equally (and nonsensically) "cinematic." The movie is like a dog with the broken bones of a cat sticking out. (What's lovable about the beast is the part that purrs.) The stage conventions are generally still present in some form and can be felt (as in "Who's Afraid of Virginia Woolf?" or "A Streetcar Named Desire"), but we may enjoy filmed plays anyway—even mediocre plays not very well filmed—because we enjoy hearing the "literate" dialogue of the theatre and seeing stylish "theatrical" performances.

Movies made from plays give actors the kind of roles they have been trained to play; they are actors, delivering their goods to us. It is *their* show, as on a stage, and although this may cause the movie to seem clumsy and may undermine it as a possible work of movie art, the power of personality often succeeds in making that clumsy movie more lively and more satisfying than a movie in which the actors are subdued and controlled for the sake of the director's conception. A play gives an actor a role he can work up and make his own, and this is usually still the case when the play is filmed—something that is rarely possible in movies derived from other material. When a play is filmed, if most of a stage-version company is retained but its star is replaced by a film actor, the movie version often goes flat, just because the film actor does not work up his role and dominate the material in the way that it was dominated on the stage, and though subjugating oneself to the material may *seem* like better film acting, the vitality that made the play effective on the stage is missing. The problem for the movie director with a stage cast is to tone down the stage performance and work it into the production so that it doesn't seem grotesque on the screen, without losing the drive and individuality that make actors exciting—and that movies need as badly as the theatre does. (A major reason for the decline of interest in theatregoing may be that so few of the great magnetic personalities are still working in the theatre. The stars have left the stage for the movies.) Most of us—particularly those of us who grew up outside major theatrical capitals—probably got our experience of the theatre from the movies more than from plays; seeing famous stage personalities repeat their roles on the screen was often our only way of seeing them. Plays on film gave us a kind of sophistication—a knowledge of what it means to turn a phrase or time a gesture—that kept alive a civilized tradition in the dispersed culture of a big country, and those of us who walked home from the movie house on dirt roads needed it. But, beyond that, I think play adaptations are one of the many *kinds* of movies and should simply be accepted as such. Some of the most enjoyable movies ever made— such as George Cukor's "Dinner at Eight"—seem appalling if they are thought of in purist terms as cinema, but they are well-made movie adaptations of plays. I *like* filmed theatre; I think there is a charge and a glamour about filmed plays and revues and vaudeville and music hall that one rarely gets from adaptations of novels or from those few screen "originals." Filmed plays are often denigrated,

somewhat dishonestly, by people who learn a little
cant about what is said to be proper to the film
medium and forget about the pleasure they've been
getting from filmed plays all their lives. Some of
them don't realize (though early movie audiences
did) that, for example, the Marx Brothers comedies
came direct from the stage, and that W. C. Fields
was doing his stage routines on the screen, just as
Chaplin and others before him had done. Reviewers
sometimes complain about filmed plays' not being
movies—as if they'd got on the screen illegally—but
most people, I think (except for the men who like
only Westerns and who have probably never developed an appreciation of the delights of repartee
or performance), enjoy theatre on film.

The movie version of Chekhov's "The Sea Gull"
is a disaster, not because it is a filmed play but
because it is a badly filmed play. And it's a disaster
in spite of the fact that Chekhov might seem to offer
fewer problems for screen adaptation than most
dramatists, since his plays are not rigidly structured
in terms of stage conventions. They're already open:
the characters drift in and out casually—gather for
lunch, break away, wander off. The drama is not
concentrated in dialogue that builds up tensions; the
drama develops indirectly—one might say undra-
matically—through the rhythm of glimpses and details. We don't see the beginning of a dramatic
action and follow it through. Rather, we are among
people whose patterns of relationship have long
since been formed, and how they behave on this day
is how they always behave. Unlike dramatists who
try to show us what is inside their characters (and is

customarily hidden), Chekhov lets the weaknesses and follies of his characters and the things that defeat them appear right on the surface—a surface that the camera could record easily and admirably. In "The Sea Gull" we observe a group of people who feel sorry for themselves, regretting their positions in life and their lost opportunities. It opens with a classic demonstration of self-pity and self-dramatization: a young man asks a young girl, "Why do you always wear black?" and the girl replies, "I am in mourning for my life." The milieu is that of educated middle-class and professional people—mixed with bohemians—just before the turn of the century. They're beset by financial problems, unrequited love, unrealized aspirations; they indulge in unhappiness and nostalgia and despair. It's a slightly stylized milieu, in which they speak their thoughts aloud, but each character knows the others too well to listen to or care about what the others say—though each is miserable at times because the others don't care enough about him to listen to him. This dramatic device (a naturalistic form of soliloquy that does not require either clearing the stage or having an actor turn aside to the audience) is also a slightly stylized psychological device, suggesting the self-absorption and isolation that are part of the texture of the characters' lives. They have poured out their hearts too many times, and nobody is listening. It takes subtle direction to orchestrate the weariness of lovers who have been dallying together adulterously for decades, the boredom of people who play cards together every night and have heard each other's anecdotes over and over, the modulations of familiarity and indifference of those who know each other's limitations. The play should be lyrical and delicately comic, and, finally, melancholy and forlorn, when, after observing the trivial daily concerns of superficial people who keep complaining that they have wasted their lives, we begin to see that what they've been saying is true and that we've been watching them make it true. The play is a graceful comic elegy on human weakness; they're almost all like that absurd girl in mourning for her life.

"The Sea Gull" is a strange, not fully achieved drama that proceeds by gentle understatement in such a relaxed way that it already seems "cinematic," but under Sidney Lumet's coarse and careless direction it's sombre and ridiculously stagy. In the movie, people come and go more rigidly than on a stage; they're practically swept away when they have spoken their lines. Lumet brought one great play, perhaps our greatest—"Long Day's Journey into Night"—to the screen with marvellous success, but the driving energy and determination that worked for O'Neill are not what is needed for Chekhov. One must have a feeling for the beauty in comedy. Chekhov makes the ordinary melodrama of our lives poignant and comic; Lumet turns Chekhov's poetic conception back into ordinary melodrama— which makes it seem inadvertently funny. Lumet's virtues as a director are hardly put to use—except for his gift for casting. There are marvellous actors here, and now and then almost all of them demonstrate how good they can be, but they can't sustain their roles or blend them without help from the director, because in a movie—with shooting spread over weeks—only the director, finally, can be responsible for the coming together of the pieces. We must see how separate the characters feel yet how closely bound they are by ties of inertia and frustration, and in Chekhov this is all accomplished by subtlety, refined humor, attention to detail—by just what Lumet notoriously lacks as a director. His method is simply to shoot the play as if it were a film script, and, given the kind of informal scenes-of-country-life play it is, this might have worked if he had had patience and if he had really paid attention. But he treats Chekhov the way the characters treat each other. Technically, the movie is slovenly. The color and the grain don't match from shot to shot, and the sound level varies. There are totally dead spots in the direction. The actors' vocal inflections aren't properly modulated, and sometimes their faulty enunciation stops the show; for example, the director permits Simone Signoret to say she's always on the *"qui vive"* so that people in the audience can be heard asking, "TV?" (It's not such a glowing example of the translator's art that it's indispensable.) And the translation has Trigorin say to Nina that he'd like to be inside her for an hour, when all he means is that he'd like to see things through her eyes for an hour. Details, only details— but in Chekhov the details are everything. Mess them up, neglect them, and the musical conception falls apart. On the other hand, Chekhov himself is responsible for the rather vacuous and conventional symbolism of the title; it was hardly a master stroke to have the characters drag that damned stuffed bird around the stage. One might have hoped that the

movie would dump some of the repetitive obviousness of the symbolism and would improve on the
appearance of the customary prop bird—which
looks as if it had never flown except when the prop
man threw it into the theatre basement. The audience laughs when Lumet makes the transition from
Act III to Act IV with a title announcing that two
years have passed, and it does seem ludicrous. Here
he has run afoul of a new movie problem. Nobody
else has solved this problem, either, which is an
even worse problem in movies derived from novels.
In "Far from the Madding Crowd," as events years
apart followed one another like the events in a day,
the passions and obsessions appeared to come out
of nowhere and were melodramatic and meaningless.
The old movie shorthand of dissolves and montages,
devised to impart the news of a lapse of time, has
been eliminated as "corny," but there is as yet no
substitute. Partly as a result of this mechanical problem, audiences at "Far from the Madding Crowd"
didn't get involved in the story, and so people said,
"Nobody's interested in that kind of novel anymore." When the audience laughs at the time-
passing title in "The Sea Gull," it may think it's
laughing at an old-fashioned device, but probably
it's laughing because of an unsolved mechanical
problem.

I think that if one is prepared for the disgraceful
production, one may be able to go to the movie and
enjoy it. There are several reasons for doing so, the
most spectacular being Vanessa Redgrave. Chekhov
should be played by ensemble actors, but in consequence of Lumet's banal direction the actors seize

their roles and play them separately, as in more conventional drama. Lumet has the wrong thing going for him in this movie—the interest we have in seeing actors show what they can do—but at least that gives him *something* going for him. Vanessa Redgrave is extraordinary-looking, and she is an extraordinary actress. As Nina, the young, inexperienced, somewhat pretentious country girl who wants to go on the stage, she is grave and girlish. It's a great role, which she has also played on the stage, and, if anything, she's almost too brilliant in it; she's so inventive she does too much. Beautiful and electrifying—like the young Katharine Hepburn, whom she sometimes resembles here—she has everything to make a great actress, and, of course, with her physical appearance and her height, she must play great heroines or great eccentrics or she cannot be used at all. But perhaps she doesn't yet have the simplicity of soul that would unify her talents. She does so many marvellous things that at times they cancel each other out; she cannot yet make each gesture count, the way Duse (on film) could and Garbo could—the way that said their whole being was expressed in that gesture. But already she seems able to do just about everything else. Her spotty performance gives one a painful sense of the missed opportunity, because it should be one of the great filmed performances (like Vivien Leigh's Blanche DuBois) and it's probably not her fault that it isn't.

James Mason, who is unusual among movie actors in that he seems to get better all the time, is remarkably fine as Trigorin, the "minor" novelist in the Russia of giants, and because he is such a quiet, almost passive actor, he seems more at home in Chekhov country than the rest of the cast does. David Warner takes the gauche young romantic hero, Konstantin, perhaps too seriously, and makes him so gauche he's no longer romantic. His performance lacks irony. Gangling and quizzical, he proves monotonous, possibly because his role as the callow, unstable young writer who wears the guise of unappreciated genius is not really well conceived in the original, and partly because he is photographed in such exhausting closeup that after a while one may begin to wonder if he's supposed to be desperately earnest or just nearsighted. Harry Andrews has a great moment or two, initially, in the role of the crotchety old Sorin, but then he overdoes it. Sorin is one of those deathtrap roles that are too easy to play and hence impossible to play; it's the archetype of all those Lionel Barrymore old codgers that made one groan. Denholm Elliott, Kathleen Widdoes, and Eileen Herlie all have some moments, but Simone Signoret is miscast in the pivotal role of Arkadina. There are no rules to guide one in cross-culture casting, and sometimes an actor who has another language background can be brilliantly effective (as Max von Sydow was in "Hawaii"); one can't tell for certain whether it will work until afterward. Still, it does seem that one could have predicted that in a play so dependent on vocal nuances a French mother with an English son and brother would disrupt the extended-family ambiance and that Signoret's accent would give her lines the wrong shadings and emphases. What has actually happened is even worse. Because Signoret's style isn't in tune with the others' and because her lines sound heavy, Arkadina loses her charm and becomes the villainess of the piece—a selfish, stingy, son-devouring Freudian mother. And every time this monster speaks she stomps on the remnants of the fragile play. But it's interesting to see actors wrestling with real roles, even when the actors are wrong for them. Simone Signoret is bad, but she is still Simone Signoret. And "The Sea Gull" is a terrible movie, but it is a movie of "The Sea Gull."

January 11, 1969

Baggy Pants

"The Night They Raided Minsky's" is another of those movies that (like "I Love You, Alice B. Toklas!" and "Greetings") are enjoyable if you don't go expecting too much, but there's so much talent involved in it that it should have been a classic movie musical (like Comden and Green's "Singin' in the Rain"), not just an erratically entertaining one. "Minsky's" is a backstage-onstage musical—a genre which is often disparaged, because the songs and dances are not integrated in the story, as in the "Oklahoma!" or "West Side Story" kind of musical, but which I much prefer. The best movie musicals are usually wisecracking and irreverent, and a little seedy, with chorus girls past their bloom. "Minsky's" has a wonderful chorus line—a row of pudgy girls with faces like slipped discs. They dance behind the beat, and when the fat tenor lifts his tired arm in a gesture it's as dispiriting as a flag being raised to half-mast. The parodies of burlesque dances have been skillfully staged by the choreographer, Danny Daniels, who has also designed a beautiful little example of the interpretive dancing of the twenties for Britt Ekland. The costumes, by Anna Hill Johnstone, are authentic in the true sense: they derive their satirical charm from theatrical history.

Charles Strouse and Lee Adams have, with miraculous self-effacement, composed songs that are hardly likely to become hits. But "Minsky's" doesn't hold to its own best style. What's bad about the movie is not that there is plot in it but that the plot doesn't develop out of the great possibilities in the material. What takes place onstage has been worked out with a consistency of approach; the rest hasn't, and much of it is thin invention. Burlesque was built on the comedy of gullibility almost as much as on sex, and I wish something had been made of this special appeal to audiences of greenhorns who were wising up. The film's evocation of the lower East Side early in the century seems an irrelevant exhibitionism of movie skills, and just too clever, but it would not be irrelevant if the film showed that burlesque was a vital, popular theatrical form for workingmen (who often got better theatre than the refined audiences uptown, who discovered burlesque comics years later). We need to see the innocence of burlesque under the tawdriness. Was this kind of ritual theatre—for burlesque is as repetitive and as preordained as a Punch-and-Judy show—integral to the period, and is that why burlesque "died"? Those who made this tribute to burlesque don't seem to have had enough confidence in the richness of their subject. If the director (William Friedkin) and the writers (Arnold Schulman, Sidney Michaels, and Norman Lear) were just going to spoof burlesque, they should have skipped the historical material. The way it's used makes the past seem cute, and that degrades us all. And the period montages become fatiguing, because their purpose is so shallow;

they're finally on a par with the divers springing back to the board in the old Pete Smith shorts. When we have had enough of the tricks and are ready to get involved in something, they're still going on.

This tribute to burlesque lacks an organizing idea—an idea of the kind that "Singin' in the Rain" and Kaufman and Hart's play "Once in a Lifetime" found in the transition of movies from silents to talkies. And there is an idea close at hand—so close that the movie keeps stumbling into it, but then out of it again. The lives of the performers offstage seem to be burlesque, too, yet the movie never quite takes hold of this idea of the unity (and diversity) of onstage and offstage life, which, basic to many backstage stories though it is, offers possibilities that are limited only by the movie-makers' talent and depth of perception. (It may be developed with as much complexity as in "Children of Paradise" or "The Golden Coach.") There are complicated relationships between the style of a theatre and the life style of the performers, and between character and the type of performing talent one has. The kinds of people involved and how burlesque affected them— this is the material, perhaps, of a more ambitious tribute. But I think Jason Robards' performance begins to suggest it; he plays his role—the straight man of a comedy team—as sly, self-pleased, lecherous. Robards is so unusual an actor in being willing to be dislikable that he is fascinating to watch even when you're not sure—as in the stage routines here— whether he's deliberately bad or just bad. "Minsky's" does carry the onstage relationship of Robards and Norman Wisdom into their backstage lives, but somehow it misses out on elements that seem waiting to be developed, so that it isn't clear that Wisdom, the patsy in their routines, is performing in the tradition of the great stars who came out of burlesque. When I've seen burlesque, the audiences have been much more restrained than they are in this movie, but I enjoyed the audience-reaction shots, which are witty and, I assume, are also intended as burlesque. The movie has two other principal attractions—Joseph Wiseman (as the senior Minksy), giving an elegant demonstration of comic style, and Britt Ekland, who is anachronistic and can't act much, either, but who has the biggest, most warming smile since Loretta Young. Movies as not built on talent alone.

A homosexual once told me how for weeks he was afraid to speak to a man he saw regularly in his cruising terrain, because the man looked so large and powerful and masculine that the homosexual was afraid he'd be slugged if he made any overtures. Finally, he approached the man and told him how terrified he felt, and the man replied wistfully, "I wish I could find somebody I'd feel that way about." There is something ludicrous and at the same time poignant about many stories involving homosexuals. Inside the leather trappings and chains and emblems and Fascist insignia of homosexual "toughs" there is so often hidden our old acquaintance the high-school sissy, searching the streets for the man he doesn't believe he is. The incessant, compulsive cruising is the true, mad romantic's endless quest for love. Crazier than Don Juan, homosexuals pursue an ideal man, but once they have made a sexual conquest the partner is a homosexual like them, and they go on their self-defeating way, endlessly walking and looking, dreaming the impossible dream. In "The Sergeant," Rod Steiger chases after John Phillip Law so long that when he grabs him and kisses him it's the climax of the picture. Then Law slugs him and Steiger goes out and shoots himself and that's it. If Steiger had grabbed Law and been rebuffed an hour and a half earlier, he could have said, "All right, so I made a mistake," and maybe the picture could have gone on and been *about* something.

What is wrong with "The Sergeant" is precisely that it takes the Army sergeant, played by Steiger, so long to make his pass that the picture keeps going just on the waiting level and we never learn what seems essential: Is he consciously or unconsciously homosexual? We don't know anything about him except that he's fat and domineering and chases the hero. He's a middle-aged man; what has he been doing all these years? If this flirtation is one in a series, why is he so inept? (And why does he kill himself?) And if this is his first crush, what set it off? Why *this* boy? What was there about him that attracted a homosexual response? It's not merely Steiger's character that seems to be newly minted for the purpose of setting the plot in motion; the whole movie lacks resonance. The script (by Dennis Murphy) is the kind of disciplined, workmanlike writing that is meant to be spare but is actually sparse. There isn't a phrase of Army slang that one can take away; nobody in it has any more character than is absolutely essential. Every scene sticks to its bare little point, every line of dialogue stays on its impoverished course; things happen neatly one at a time. We never for a minute have the illusion that those people so obviously assembled to be "background" will go on doing what they're doing when the camera cuts away.

The sergeant is not just homosexual—he's a psychopathic personality. It would be unfair to accuse the movie of implying that one has to be crazy to be homosexual (that would be like accusing "Oedipus Rex" of implying that only kings can love their mothers), but one can legitimately ask: Why are all the other soldiers so incredibly, antiseptically straight that it really begins to look as if you *did* have to be crazy to be homosexual? In the French and German girls'-school movies of the thirties, it was perfectly obvious that lesbian feelings were implicit in the situation, but here in this *Army* situation there is nothing in the atmosphere that links up with the sergeant's homosexuality, and when everyone is this one-dimensionally "normal," and homosexuality is, to all appearances, unknown and without cause, it does begin to seem as if only a monster could have such aberrant impulses. Except for the sergeant's, there is no passion or sexuality of any kind in this sterile movie, so a heterosexual display of love would seem just as crazy. (When the nice hero and his nice girl are in bed together for the first time, she says "Hello" and he says "Hello".)

This determinedly grim and "strong" movie, directed by John Flynn at a relentlessly unvarying tempo, is not without artistic flourishes. It's "daring" in a "mature" way, and means to be taken very seriously. But wasn't the idea behind the financing of the movie that the star must be an actor the public likes and thinks is a great *actor*, so they'll know it's not for real? Why else would Rod Steiger be cast in the lead? A repressed (if that's what it's meant to be) homosexual seems to be totally outside his range; he keeps his face prissy, with his lips pursed, throughout the movie, as if waiting for his emotional outbursts, so that he can let go, but the prissy blank is a blank. Does playing a homosexual paralyze him as an actor? He gives such a tense, constricted performance it's almost as if he didn't want to convince anybody. He never looks at Law with love. (He looked at Poitier with more affection in "In the Heat of the Night.") "The Sergeant" is so insufferably "tasteful" and controlled and careful about its homosexual theme that, ironically, it has less homosexuality in it than many movies have had unconsciously or by the accidents of casting or by carelessness or indifference—"Strangers on a Train," for example, or "Purple Noon," or any of those Westerns in which the manly friendships begin to suggest something that wasn't intended. And there was that come-back-to-the-raft-ag'in-Huck-honey classic of a couple of years ago, "The Fortune Cookie," with Jack Lemmon leaving his dirty wife for his clean, sweet Negro buddy, and with the memorable closing shot of the two of them playing ball together.

January 18, 1969

Son of Little Caesar

"Mother of God, is this the end of Rico?" Little Caesar (Edward G. Robinson) asked, surprised, as the bullets hit him. The classic movie gangsters of the early thirties—Rico, and Paul Muni in "Scarface," and James Cagney in "Public Enemy"—were killed by the police or they were fingered by betrayers and set up to be murdered by rival gangs, killing each other off, as it were. Just as there is a family tree of monsters in horror films, gangster films reveal a family pattern. Kirk Douglas' Frank in "The Brotherhood" is in the direct line of descent; his gangster father was betrayed, and murdered by Luciano. In this sequel, the next generation stays in the same line of work, as thoroughly committed as vampires. Though Cagney may have played it Irish, it is understood that the ancestral home of gangsters is Sicily, as the ancestral home of monsters is Transylvania. Some characters persist through generations of horror movies, and in "The Brotherhood" Eduardo Ciannelli, who played so many gangsters in the thirties, including one modelled on Luciano himself, is now an old, involuntarily retired Mafioso. Horror films used to reprise climactic sequences to clue us in on the previous material (and for reasons of economy); we have seen enough gangland massacres to fill in Frank's background, and we provide our own reprise. We know what Frank is meant to be. His forebears were ambitious and wanted quick money and power and respect; he has got what they died for. He is the gangster as a success, entrenched in his union, his shady businesses, his protection rackets. The story goes like this: Frank's ties are to the old Mafia he grew up in, and he's uneasy about the new, modern business plans of the "syndicate" of which he is part, but his younger brother, Vince (Alex Cord), whom, of course, he has brought up, is college-educated and goes along with the new investment ideas, as does Vince's father-in-law, Bertolo (Luther Adler). When Frank discovers that it was Bertolo who betrayed his father to Luciano, he murders Bertolo, and the syndicate orders Vince to eliminate his brother. This is all implicit from the outset; we know that this Brotherhood must end in brother killing brother.

It doesn't work, dramatically. Westerns have often taken the theme of the last of the old-fashioned badmen and made us feel regret as he is defeated by the forces of progress, but they have cheated on his badness. He is a romanticized outlaw, not a man who plays dirty. However, Lewis John Carlino, who wrote "The Brotherhood" (as an original screenplay), has made Frank an old-fashioned *murdering* racketeer—the kind who orders his henchmen to execute an informer and stuff a canary in his mouth —so he is colorful but hardly lovable. We saw those early gangsters do terrible things, too, but they were cocky upstarts, bucking the established criminal world, and we were involved by their audacity;

Frank is a *settled,* middle-aged racketeer, a brutal, corrupt version of a middle-class businessman.

That plot that seems "classic" because it has seen service in so many screen classics can function only if we regret the old way of life that is passing; if we can't—and it's pretty hard to get nostalgic about the Mafia—we are numbed by a tired old story that just gets in the way of what is interesting and new in the movie. Robert Warshow, in his famous analysis of the gangster hero, said that it wasn't relevant "to point out that most Americans have never seen a gangster," and that "what matters is that the experience of the gangster *as an experience of art* is universal to Americans." I think it *is* relevant that most Americans have never seen gangsters, because although we don't see them *we know they're there,* and those early movies showed us how these people we didn't see operated. The Western's heroes were legendary, mythic, but the gangster movies were set in the present. In action films we got to see logging and mining and whaling and railroad building and drilling for oil, and in the gangster films we got to see how illegitimate business worked. And because crime is hidden from us, and far more difficult to see than ordinary industrial processes, the fictionalized accounts in the movies had the excitement of revelation. We saw how gangsters terrified small shopkeepers into paying protection, how they transported liquor during Prohibition, how they ran night clubs and prostitution, how they bribed police and worked with politicians, how they fought each other for control of territories and spread their spheres of influence. Naïvely dramatized though the early gangster movies were, they had—what the Westerns lacked—the excitement of urban contemporaneity; they showed us the dark side of democratic ambition, and the nightmare city with the network of crime like a sewer system that didn't drain. Warshow may possibly have exaggerated our psychological involvement with the imaginary gangster—"the tragic hero"—and underestimated (or not been concerned with) our curiosity and anxiety about criminal life.

"The Brotherhood" underestimates our curiosity, too—it gives us too many conventional movie situations and too little of the new business of crime. It's interesting to see that gangsters at home live by traditional values when this is contrasted with what they do outside the home; when there isn't any contrast, it's merely banal. We cared about Rico or Tony or Tom not because he loved his mother or sister but because we saw what he did to become a big shot; we saw what defined him as a gangster and what a life of crime meant. "The Brotherhood" is conscientious in its portraits of the old-timers playing *boccie* and of Frank the family man, but although little bells ring in our heads at each "insight" and tiny lights flash for the "nice details," each scene seems to be an obligatory scene that we have to get through. And when we finally get away from the "human" side of a gangster's life and see Frank at his union office, what does he do? He phones his brother. This gangster movie starves to death for lack of contemporaneity in the business of gangsterism. Movies are neglecting what they took over from the novel—our interest in the life about us—and they're not giving us the material in which the plots were grounded. The new investment plans that Frank recoils from are contemporary documentation that could be more exciting than the movies about international spy systems and evil geniuses—documentation that makes America seem more of a paranoid vision than Transylvania ever did. The syndicate proposes buying into electronics firms that are crucial for national defense, and, of course, since it will control the unions, it can eliminate competition. This makes contact with the world we live in as surely as Scarface throwing his "pineapples" did; it is, in fact, the same ruthlessness carried from the local to the national level. Were those who made the movie afraid of boring us with more data, or did they recoil, too? Is that why they tell us so little and show us even less?

My guess is that Carlino intended to make the plot work on the plane of irony—that his point was that we might well feel nostalgic about an assassin like Frank when we got a whiff of his successors. But any hope of irony is destroyed by a sentimental, juicy, big-star performance by Kirk Douglas (who produced the picture), and by Martin Ritt, who directed, cloddishly, for a tragic last-of-the-gangsters effect. Their conventional approach obscures the wicked joke that might have split the surface and forced us to laugh as the spectre of the new racketeers manipulating the nation made the old Mafia of terror and revenge seem rather endearing.

The murder of Bertolo is poorly staged, and there's a jarring break in the continuity after the murder, so we never find out how the syndicate discovered that Frank did it. Lalo Schifrin's music is thrown over so many holes and bad spots that it becomes a form of surgical dressing. Even within the rather simple terms of Ritt's approach, the casting of Alex Cord as Vince is a mistake. Douglas and Cord are not brotherly enough to produce any sense of tragedy; Frank's emotions about Vince just seem misplaced. And Cord is too rigid to be interesting as a new kind of junior-executive crook. In order to sustain the plot at even the simplest level, Vince needs to be amiable and ingratiating, but Cord is tight and cold. Not only does Ritt lack the style for irony but he keeps Frank in loving closeup so much that we seem to take up residence in the crater of Kirk Douglas' chin. Playing a Lee J. Cobb sort of role, Douglas has begun to act like him and to look like him. This is something we can easily live with, but Douglas may not find it so easy. Frank shouldn't apologize to Vince about putting on weight. That's star talk—it lets the star think he's fooling people into believing he got heavy for the role. As Frank, Douglas does the obvious well. He's a good, strong actor, but he's not an interesting actor. He has reached the point where he must be the star because he isn't subtle enough to be anything else. It's fun to see him swelling his chest and grinning happily under a floppy mustache, but actors who strut the stage so supremely confident of their virility make the best cuckolds. Douglas has become so broad and hearty an actor that every time Luther Adler wobbles his jowls or Irene Papas (Frank's wife) does something *small,* he is obliterated. Mother of God, a star, like a gangster, doesn't know what direction he's getting it from. By the time Vince shoots Frank, Kirk Douglas has already been laid out.

January 25, 1969

Overkill?

"The Stalking Moon" is a brutal horror story in a Western setting. Eva Marie Saint is rescued after ten years with the Apaches; under the protection of Gregory Peck, she escapes across country to his ranch with her half-Apache son while the boy's father—a supersadistic killer—pursues them, butchering everyone in his path. It is not difficult to keep an audience in a state of terror when a helpless white woman is running from an evil, painted savage swathed in rough fur—King Kong without Kong's nice side. There are basically two kinds of movie chases: when you're in the position of the pursuer trying to get somewhere before something you don't want to happen happens, and when you're in the position of the pursued. When you're being hunted, as in this movie, the chase can become a nightmarish experience of tension and anxiety. This nightmare is punctuated with massacres in bloody closeup, and at the end, when Peck, wounded and bleeding, has destroyed the monster, there is no one left alive but the woman and the child and, of course, Peck. For many years, big-budget Westerns have generally tried to be respectful and sympathetic toward the Indians, and now, when "The Stalking Moon" goes back to the most primitive movie image of the vicious savage, damned if it doesn't get acclaimed in *Life* for "the simplicity and fascination of a myth dredged up from the unconscious of the race." The moviemakers didn't really have to dredge very deep. And, in case we're not mythologically oriented, they've taken care to provide a little resonance. As Peck and the monster lie locked together, grappling in final conflict, the monster dies on top of Peck, and there is a lingering shot of his brown hand on Peck's shoulder. A study guide to "The Stalking Moon" has already been prepared. (Robert Mulligan, the director, and Peck also worked together on "To Kill a Mockingbird," which is used as an example of movie art in courses in high schools and colleges.) One can see a new generation of teachers treating that blasted brown paw as the movie equivalent of Maule's curse.

Eva Marie Saint is competent and shows some strength, though one waits in vain for her character to develop, and Robert Forster, as a half-breed Army scout who sets an example for the young boy to emulate, has the kind of gallant, amusing role that helps actors become stars. But the picture centers on Peck, the model American. He's a dull ideal, yet his dullness works in his favor; it makes him seem more *sound*. The role of the decent superman requires an actor like Peck—an actor of proved authority—and Peck is very good in it. Why wouldn't he be? He has played it before. Actually, he has always played it (even when it wasn't called for), but I mean specifically in "Cape Fear"—a movie built on the same mechanism of a family being stalked by pure evil, and with many of the

same details, even to the monster's killing the family
dog. Why be afraid to pull out old stops? This is
commerce, baby. If you want to show that a killer is
evil, you don't take chances with just a half-dozen
massacres; some people don't care about people, so
he'd better kill a dog. And why leave it there? Press
on. Have the old man who loves the dog become so
distraught that he wanders out and gets killed, too.
Wring it dry. "The Stalking Moon" doesn't have a
sense of shame—only a sense of what "grabs" you.
"Cape Fear" was so effective at scaring the hell out
of the audience that it was generally attacked and
disparaged back in 1962 as a pointless exercise in
terror. How is it that just a few years later the same
kind of movie can be rated "G" (for General Audiences) and recommended as a "rewarding experience"? In "Cape Fear," the stalking monster was a
character in the movie (Robert Mitchum as a reptili-
an, sadistic sex maniac). Horrible and exciting as the
movie was, it was limited in its frame of reference;
both men were white, and the setting was modern
and urban, so the movie was merely a gruesome
shocker, obviously designed to give you thrills. But
in "The Stalking Moon" we never get a clear look at
the monster (except for his dead hand), so the audience can project onto him much more easily, and
the movie is set in the eighteen-eighties and has so
many authentic-looking details that people can experience the tensions of a sadistic horror story while
feeling that they're appreciating the realism of this
picture of the Old West. The crude log cabins may
be just another example of the amazing things
they're doing with plastics these days, and the old

stagecoach may be just décor for the horror story, but people who want to elevate what they're responding to can clutch at those details and at the bits of human interest—which are décor, too. And, because the conflict is not between *characters,* they can see the film as "the struggle between the good guys and the bad," as the study guide suggests, and they can go all the way into irrationality with the study guide, which informs schoolchildren that "the duel" between Peck and the mad monster "represents symbolically the clash between the white settlers and the Apaches of the Southwest."

There has always been a basic ambivalence in the Westerns that dealt with Indian vs. white. Even when the Indians were represented as betrayed and goaded beyond endurance—and they often have been represented that way—the audience, in the crunch of the final battle, rooted for the white settlers huddled against their wagons while the flaming arrows of "the savages" flew toward them. The hero and heroine would survive, the Indians would be wiped out or driven off. This ambivalence is the plague of the Western: ultimately, the whites are the good guys and the Indians the bad guys. If we were appalled during the Second World War by all those movies that turned the issues of the war into a simple contest between us (good, decent, human) and them (evil, cruel, treacherous, fanatic, psychopathic, inhuman), and if we refuse to go to see something like "The Green Berets" because the standard movie reduction of the issues to good and evil and the dehumanization of the enemy are repulsive to us, then maybe we should ask: What's going on in "The Stalking Moon," with that Apache in his bestial garb? Because if he's a symbol, I don't think it's for the Apaches of the Southwest. I think he's a stand-in.

To return to what *Life* says about the movie: "It is an examination in archetype of good and evil locked in a death grapple. It has the simplicity and fascination of a myth dredged up from the unconscious of the race. It is, in this simplicity, what movies are all about." People may think this is what movies are all about because this conflict between good guys and bad guys is what moved them as children and they may have the desire to be gripped the same way when they go to movies as adults. They feel it's the real thing—"pure movie"—when it's a basic morality play. If the monster were not an Apache in a bearskin but a Jew dressed in money, that could tap "the unconscious," too. And if the monster were a naked black man carrying a spear, the movie could score a knockout at the "unconscious" level. The Apache has been stripped of all humanity in order to make him function as pure bad guy, and then we are told that the child must make a *choice* between the cultures of his mother and his father, as if between his good and evil heritages. The child's soul is being battled for, and his final winning over to his mother's culture becomes the moral aim of the picture. The implication is that if his Indian side wins, his future will be murderous and the country will be in turmoil, but if his white side wins, all will go well for the country.

311

(The adult half-breed who has taken the right road sacrifices his life for the whites.) What *is* this crazy movie about? In a movie in which an artist is in control, we can try to examine what he's doing, but in this kind of factory picture, with its conflicting intentions and its compromises and its sanctimonious think pieces about the future of America, we can't tell what's going on, because it doesn't represent *anybody's* point of view. Yet in dropping the usual sympathies and explanations, in treating the Apache as evil incarnate, it's very much of this time and of the tendency now to think that we're cutting through to the truth—if not of what happened, of how people feel. Oversimplification seems to be in style. It's easy to make fun of the equivocation in the more flexible and more historical approaches of recent Westerns, but I wonder if we should be so eager to sweep away the modern movie tradition of showing that issues of good and evil are not clearcut, that dehumanizing the enemy is often a way of justifying our own inhumanity.

The plot of "The Stalking Moon" doesn't grow organically from the material and it never takes up the subject right at hand—what the white woman has experienced in her ten years of captivity. It's just a plot rigged to scare us and keep us scared. And it does—even though we can see perfectly clearly that if the woman at her moment of liberation, when she says she must leave the area immediately, were asked "Why?" and explained, she could be given a military escort and the movie would be over. At every step, the plot proceeds fraudulently just to prolong the movie: Forster shouts when he should shoot, the Apache abducts the woman to no particular purpose, Peck waits too long to fire, and so on. The movie isn't directed well enough to conceal the improbabilities, and Mulligan doesn't have the aptitude for violence of an Arthur Penn or a Sam Peckinpah—directors who can give violence meaning. But this kind of movie can be "effective" even when it's poorly done, because it hits below the belt. And to be violently teased simply isn't enough reason to go to a movie. It is not enough for the aim of a movie to be to "grab" you and hold your attention. If that is its only aim, it offends even as it succeeds, because you resent the manipulation. I resent the assumption that we are so bored and corrupt that we will be pleased whenever we are not bored. Since I am not bored outside the theatre, why should I go in to see a movie whose only purpose is to keep me from being bored? I don't think the basic morality play *is* what movies are all about. On the contrary, I think it is what movies in the past have too often been about. Maybe we shouldn't be so eager to dredge up myths—Pop versions of old wives' tales—from what so many people now call the unconscious when they probably just mean pulps and comics and old movies. Because, of course, these myths are formed of fear and prejudice. Old movies are full of them because the easiest, fastest way for commercial entertainment to appeal to a mass audience is to touch soft spots. I have been very harsh on this movie, and perhaps, like "The Stalking Moon," this is overkill, but movies, along with the other arts, can open us to complexities, and I don't think we should applaud this kind of infantile, primitive regression.

February 1, 1969

Saintliness

We are so often bathed in emotion at the movies by all those directors whose highest ambition is to make us feel feelings that aren't worth feeling that the cool detachment of Luis Buñuel has a surprising edge. Buñuel doesn't make full contact with us, and the distance can be fun; it can result in the pleasure of irony, though it can also result in the dissatisfaction of feeling excluded. His indifference to whether we understand him or not can seem insolent, and yet this is part of what makes him fascinating. Indifference can be tantalizing in art, as in romance, and by keeping us at a distance in a medium with which most directors try to involve us he deliberately undermines certain concepts that are almost axiomatic in drama and movies—especially drama and movies in their mass-culture form. Buñuel, who regards all that tender involvement as "bourgeois morality," deliberately assaults us for being so emotional. His most distinctive quality as a movie-maker is the lack of certainty he inflicts on us about how we should feel toward his characters. Buñuel shoots a story simply and directly, to make just the points he wants to make, though if he fails to make them or doesn't make them clearly he doesn't seem to give a damn. He leaves in miscalculations, and fragments that don't work—like the wheelchair on the sidewalk in "Belle de Jour." He's a remarkably fast, economical, and careless movie-maker, and the carelessness no doubt accounts for some of the ambiguity in the films, such as the unresolved trick endings that leave us dangling. From the casting and the listless acting in many of his movies, one can conclude only that he's unconcerned about such matters; often he doesn't seem to bother even to cast for type, and one can't easily tell if the characters are meant to be what they appear to be. He uses actors in such an indifferent way that they scarcely even stand for the characters. Rather than allow the bad Mexican actors that he generally works with to act, he seems to dispense with acting by just rushing them through their roles without giving them time to understand what they're doing. Clearly, he prefers no acting to bad acting. The mixture of calculation and carelessness in his ambiguity can be maddening, as in some of "Viridiana" (1961) and in most of the slackly directed "The Exterminating Angel" (1962). But sometimes what makes an artist great and original is that in his lack of interest in (or lack of talent for) what other artists have been concerned with he helps us see things differently and develops the medium in new ways. Like Borges, who won't even bother to write a book, Buñuel probably doesn't think casting or acting is important enough to bother about. And casting without worrying about whether the actors suit the role—casting almost *against* type and not allowing the actors to work up characterizations can give movies a new kind of tone. Without the conventional emotional resonances that actors

acting provide, his movies have a thinner texture
that begins to become a new kind of integrity, and
they affect us as fables. Most movies are full of
actors trying to appeal to us, and the movies themselves try so hard to win us over that the screen is
practically kissing us. When Buñuel is at his most
indifferent, he is sometimes at his best and most
original, as in parts of "Nazarin" (1958), which
opened here last summer, and in almost all of his
newly released—and peculiarly exhilarating—
"Simon of the Desert."

Other movie directors tell us how we should feel;
they want our approval for being such good guys, and
most of them are proudest when they can demonstrate their commitment to humanitarian principles.
Buñuel makes the charitable the butt of humor and
shows the lechery and mendacity of the poor and
misbegotten. As a movie-making comedian, he is a
critic of mankind. One can generally define even a
critic's position, but there is no way to get a hold on
what Buñuel believes in. There is no characteristic
Buñuel here or heroine, and there is no kind of
behavior that escapes his ridicule. His movies are
full of little sadistic jokes that we can't quite tell
how to take. The movie director most influenced by
de Sade, and the only one still at work who had
close ties to the Surrealist movement, Buñuel has
gone on using the techniques of the Surrealists in the
medium that once seemed their natural habitat. We
may not really like his jokes, yet they make us
laugh. A perturbing example that comes all too
readily to mind: When Jorge, in "Viridiana," frees a
mistreated dog that has been tied to a cart and then

we see another cart coming from the opposite direction with another dog tied to it, is Buñuel saying that Jorge is a realist who does what he can, or does Buñuel really mean what the audience, by its laughter, clearly takes the scene to mean—that Jorge's action was useless, since there are so many mistreated dogs? This "joke" could be extended to the "comedy" of saving one Jew from the ovens or one Biafran baby from starvation, and I think we are aware of the obscenity in the humor even as we laugh—we laugh at the recognition that we are capable of participating in the obscenity. His jokes are perverse and irrational and blasphemous, and it may feel liberating to laugh at them just because they are a return to a kind of primitive folk comedy—the earliest form of black comedy, enjoyed by those who laugh at deformity and guffaw when a man kicks a goat or squeezes an udder too hard. Buñuel reminds us of the cruelty that he feels sentimental art tries to hide, and we respond by laughing at horrors. This is partly, I think, because we are conscious of the anti-sentimentality of his technique —of his toughness and his willingness to look things in the eye.

Some of his recurrent jokes are really rather private jokes—the udders and little torture kits and objects turned into fetishes—and Buñuel throwing his whammies can seem no more than a gigantic, Spanish Terry Southern. Bad Buñuel is like good Terry Southern—a putdown and a crackle. Sometimes when we laugh at a Buñuel film we probably want to sound more knowledgeable than we are; we just know it's "dirty." Yet this is the vindication of the Surrealist idea of the power of subjective images: we *do* feel certain things to be "dirty" and some kinds of violence to be funny, and we laugh at them without being able to explain why. Buñuel gets at material we've buried, and it's a release to laugh this impolite laughter, which is like laughter from out of nowhere, at jokes we didn't know we knew.

Once, in Berkeley, after a lecture by LeRoi Jones, as the audience got up to leave, I asked an elderly white couple next to me how they could applaud when Jones said that all whites should be killed. And the little gray-haired woman replied, "But that was just a metaphor. He's a wonderful speaker." I think we're inclined to react similarly to Buñuel—who once referred to some of those who praised "Un Chien Andalou" as "that crowd of imbeciles who find the film beautiful or poetic when it is fundamentally a desperate and passionate call to murder." To be blind to Buñuel's meanings as a way of being open to "art" is a variant of the very sentimentality that he satirizes. The moviegoers apply the same piousness to "art" that his mock saints do to humanity: both groups would rather swallow insults than be tough-minded. Buñuel is the opposite of a flower child.

"Simon of the Desert," a short (forty-five-minute) feature made in Mexico in 1965, just before he made "Belle de Jour," is a playful little travesty on the temptations of St. Simeon Stylites, the fifth-century desert anchorite who spent thirty-seven years preaching to pilgrims from his perch on top of a column. It is, in both a literal and a figurative sense, a shaggy-saint story, and (unlike much of

319

Buñuel's work) it is charming. The narrative style of "Simon" is so straightforward and ascetically simple that it may be easier to see what he is saying in this film than in his more elaborate divertissements about saintliness turning into foolishness—"Nazarin" and the complicated, allusive "Viridiana," which was cluttered with Freudian symbols. Buñuel seems to have a grudging respect for Nazarin and Simon that he didn't show for Viridiana, whom he made sickly, chaste, and priggish. "Viridiana" seemed dramatically out of focus because Buñuel didn't even dignify her desire to do good, and so the film had to depend on the pleasures and shocks of blasphemy—probably not inconsiderable for insiders, but insufficient for others. The tone of "Simon" is almost jovial, though the style is direct—just one incident after another—and as bare and objective as if he were documenting a scientific demonstration; even the Surreal details (like a coffin skittering over the ground) are presented in a matter-of-fact way. Buñuel has himself in the past given in to temptation: with more money than he was accustomed to, he fell for the fanciness of all that French *mise-en-scène* that made his "Diary of a Chambermaid" so revoltingly "beautiful." But there's very little money in "Simon," and there was, apparently, none to finish it; the bummer of an ending was just a way to wind it up.

Simon (Claudio Brook) performs his miracles, and the crowds evaluate them like a bunch of New York cabdrivers discussing a parade: whatever it was, it wasn't much. He restores hands to a thief whose hands have been chopped off; the crowds rate

320

the miracle "not bad," and the thief's first act with his new hands is to slap his own child. The Devil, in the female form of Silvia Pinal (much more amusing as the Devil than she was in her guises in other Buñuel films), tempts him, and, at one point, frames him in front of the local priests, who are more than willing to believe the worst of him. Simon is a saint, and yet not only are his miracles worthless—they can't change men's natures—but even he is dragged down by his instincts. Buñuel is saying that saintliness is sentimentality, that, as the platitude has it, human nature doesn't change. This is not, God knows, a very interesting point, nor do I think it has the slightest validity; the theme is an odd mixture—a Spanish schoolboy's view of life joined to an adult atheist's disbelief in redemption. This outlook creates some problems when it comes to responding to Buñuel's work.

There are probably many lapsed Catholics who still believe in sin though they no longer believe in redemption, who have the disease though they have lost faith in the cure. In this they are not much different from the Socialists who still accept the general Socialist analysis of capitalism without having much confidence in the Socialist solutions. But psychologically there is an enormous difference between those who regard man as the victim of violent instinctual drives and those who live by a belief in justice and decency, even without any real conviction that society will ever be better. The pessimistic view can be so offensive to our ameliorative, reforming disposition that it's almost inconceivable to us that an artist whose work we respond to on many levels can disagree with us at such a funadmental level. And so with Luis Buñuel in films, as, in literature, with D. H. Lawrence and T. S. Eliot and Pound, we often contrive to overlook what the artist is saying that is alien to us. Because Buñuel is anti-Church and is a Spaniard at odds with Franco, because he satirizes bourgeois hypocrisy, there is, I think, a tendency to applaud his work as if this were all it encompassed. At the movies, when we see horrors we expect the reformer's zeal; that is the convention in democratic art, and perhaps we project some of our outraged virtue onto Buñuel's films. We feel free to enjoy his anarchic humor—which is often funniest when it is cruelest—because we can feel we're laughing at Fascism and at the human stupidity that reinforces Fascism. But though his work is a series of arguments against the Grand Inquisitor's policies, his basic view of man is the Grand Inquisitor's. Buñuel attacks the Church as the perverter and frustrater of man—the power trying to hold down sexuality, animality, irrationality, man's "instinctual nature." He sees bourgeois hypocrisy as the deceptions that men practice to deny the truth of their urges. His movies satirize the blindness of the spiritual; his would-be saints are fools—denying the instinctive demands not only in others but in themselves. Surrealism is both a belief in the irrationality of man and a technique for demonstrating it. In his "Land Without Bread," Spain itself—that country that seems to be left over from something we don't understand—was a Surreal joke, a country where the only smiling faces were those of cretins. Like other passionate artists who fling horrors at us, Buñuel is an outraged lover of man, a disenchanted idealist; being a Spaniard, he makes comedy of his own disgust. He can't let go of the Church; he's an anti-Catholic the way Bogart was an anti-hero. He wants man to be purged of inhibitions, yet the people in his movies become grotesque when they're uninhibited. And when his saintly characters wise up and lose their faith, he can't show us that they're useful or better off, or even happier. He is overtly anti-romantic and anti-religious, yet he is obsessed with romantic, religious fools. He has never made a movie of "Don Quixote," but he keeps pecking away at the theme of "Don Quixote," and gets himself so enraged by the unfulfillment of ideals that he despises dreamers who can't make their dreams come true. In "Viridiana," he twisted the theme into knots—turning in on himself so far that he came out the other end.

How can Buñuel in "Simon of the Desert" make a comedy out of a demonstration of what liberals have always denied and yet make liberals (rather than conservatives) laugh at it? It's as if someone made a comedy demonstrating that if you divided the world's wealth equally, it would all be back in the hands of the same people in a year, and this comedy became a big hit in Communist countries—which, however, it might very well do if the style of the comedy and the characters and details were the kind that the Communists responded to. And it might become an underground hit if it had jokes that brought something hidden out into the open: Buñuel's Freudian symbols and blasphemous gags alienate the conservatives and, of course, please the liberals. And then there is the matter of style. Buñuel doesn't pour on the prettiness, he doesn't turn a movie into a catered affair. There is such a thing as mass bourgeois movie sentimentality; we are surrounded by it, unundated by it, sinking in it, and Buñuel pulls us out of this muck. "Simon" is so palpably clean that it's an aesthetic assault on conservative taste. It's hard to love man; Hollywood movies pretend it's easy, but every detail gives the show away. Buñuel's style tells the truth of his feelings; the Spanish stance is too strong for soft emotions like pity. Though, as in "Diary of a Chambermaid," he can be so coldly unpleasant that we are repelled (and happy to be excluded), he never makes people pitiable lumps. And though he may turn Quixote into a cold green girl or a dithering man, in his films the quixotic gestures of the simple peasants are the only truly human gestures. A dwarf gives his inamorata an apple and his total love; a woman offers Nazarin a pineapple and her blessing. Nazarin is so stubbornly proud that it's a struggle for him to accept, and Buñuel himself is so proud that he will hardly give in to the gesture. Humility is so difficult for him that he just tosses in the pineapple ambiguously—he's so determined not to give in to the folly of tenderness that he cops out.

At the end of "Simon of the Desert" Simon is transported to the modern world, and we see him, a lost soul, in a Greenwich Village discothèque full of dancing teen-agers. This is a disastrous finish for the movie—a finish of the careless kind that Buñuel is prone to. The primitive Mexican desert setting situates the story plausibly, but New York is outside the

movie frame of reference, nor does this discothèque conceivably represent what Simon's temptation might be. What Buñuel intended as another little
joke is instead a joke on his gloomy view. "It's the
last dance," the Devil says, though what is presented
to us as a vision of a mad, decaying world in its
final orgy looks like a nice little platter party.

February 15, 1969

The Lady from Across the Sea

"Once, I loved a woman named Lola," sang the melancholy diamond merchant in Jacques Demy's "The Umbrellas of Cherbourg," played by the very actor who had indeed been the young drifter who loved her and lost her in Demy's first film, "Lola." Now Demy has taken her from the realm of memory and brought her to Los Angeles in his first American film, "Model Shop." Lola is again played by Anouk Aimée, and Demy may think she's the same woman at a later stage of her life, but she has an entirely different character. Lola then was simple and open, an untalented and not too bright cabaret dancer, a vulnerable, sentimental, wholly lovable girl. The movie "Lola" was like an adolescent's dream of romance, formed from old movies; it was life rose-tinted, a lovely, quirky mixture of French-movie worldliness and wisdom and defeat circa 1939 and the innocent cheerfulness of the Gene Kelly-Frank Sinatra M-G-M musicals of the forties—"Anchors Aweigh" and "On the Town"—with their generous, shy sailors, kind to kids and looking for love. The movie gently mocked romantic movie effects, which it employed more romantically than ever. A mother fainted when her long-lost son came home, the cabaret girls wept when Lola and the father of her child were reunited, and there were faint quotation marks around everything. The implausible meetings and partings of old movies became motifs, and corny old devices were transformed into conceits. Lola, in top hat and boa for her night-club act, was herself a quote—an homage to Dietrich's "Lola Lola" of "The Blue Angel," but only to the effervescent and harmless half.

The new Lola of "Model Shop" is elegant and imperious and refined, and Anouk Aimée, dull and ethereal, appears as a mysterious and glamorous lady in white. When Demy used the device of the mysterious stranger in white before (Jeanne Moreau as Jacky in "Bay of the Angels," and Michael, in his white suit and with his big white convertible, in "Lola"), it had an air of deliberate artifice, of toying with a movie cliché; here it's as if Anouk Aimée had become a big guest star requiring special star treatment, and the clichés are just clichés. Lola, who is stranded in L.A., working in a "model shop" (i.e., posing for men who take "dirty" pictures), appears in stunning, simple white, gets into a long white car, and drives to a palatial residence (mysterious, too, since the movie never explains what she is doing there), and it's all just stardust. The quotation marks are gone. Poor little Lola has become a high priestess of wisdom, a *dea ex machina,* dragged in to give George, the hero, the will to go on—the "purpose and direction in life" of hoked-up drama. The new trying-to-appeal-to-youth movies are full of this synthetic "finding yourself."

I think it is not George (Gary Lockwood), a young architect with a yearning to be creative, who

327

needs Lola's help, but Demy. Out of one can only guess what anxieties about his American début, he has borrowed illegitimately from his own past; he has violated the conventions of his own creations. What made "Lola" so enchanting a movie was its exquisite escapism; Demy had created his own fantasy world from the movies. Characters suddenly got rich or were stranded on an island, like a movie hero; Lola's dreams came true—and not just her dreams but her *illusions*. The charm of this world was that it was consciously unrealistic, a poetic world in which illusions were vindicated. Lola, abandoned by her sailor lover, brings up their son in the best sentimental, good-hearted-bad-girl movie tradition, believing all the time that her man will return, and in the structure of this fairy tale, because she sustains her faith in this illusion, he does return, fabulously rich and still in love with her and eager to receive his child, and they drive off into a bright future as the other cabaret girls weep in unison at the soul-satisfying beauty of it all. There are certain happy endings in movies which become in themselves a comment on movies and on how we want from movies what we don't get in life. The most famous of these is the final sequence in F. W. Murnau's "The Last Laugh"—the happy ending the producer insisted on—in which a sudden bequest transforms Emil Jannings into a millionaire after he has reached the abyss of humiliation as a lavatory attendant; we don't for a minute believe in this ending—it becomes an ironic demonstration of what life isn't, and of how the movies can improve on life. The ending of "Lola"—which is integral to

Demy's whole conception—is another classic consummation; it is all our movie dreams rolled into one and come true, and it has romantic magic. Now Demy is trying to steal some of that magic, but when he takes Lola out of the fairy-tale frame of reference, instead of letting her live happily ever after, he collapses the dream and we are just embarrassed and—aesthetically—disappointed. His explanation in "Model Shop" that Lola's husband went off with Jacky, the compulsive gambling lady of "Bay of the Angels," is so facile and yet so basically silly and misconceived that one begins to wonder about where an artist can go from the stylized naïveté of "Lola" and "Bay of the Angels" and "The Umbrellas of Cherbourg." Demy fell into mechanical coyness in "The Young Girls of Rochefort," and he loses the beauty of naïveté in the ordinary, clumsy naïveté of "Model Shop." It is always embarrassing when an artist's new work makes true what one has been denying about his earlier work. I hope these last two films won't be taken as proof that his first three were as stupid and sentimental as some people found them, but I have an awful memory of playing hopscotch with a little girl who said I stepped on the line when I didn't, and then, when we agreed to discount that one and do it again and I *did* step on the line, said, "See? That proves you did it the first time."

It would be cruel and pointless for me to dwell on the inanity of "Model Shop" if it were not a film made by an artist for whose work I have deep affection. One's first reaction to the deadening *thoughts* of the characters in "Model Shop" is that

329

maybe they wouldn't sound so bad sung to Michel Legrand's music. Still, the music didn't save "Rochefort." And I don't think it's Los Angeles, or even the awkwardness that results from Demy's working in English, that does him in. His movies have always been influenced by Hollywood, and, in a sense, he has reached the promised land of his characters. If he doesn't know where to go from there, it's probably because he was influenced by a *romantic* view of America, from the movies. Los Angeles should have helped him renew himself, because it was obvious from "Rochefort" that he had—momentarily, I hope—run dry, but instead he is drawing upon the exhausted past. And what was sweet and lush and graceful then seems just softheaded now. When he extended the artificial world of "Lola" with the fresh artifices of "The Umbrellas of Cherbourg," the results were charmingly attenuated. The recitative helped to formalize the romanticism, just as the harmonies of color and the matching costumes and wallpapers did. But now, when he presents a non-formalized view of Los Angeles in pretty pastels, the prettiness undercuts the story he's telling. There is something ingratiating about his love affair with Los Angeles, which, in the manner of a truly personal filmmaker, he makes over into his own milieu, so that it looks like a lovely seaside town, the harsh bright sunshine turned delicate and white, the buildings pleasantly ramshackle. But Demy is a lyricist in a setting where lyricism seems absurd, and his all too conventional now-generation-in-rebellion story makes no sense in this devulgarized setting. Demy's feeling for the young is probably more genuine than that of the finky sycophantic movie companies that are now so busy making shallowly sympathetic movies about youth and alienation, but because he doesn't have roots in American life his view is just about as shallow. His tact as a director saves him from the worst mistakes, but his way of looking at American youth is amateurish and without depth; he takes too much at face value. He doesn't have the toughness of mind to see anything funny in the hero's girlfriend who wants him to commit himself to life by letting her have a baby, or to see anything ironic in the rock musicians' casting themselves and selling themselves in the life style of sweet Jesus. And although he may have inadvertently got on to something in creating a new hero—the flabby American—he doesn't seem to know what to do with him. George mumbles platitudes about the draft and life in general, but he is just Roland, the dreamy drifter of "Lola," all over again—the character who returned in "Cherbourg"—and if Demy keeps going in this self-derivative way, George may come back from the Army to tell us, "Once, I loved a woman named Lola."

February 22, 1969

He Walks in Beauty

Omar Sharif is a caricature of a movie star, but he is also truly a movie star. Long ago, artists put fraudulent profiles on coins—flattering their monarchs while telling themselves that symmetry was a matter of artistic license. And nature imitates even the lies of artists. Like Candice Bergen, Sharif is a movie star by an act of nature. Perhaps stars like these could be bred, like broad-backed circus horses, or minks. This kind of star-by-nature may even satisfy a gambling streak in the audience; movies become a kind of lottery, a game in which some people just naturally win. Sharif, the new romantic "great lover" of the screen, is a walking love scene, though he plays moments of passion as if he were straightening his collar, and lacks even the dedication of a fop. Archduke Rudolf, his role in "Mayerling" is a dissolute voluptuary redeemed by his love for an innocent young girl. Debauchery is one of the oldest movie staples, and it doesn't take much talent, but Sharif cannot simulate the fire of sensuality or the volatile nature that would make this conception plausible. In the earlier "Mayerling," Charles Boyer hung a cigarette on his Hapsburg lip and grabbed a girl's leg and the movie took off; with Sharif the story works a different way. He is presented as a

morphine addict who is in love with his mother, and
still he is totally unsensational; if he does it, it must
be the decent thing to do. Sharif is the least dashing
and explosive of romantic stars; there is nothing
bottled up in him, not even a hint of repressed
emotion. He is so placid an actor that he seems to
ruminate before he speaks—and he doesn't hurry
through his words, either. Yet his handsome, soulful
face is a token of all romantic heroism, and his
pained little smile an emblem of doomed romance.
In keeping with the sixties, Rudolf, the heir to the
throne, is now a secret revolutionary, and he is
introduced to us among the students arrested during
a demonstration. He is incognito, of course. The
movie combines the sixties stuff with the oldest
dodge from operetta, and, with a star who is incapa-
ble of transgressions, this new "Mayerling" becomes
a muted version of "The Student Prince." Movies
are such a wonderfully adaptable medium.

Sharif became the hero in "Lawrence of Arabia"
because the audience, caught in the midst of a confusion of motives and problems and dimly remembered history, simply took its bearings from his
sparkling eyes and decided that he must be the good
guy. Seven years have passed, and his eyes don't
sparkle much anymore, but they make tears beautifully. And, dull as he is—with his sucked-in cheeks
for "spirituality," and the greenish tinge to his skin—
he is the perfect royal loser. Rudolf seems the part
he was born to; that he can't *play* it is almost beside
the point, he is so perfectly cast. At home in the
role, he is rather livelier than usual. Perhaps that is
just the actor's pleasure in being exhibited to best

advantage in so many splendid uniforms. He sets the tone and dominates the movie; he may be gentle, but he is surrounded by actors of such overpowering passivity that he almost passes for energetic. The vitality level of the whole cast is so low that no one speaks above a murmur; it's as if the film had been shot in a public-library reading room. And he is protected against competition; I don't believe that there is another handsome young man visible in the whole of the Austro-Hungarian Empire—and we do seem to see most of it. In only one sequence is Sharif cancelled out. When he attends the ballet, the director crosscuts between the dancers and the romance, and one longs to stay with the dancers. Not just because the ballet is elegantly staged and photographed, with suggestions of Ingres in the design and color, but because the trained intensity of the dancers compels attention, and the actors are slack and dispiriting.

It's fortunate for other stars that Sharif is around to play these noble noodles, or the others might get stuck with them. Big new stars—a Gable, a Bogart, a Burt Lancaster, or a James Coburn or Steve McQueen—are often not in the accepted "handsome" mold. They break it and change it, but if it is their bad fortune to be cast later in vacuous, conventional roles, they become stuffed shirts. Of course, because they are not in the accepted handsome mold, they are generally getting on in years by the time they reach stardom, and so they are often much too old to play the pretty-hero parts that are wrong for them anyway. Sharif, who began by being unable to do anything *but* play a sweetheart, can drain these roles off, and these roles, which would be poison to others, keep him a star. Sharif doesn't try to act, so he isn't gauche, and he is never vulgar (that would take energy), and he is convincingly male, so he isn't embarrassing the way British actors can be. The trouble with all these virtues is that they're largely negative and they don't add up to much *entertainment*. The name Omar Sharif may sound like a put-on—a mate for Theda Bara—but Sharif himself is almost painfully straight.

Sharif's co-star, Catherine Deneuve, is pallid and demure as Maria Vetsera. What is required of her is a reprise of the enchanted heroine of "Elvira Madigan" and of Danielle Darrieux's celebrated sexy loveliness in the role of Maria, but she is too obviously carefully handled and arranged. One can almost feel the presence of all those off-screen hands fussing over her, determined to make her the most fragile, haunting thing ever—a perfect little figurine in a gifte shoppe, like Grace Kelly—and so, instead of having the sense of discovering the ecstatic qualities of her face for ourselves (as one did in her earlier films), we begin to look upon her as expensive merchandise and to notice the defects. She may share this dismay; at times there is a suggestion of puckish amusement about her, which could be a reaction to the poised and humorless Sharif and the lavishness of the production. And James Mason, as Emperor Franz Josef, hardly seems strong enough to function as a repressive Oedipal force. I like his quiet walk and the way he seems just to slip into a character, but he's too weak for *this* character. The picture didn't tell me what my encyclopedia did—that Rudolf's position as crown prince was really absurd. He died at Mayerling in 1889; his father's reign, which began in 1848, went on until 1916. Mason doesn't begin to suggest that kind of staying power, and one wonders why his son doesn't hang on a bit. The choice of Ava Gardner—a star famous for beauty and underacting—to play Sharif's mother, the empress, seems almost inspired. They are of the same lineage; spawn of the movies, they even resemble each other, and one would have to work hard to dislike either of them.

The production *is* lavish, and one can't call the expenditure a waste, exactly, because it keeps one from getting impossibly bored—there's always a change of locale coming up, and new uniforms and gowns. We may not see much evidence of emotion, but Sharif keeps making declarations of love, and he's such a nice man that we can't believe he would lie. And the writer-director, Terence Young, is careful to give us something to look at in the backgrounds; the romance is swathed in décor, and it's lovely décor. Though the picture feels much longer than it is, you do come out with the feeling that you've had a lot of movie. It's dull, but it's pretty and inoffensive.

Lee Marvin and Toshiro Mifune are the stars of "Hell in the Pacific," and there's nobody else in the movie—just this American soldier and this Japanese soldier stranded on a Pacific island during the Second World War, and neither speak a word of the other's language. Doesn't that make you eager to see it? Surely you can hardly wait for its pungent thought-for-today. Haven't you always longed for a movie full of Toshiro Mifune grunting and Lee Marvin muttering to himself? Marvin actually has a few lines of dialogue—talking to himself, of course—and is rather funny. And near the end there is a sexy moment when the two men shave and look at each other's smooth face—which might have made a promising beginning for a comedy. But "Hell in the Pacific" is about—you guessed it—brotherhood and communication, and it's made for star turns not only by the actors but by John Boorman, the director, and Conrad Hall, a clever, showy cinematographer who thrusts opulent, empty imagery at us. Hall can't just shoot a picture; he has to make it a tour de force. After his flashy, overdramatic work in "Cool Hand Luke" and "In Cold Blood," one might think that a talented director like John Boorman would know better than to use him, but I fear that the situation is just the reverse—that Boorman, who got caught up in directorial flashiness in "Point Blank," is so determined not to risk banality that he is going further into the clever, commercial forms of ersatz art, in which the only aim is to be strikingly effective. Together, he and Hall make the Pacific island a pile of sequins. And Hall's tricky little camera études deserve Lalo Schifrin's I-can-do-anything-anybody-can-do music. When John Boorman and Conrad Hall and Lalo Schifrin all found each other, the shocks of recognition must have been deafening.

March 1, 1969

The Small Winner

Some years ago, Jean-Luc Godard described François Truffaut's films as "rigorous and tender." I don't think this any longer applies. Truffaut's new film, "Stolen Kisses," is charming, certainly, and likable, but it's too likable, too *easily* likable. It won the Grand Prix du Cinéma Français (which, like the Academy Award here, is given by the industry) and the 1968 Prix Méliès (which is given by the critics), and it may become Truffaut's biggest popular success in America. The timing for its arrival is perfect; people are, no doubt, starved for a romantic comedy that says it's good to be alive. But "Stolen Kisses" isn't rigorous, and without rigor the tenderness is a little flabby. "Stolen Kisses" is a series of improvisations on the young manhood and love life of Antoine Doinel (Jean-Pierre Léaud), who was first presented at twelve, suffering from the callousness and injustice of the adult world, in "The 400 Blows," and later appeared as an adolescent in Truffaut's episode of "Love at Twenty." When I saw Antoine in "The 400 Blows," I thought he was basically a healthy and resilient child who wasn't too badly off—not as badly off as the picture made him out to be. But I didn't think Truffaut saw it that way, and the frozen frame at the end, with Antoine looking at the sea, suggested that his future was hopeless. Now Truffaut has made him so healthy that I can't believe that that sensitive boy could have become so *trivially* healthy. The child's desperation has disappeared, and the adult world is now a collection of harmless eccentrics, some of them unfortunate but most of them—well, lovable. Truffaut has turned Antoine into the sad sack who wins. In earlier periods of the movies, the Chaplinesque figures were generally losers, but now—"The Graduate" led the way—the traditional loser types have become small winners.

The New Wave showed that it was easier to make films than the older generation had indicated, but there is a danger in this easiness which "Stolen Kisses" makes apparent: the possibility of losing the sense of illusion. This movie is so lightly done that the improvisatory style undercuts not merely the believability of the characters and incidents but the very beauty and mystery of movie art itself. The throwaway quality—the ease with which the story seems to make itself up as it goes along—is meant to be the picture's charm, and to some degree it is, but when we can see how it is all done, we may also lose interest. The feat of a master of improvisation would be to achieve the looseness and texture of "life" and the "magic" of movie art simultaneously—to tell a story as if it had been found. Truffaut fails to give us the feeling that he has discovered just what he needed. "Stolen kisses" seems not a found story but a planted story, and so superficially and clumsily rooted that we are conscious of the filmmaking process and of the players trotting around the streets of Paris playacting for the camera. From the very first shots, when Antoine is being discharged from the military, his face in closeup is reacting to onlookers rather than to the man he is listening to, and all through the movie there's an imprecision in the material, and especially in the editing, that makes us aware of the casualness of the movie-making. And in this informal atmosphere of just-pretend acting, and with a story that is surely meant to be taken only as the excuse for a movie, such directorial interjections as closeups of the twisting hands of a homosexual are surprisingly cheap. There are so many playful false leads that one keeps thinking the movie is heading somewhere, instead of enjoying where it's at. When it's good, it has something of the idiosyncratic freedom of a Sacha Guitry comedy like "Assassins et Voleurs." There is a delightful little documentary interpolation on the speedy mail service, a lovely moment when the heroine (Claude Jade) teaches the hero a method of buttering toast, a bit of lunatic comedy when a husband, trying to simulate outrage, throws the flowers from a vase instead of throwing the vase. And, best of all, there's a marvellous character invention: Michael Lonsdale as M. Tabard, who can't understand why people don't like him and thinks there must be a conspiracy. But when it isn't good it falls back on being "beguiling."

Traffaut's aim has become, it appears, purely to please. Perhaps this is what Truffaut has really learned from Hitchcock. In his book on Hitchcock, whenever Hitchcock explains how something was calculated to tease and please the audience, Truffaut interprets the explanation as if this were the meaning of art. It can, however, be the meaning of commerce, and of emptiness. We can all surely put up with love-in-bloom, and I don't mind boulevard farce, but this movie keeps slipping in and out of the form, and it lacks the *crassness* of boulevard farce—which can be a kind of rigor. Truffaut doesn't bother to create even the central character; he uses Léaud as he used Jeanne Moreau in "The Bride Wore Black"—for what the actor already is. In "Stolen Kisses" Truffaut seems to start with the assumption that we already love his little Antoine and will find his ineptness and incompetence adorable. But I liked Antoine for his strength, and that is gone. Léaud has grown up for us in Godard's films, where he seems more the Antoine we knew as a child than he does in this Truffaut film. Truffaut makes him childish and diminutive, and less than the child he was. When Léaud becomes intense in one sequence—looking in the mirror and chanting the names of his two loves—he is too strong for this film, and leaves it in ruins behind him, because the idea of "Stolen Kisses" is an anti-passionate, anti-serious twentieth-century *éducation sentimentale*. It's a carefree view of romance; when a man declares undying love for the heroine, she observes, "He must be crazy." But it's a careless and, oh, so forgettable movie—almost a disposable movie. Truffaut himself appears to be such a small talent in "Stolen Kisses" that it may seem like overreacting even to put it down because it's so inoffensive in every way except in being so inoffensive.

"Three in the Attic" is a sophomoric sex comedy—a sex-exploitation picture with the basic values and outlook of a rather square fraternity boy—but a pretty good case can be made for collegiate lowbrow humor when it's blatant about its purposes, and not coated with the archness of Old Broadway. Christopher Jones' Paxton Quigley is the opposite of Dustin Hoffman's Benjamin; he's closer to those wierd neo-Nazi blond boys who were whacking each other with towels in "The Graduate." He's a tough and wily seducer, and Jones himself is a wily actor; he looks like James Dean, but he doesn't look hurt or wounded, and his character here doesn't seem to ask for sympathy or protection. Dean was always "misunderstood," but it's just about impossible to misunderstand Jones. He's the American as a young dog. In a sense, he's the American as enemy—the unredeemed self-centered, carnal frat boy—but if you have watched something like "The Experiment" on television or have been going to recent youth-oriented movies, Paxton Quigley's single-minded preoccupation with sex seems as refreshing as Andy Hardy's naïveté; he's too busy groping somebody to be searching for himself, and he isn't creative. As soon as a moviemaker serves up a self-righteous hero who is a tender idealist worrying about his soul, he thinks he's making art and a statement about our time, but this movie seems to be made without pretension or hypocrisy. "Three in the Attic" is coarse-minded without being tough-minded, but that coarseness nevertheless has something liberating in it. The "Beach Party" movies may have shown a lot of wiggling and a little flesh, but the principals—Annette Funicello and Frankie Avalon and all—were pure and smirky. "Three in the Attic" is new-style corny Americana without the coyness and prissiness. There is too much soft-focus lyricism and leaping about, the last third is poor, and some of the trying-to-be-bright lines are real thudders, but it does have an openness of attitude that is a pleasant change in youth-exploitation pictures.

"The Night of the Following Day" is a very bad kidnapping-for-ransom movie, and the audience laughs at it, but the audience also laughs with it and somehow seems to be having a good time. It is taken from another of those Lionel White pulps (Stanley Kubrick used one for "The Killing," and Godard used one as some kind of starting point for "Pierrot le Fou"), and I have a hunch that it may be taken up and turned into a "classic" crime picture— particularly abroad, where people won't be able to *hear* the worst of it. Hubert Cornfield, the writer-director, points the camera up a girl's skirt. Wow! What technique! Cornfield is a former graphic designer who in the past has joked in interviews about producers' calling him an "arty director," but even producers can be right now and then. "The Night of the Following Day" is that mixture of the fancy and the stupid which makes a movie an art movie in the worst sense. The film is handsomely designed in gold and brown and blue and black, and has the characters silhouetted against white walls; the scheme is so stylized that the hero and his girl have gold hair. The opening looks promising, but then the characters start to talk a pseudo-casual gangster jargon; this sub-banal way of talking is very likely a deliberate attempt to be cool, but the actors' faces are so blank and their language has so little relation to the design that it sounds funny. Aiming at coolness is not only not a very high aspiration, it's a risky one. From scene to scene, the actors don't seem sure whether or not to take the movie seriously, and the audience shows the same uncertainty about the actors.

The reaction of the audience is so ambivalent that the movie may gain a certain fame from this alone. And Cornfield did something that has turned out to be awfully shrewd: in two of the cardboard-cutout roles he cast Marlon Brando and Richard Boone— actors who have such phenomenal audience rapport that the audience is *with* them even when they're doing nothing, and doing that badly. I don't think that Brando has ever been worse or less interesting than in this movie—not even in "A Countess from Hong Kong"—yet Brando is, after all, our great *original*. And the audience is so drawn to his singularity that it seems happy just to watch him do some dumb little thing, like stare at his girl when she's all doped up and pretending not to be. And Richard Boone, with his big, scowling, humorous face, is so familiar from all those years on television, and is such a cartoon of a tough, no-good guy, that the audience goes along with him, too. The only acting in the picture is done by Rita Moreno, who plays the ticky little drug addict and gives an expert stylized performance. But though probably almost no one accepts Brando and Boone in their roles, their very presence evokes a special empathy—not simply because they're stars but because their edge of irony about what they're doing and their uncertainty about how to play the comic-strip gangsters make the difference for the audience between just laughing at the picture and laughing both ways. The bad movie begins to seem a joke that we're all partly in on. Kidnapping would seem to be an ideal subject for a movie thriller, because tension and suspense are practically guaranteed, but I don't think there has ever been a good kidnapping-for-ransom movie. I don't know why, any more than I know why when opera singers go into the movies the baritones can act but the tenors can't.

March 8, 1969

School Days, School Days

From the advance rave quotes, I gather that many reviewers believe that "If . . ." will be a great success with youth and that it is a masterpiece. One may suspect that in some cases the evaluation is based on the prediction. I think "If . . ." will be a success, but I think it's far from a masterpiece, and I should like to make this distinction, because so many people are beginning to treat "youth" as the ultimate judge—as a collective Tolstoyan clean old peasant. They want to be on the side of youth; they're afraid of youth. (And this is not irrelevant to the subject of "If . . .") If they can be pushed by clever publicity into thinking "youth" will respond to a movie, they are then instrumental in *getting* "youth" to respond to it. Movie companies are using computerized demographic studies and market research to figure out how to promote movies. Here, taken from *Variety,* is the report on the technique adjudged most suitable for "If . . ." by the same new "scientific" group at Paramount Pictures (a subsidiary of Gulf & Western) who worked out how to sell Zeffirelli's "Romeo and Juliet." The report predicted that "If . . ." will repeat its British success in the United States *"if it is given the same kind of intensive marketing support that made it such a hit in its première engagement* in London," and described the key element as "a very extensive screening program for critics, writers, radio and TV commentators, educators, and members of government," continuing, "We went out of our way to pursue every means of reaching the public through newspaper editorials, radio and television panels or discussions, magazine features and lectures before important opinion-making groups. The outpouring of 'breaks' in all communication media was phenomenal and most unusual in that [the film] was treated as a news event away from the usual coverage of motion pictures." It's easy to recognize the standard advertising campaign aimed at the mass audience—the big ads and the appearances of stars and movie-makers on the TV talk shows—but we are still novices when it comes to an advertising campaign that feeds the appetite of the media for something new and exciting, and we may not spot techniques directed at the selective, educated audience. Obviously, these techniques couldn't work if the film didn't have something in it for people to react to, but if it does, the publicity people can build up a general impression of urgent, clamorous response. It's no accident when all those rave reviews come out before a picture has opened; the early reviewers get the taste of triumph as they rush to be the first to jump on the bandwagon. And when this atmosphere of consensus about the importance of a picture is built up, anybody who doesn't go along begins to seem "out of it"—"not with it." "If ..." has been so well sold that people were discussing it in the *Village Voice* weeks before it opened; that's real marketing, and it means that the whole underground press has been alerted by now. "Youth" will "discover" another movie; in a flash forward, one can already hear the discussions on WBAI. Once this process has begun to work and the publicity has caught on, the film *is* important; people want to see it because they are hearing about it wherever they go. The publicity men have manufactured "news," and the mass media don't want to be scooped and left behind.

The joke about all the rave quotes from the networks and *Cue* and *Life* and the *Ladies' Home Journal* and *Playboy* and *Look* ("I'll be talking about 'If . . .' forever") and the rest is that the hero of "If . . ." is firing a machine gun at everything they represent. They are turning "youth" on to armed revolt, and the market-research people and the press are so eager to sell to "youth" that they'd probably include a machine gun with the admission ticket if it were economically feasible. This may be one of the contradictions in capitalism that Marx did not foresee: the conglomerates that control the mass media are now selling "youth" the violent overthrow of the Establishment for the suicidally simple reason that they can find and develop a demand for it.

"If . . ." deals with a schoolboys' revolt on the model of Jean Vigo's 1933 film "Zero for Conduct." I think it will have psychological appeal here because it's a revolt of the privileged and provides a basically psychological rationale for student revolution. The battle cry is for freedom and nonconformity and an end to stupidity, rigidity, hypocrisy, and cruelty. The violence is thus given a psychological meaning and justification: it's to explode the repressive system, to liberate men from all the dull nastiness that the corrupt school represents. And because this kind of psychological rationale for student revolt is probably close to how students at American high schools and colleges feel, and because hatred and disgust for the old system provide a simpler, more basic justification than political and social and economic issues do, I think they'll respond. Lindsay Anderson, the director of "If . . ." gives the rebels a cause.

"If . . ." may have a potential appeal for young people, but I rather doubt whether it would reach much of an audience without a brilliant selling job. It has a bleak, pseudo-documentary solemnity that is about as attractive to Americans as blood pudding. Anderson's movies—"This Sporting Life" and "If . . ."—draw their considerable power from what one can only assume is unconscious and semiconscious material. Anderson is a major talent (partly because he isn't interested in doing anything minor), but to be successful in the theatre or in movies it is not enough to be talented; one must have a certain *kind* of talent. We may admire sequences in an Anderson film, but his talent really isn't likable, and even his best sequences are often baffling—heavy with multiple meanings that he doesn't appear to think need sorting out. Yet though the material may be staggeringly private, if disguised, the manner of the presentation is coldly realistic and precise; the style is so controlled one might assume the content was, too. At first, and for a considerable stretch, "If . . ." appears to be a clinical exposé of the horrible organized bedlam inflicted on English boys in the name of a gentleman's education. The film is especially fixated on the cruelties that the students perpetrate against each other, and one may suppose that all this lingering attention to scenes of juvenile sadism and flogging and homoeroticism and the allusions to the rot and collapse of the British upper classes are in the service of reform. The detailed (and I think obsessively dwelt-on) material about the school deceives one about where the movie is heading.

In "Zero for Conduct," the schoolmasters and the other adults were presented non-realistically, the way the derisive, imaginative children perceived them—the principal a bearded dwarf in a top hat (in 1933 the beard meant the opposite of what beards mean now), another school official a tall, skinny spy sneaking around. Though to Americans the film might seem marvellously innocent and poetic, a charming satíric fantasy, with the black flag of anarchism that a child raises on the roof no more than an emblem of youth's desire for liberty, the film was taken much more seriously in France, and was banned there until after the Liberation. The rebellion of children is, in a sense, the first—the primary—rebellion, and is the model for future rebellions, as the school is children's first experience of an *institution*. Vigo's school was like a prison. (Political rebels—especially, the bomb-throwing kind—spent their lives in and out of prisons, and Vigo's father had actually spent part of his childhood in a children's prison.) The words that the child who instigates the revolt speaks to the teacher tormenting him (*"Monsieur le professeur, je vous dis merde!"*)

which sound like what every schoolboy on occasion longs to say to his teachers, had a more specifically dangerous meaning in France. Vigo's father, the almost legendary anarchist leader Almereyda, had been one of the instigators of the mutiny of the French Army during the First World War—the only historical example of an army's mutinying in the face of the enemy. The words *"Je vous dis merde"* had been Almereyda's challenge to the government in the headlines of his newspaper, *La Guerre Sociale.* (His name was itself an anagram of *"y a [de] la merde."*) When "Zero for Conduct" was attacked in France as violent, perverse, and obscene, there was no doubt that, as André Bazin said, "for Vigo the school is nothing less than society itself." Anderson's model for "If . . ." is a key film both aesthetically and politically, and Anderson's school, following the same plan, seems meant as a mirror of society, and his conscious aim in all that stuff about rigidity and sadism and the rot of the upper classes seems to be to demonstrate that our society drives us to violence as the only solution— that it is the only pure act that can come out of all this. Anderson's adults are grotesques, but, unlike Vigo's, they are presented literally, and may even be intended to be taken realistically, as proof of the effects of stultifying traditions. They will probably be taken by most adults in the audience as evidence of conditions that must be improved, and by at least some students as evidence that the only thing to do is blow everyone up—after all, killing them isn't like killing real people, because they don't seem to have any honest emotions. "If . . ." is intended to be a revolutionary epic, and there are so many strong, coldly repellent scenes and such a powerful (even if possibly displaced) sense of anger that sequences that individually fail to move us accumulate steadily until the sheer grinding tendentiousness may make the climax pass for inevitable.

Vigo's vision was "poetic" partly because of its consistency and our instant recognition of its meanings. We responded immediately to the juvenile conspirators, who were not the innocent children seen by adults whose own childhood has become a sentimental memory but, rather, children seen by a director so young and so close in temperament to childhood that they seemed to be children as they saw themselves. The movie could leap along and we could make the connections, and the Surreal touches were intensifications of vision that reawakened our own old feelings. But Anderson's Surreal touches and episodes simply don't work; they just seem to be odd things happening, and one's reaction is "Huh?" I rather doubt whether one can successfully use Surreal distortions in such a humorless, tight style. Vigo, like Buñuel and Godard, could be wildly funny, and could do startling, imaginative things and make them seem perfectly natural. Anderson doesn't have the right tone; he's a scourge, not a poet, and the picture is clogged by all the difficult, ambitious things he attempts and flubs. Yet the visual style provides a kind of unity (despite the changes from color film to black and white, which I assume were the results of accident and economy—I assume that when the light wasn't adequate for using color film, they went on shooting with black and white), and Anderson's tone of cold, seething anger unifies the film, too. But we don't really know—immediately and intuitively—why he is showing us what he is showing us. This kind of picture should hold together emotionally and intellectually much better than it does, yet Anderson precludes such criticism by setting up as the No. 1 target the disgusting, hypocritical headmaster, who is calling for reason when he gets it—*ping!*—right in the middle of the forehead.

The basic inconsistency—the true craziness—of Anderson's vision of youthful revolution is that he is full of bile about youth. Vigo's children were united by the high spirits that were bursting out of repression (they saw one of the teachers, who had kept *his* high spirits, as a clown, and an ally), but Anderson devotes most of his energy to the meanness of the students, and it is really not a rebellion of the young that he shows us but a rebellion of a self-chosen few—three boys (and a girl picked up along the way) who set fire to the school on Speech Day and start sniping at those who flee the fire, including the rest of the young. Anderson's concept of destroying the prison is to kill the inmates. The conspirators are cleaning out the whole mess, apparently—killing everybody, because nobody's fit to live. The last shot is a glamorous, approving closeup of the hero as he fires away, like Robert Taylor aiming at "the Japs" at the end of "Bataan." Anderson had dehumanized the other people as shamefully as Hollywood dehumanized "the Japs" during the war years, and has set up these few as the judges and purifiers of humanity. It's as crazy, in its way, as it would be to make a movie hero of that demented boy at the University of Texas who climbed to the top of a tower and fired at everyone in sight, and yet because these kids *are* students at school and are firing away I think they will be taken as youth driven to clean out the dead wood.

Anderson may think he has made a movie about revolutionary youth and freedom, and I guess that's what David Sherwin thinks he was putting into the script, but though they may think it's there, it isn't. We can read the signals, all right—the poster of Che and the hero's forbidden mustache and his playing the "Missa Luba"—but are we to believe the signals or the style of the film, which is constricted and charged with inconsistent, ambivalent feelings? We could tell what "Zero for Conduct" stood for because the movie was free and liberating, but the material about the revolt *feels* added to "If ..." because we haven't sensed a movement toward freedom. Anderson is skillful at scenes of sadism, but when he wants to suggest that his nonconformist heroes have some of the joy of life that the others haven't, he becomes as banal as a TV director and shows them speeding lyrically through the green countryside on a stolen motorcycle. And, because one of his arguments against the school is the homoerotic atmosphere, he apparently feels it is necessary to show that his hero has "healthy" appetites—and does so by presenting him in a sexual scrimmage with a girl who is harder and tougher than the boys. The ways in which Anderson tries to illustrate the desire for freedom are so mechanical and carry so little conviction that I think one may

354

conclude that the heroes are shooting because he needs to discharge his rage—which may be closer to why the boy in Texas was shooting than it is to a revolution. Anderson seems to have lost sight of what was so apparent in Vigo's view, and what was so funny in it—that school is a *child's* mirror of society. Vigo's vision was a comic metaphor; Anderson's movie has no wings, and his literal-mindedness about the school leads to the climax of shooting up the people in the school. Vigo did not confuse the children's view with "reality." Anderson does, and what makes the film such a can of wriggly worms is that his confusion will probably be the basis of its appeal. It's so convenient for older students to use a child's experience of institutions and to take the school for the Establishment. The conglomerates and the mass media may go on playing their dangerous turning-on games as long as the clowns and academics and liberal institutions, rather than the real centers of power, are the targets.

Considering the problems of adapting such a distinctive comedy style as Muriel Spark's, and such a special vision as that of her short novel "The Prime of Miss Jean Brodie," to the screen, Jay Presson Allen's adaptation is a good try. Most of the problems are just about insoluble. Miss Brodie (Maggie Smith), the spinster lady in Edinburgh in the thirties, the romantic crackpot who wants to inspire rather than teach the little girls, has become more heroic and embattled, and more bizarre. When Muriel Spark's witty caricature of the teacher is moved to stage and screen and enlarged to be the

complete person, she becomes a witty monster. And
because she has the comedy lines (by which the
author exposed her) to speak, she, of course, plays
them for laughs. Instead of being unconsciously
outrageous, she is deliberately outrageous, but I
doubt whether the role would "play" any other way,
and Maggie Smith, with her gift for mimicry and
her talent for mannered comedy, makes Jean Brodie
very funny—absurdly haughty, full of affectations,
and with a jumble shop of a mind. She becomes a
mock-heroine (a bit of an Auntie Mame), and we
enjoy the funny things she says and does. There
probably wouldn't be any play or movie—or much
fun, either—if she weren't played as a glorious ec-
centric, but after we've been invited to fall in love
with her, it seems to me we rather resent it when she
is cut down and becomes a mocked heroine. We
think, Well, after all, she did give those kids more
pleasure and excitement than they got from the
other teachers. We want to be on her side, and we
simply don't believe all that stuff about her trying to
put Jenny into bed with the art instructor, or about
Sandy's affair and revenge, and we don't believe
that her Fascist fantasies could be so serious. It's a
great showy role for an actress, but my guess is that
there's no way of interpreting it that would seem
right. The distortions that come about when a character in a novel becomes a star turn on the stage or
the screen are only part of the problem. The material, literate and charming and good as it is, may be
fundamentally unsatisfying (I didn't believe the
resolutions in the book, either); but the material is

so compelling that, I think, despite the flaws—of book and play and movie—we are always engaged.

There are changes from the book—such as combining Mary McGregor with the girl who went off to Spain, and a melodramatic confrontation scene at the end—that are dismaying, despite the fact that one can see perfectly well why they have been made. And though we expect the movie to lose the reverberations that the teacher and the girls have in each other's lives, what is also lost in the movie, surprisingly (it was present in Mrs. Allen's stage version), is the sense of the girls as a clique. This is probably the fault of Ronald Neame's direction. The movie gives one the sense of filmed theatre—partly, no doubt, because Muriel Spark doesn't provide much *extra,* her defining lines of dialogue and description being almost as concentrated as a dramatist's, and partly because Neame works in such a conventional style. The movie doesn't seem to have any resonance, but the virtue in his conventionality is that he respects the actors and gives them individual opportunities to hold our attention. Celia Johnson has a genuine triumph as Miss Mackay, who in the film becomes Miss Brodie's true adversary; the force of talent transforms the material. The casting in general is superb—unusual care has been taken with the small parts. (The school secretary aroused more memories of school for me than anything else in the movie.) And Robert Stephens, with that oddly bruised voice, makes the art instructor much more believable than he was in the book—where he seemed to come out of the same fantasy world as Miss Brodie's lost lovers. He and Maggie Smith have an intimacy when they talk together in one scene that almost makes their love affair convincing; he is the only character in the film with whom she isn't domineering, and that is as it should be.

March 15, 1969

Index

ABOUT THE AUTHOR

PAULINE KAEL is considered by many the most influential movie critic in the United States today. In Berkeley, California, she made weekly broadcasts on the Pacifica network and managed the first twin art-film house in the United States, which she supplied with thousands of program notes that were later used by film societies throughout the country. Miss Kael's criticism appears in a variety of magazines, including LIFE, HOLIDAY, VOGUE, THE ATLANTIC MONTHLY, MADEMOISELLE, SIGHT AND SOUND, PARTISAN REVIEW and FILM QUARTERLY. She contributes film criticism to THE NEW YORKER and is at work on a study of *Citizen Kane*. In addition, she has made experimental short films.

Miss Kael lectures frequently at universities and film festivals in this country and Canada. Her home is now in New York City.

BANTAM BESTSELLERS

OUTSTANDING BOOKS NOW AVAILABLE AT A FRACTION OF THEIR ORIGINAL COST!